IMAGES
of America

PARKER

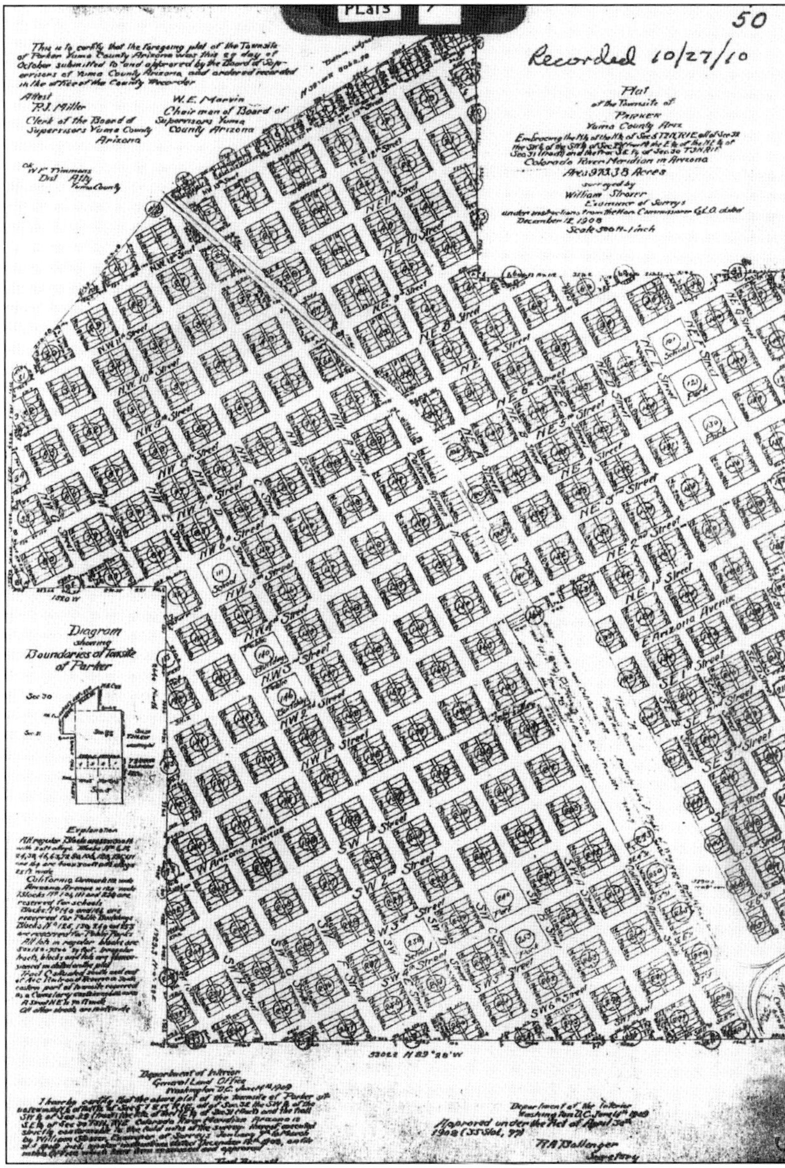

On April 30, 1908, the U.S. Congress (35 Stat 77) authorized the town site of Parker to be reserved and set apart and to survey, plat, and sell the tracts so set apart in such a manner as the secretary of the interior may prescribe. On June 10, 1908, the Secretarial Order establishing the town site of Parker was issued, followed by the Order of Reservation for the town site issued by the General Land Office on June 18, 1908. For six months, from December 1908 to June 14, 1909, instructions for the survey were issued, and the survey and plat of the town site were completed, approved, and certified. On October 24, 1910, the plat map was submitted to and approved by the Yuma County Board of Supervisors, which ordered the plat to be recorded for the town site of Parker. On October 27, 1910, the plat was recorded on docket 1, page 50, in Yuma County, Arizona.

ON THE COVER: Nellie Bush stands at the helm of the ferryboat *Nellie T*, which was named in her honor by her husband, Joe. (Courtesy Arizona Historical Foundation.)

IMAGES
of America

PARKER

Deanna Beaver and
the Parker Area Historical Society

Arizona Historical Foundation

ARCADIA
PUBLISHING

ISBN 978-0-7385-5638-3

Published by Arcadia Publishing
Charleston, South Carolina

Printed in the United States of America

Library of Congress Catalog Card Number: 2008920087

For all general information contact Arcadia Publishing at:
Telephone 843-853-2070
Fax 843-853-0044
E-mail sales@arcadiapublishing.com
For customer service and orders:
Toll-Free 1-888-313-2665

Visit us on the Internet at www.arcadiapublishing.com

To Parker's founders: the men, women, and children who with great fortitude built this community to pursue the American Dream of life, liberty, and the pursuit of happiness

CONTENTS

Acknowledgments

We thank the current officers and directors of the Parker Area Historical Society—Leroy Shontz, Jessie Siebert, Linda Kruse, Deanna Beaver, Marilyn Goar, Florene Parks, John Stine, Leroy McVey, and Don Sullivan—for their perseverance and dedication to keeping Parker's history alive.

Our gratitude goes to the following former officers and directors, who tirelessly supported the society by donating their time and energy: Janet and Woodie Winans, Bob and Sheryl Drew, Del and Aliene McMinn, Bud and Sharon Champion, Dennis Wilskey, Fred Siebert, Joyce West, and Elizabeth Solper.

All images featured in this publication come from the Parker Area Historical Society (unless cited otherwise) or from private collections held by Parker descendants. The society expresses gratitude for the use of private collections provided by the following: the Marion Beaver family, including his wife, Patricia, and children Roberta Hoffman, Marilou Fellman, Jo Andress, and Dan Beaver; the Alfred Preston children, Diana Baker and Allan Preston; Barbara and Wayne Holdread; the Lois Terry–Patrick family, including her husband, Raymond, and children Coni Interlicchia, Kelly Wilson, and Mitchell Patrick; Art Fox and Ruby Finley-Fox; Marion Hendrix-Shontz and Tammy Hendrix-Thorn; the Parker Area Chamber of Commerce and director Randy Hartless; Ellen "Billie" Fuqua-Dick; the Bill Brennan children, Nell Dick, Mark Brennan, and Robert Brennan; John "Jackie" Garner; Buni Harvey-Hooper; Frank McVey; D. L. Wilson; Carl Wickes; Theodor Isler; Mike Mack; Liz Herbst; Michael Newman; Lake Havasu Masonic Lodge; Parker Unified School District and Supt. Kevin Uden; Cliff Edey; Brad and Liz Soden; Steve Robinson; Wanda Robinson; Carl and Kathy Roland; the daughters of Joan Bighead, Jacquie Gunning and Diane Bighead. Appreciation is extended to the *Parker Pioneer*; John Gutekunst; Joan Travis; Don and Kathy Sullivan; Town of Parker; Mario Ponce; and Candy Critchlow-Cockrell for the invaluable assistance provided during the development of this book.

Special thanks go to the Arizona Historical Foundation for allowing the use of the cover photograph of Nellie T. Bush. Additional gratitude goes to Jared Jackson, Arcadia Publishing acquisitions editor, who kept this project moving along with constructive suggestions and encouragement. Thank you so much, Jared. We finally finished it!

Deanna Beaver, a local Parker historian, provided the text for this Images of America book. Deanna is a passionate self-taught historian and genealogist beginning as a Parker High School student, thanks to several former teachers: Fred Siebert, Ron Curnutt, and Alex Martinez. Additionally, Deanna credits her then-future mother-in-law, Esther Beaver, for instilling her love of history through her trivia competitions. As a member of the Havasu chapter of the National Society of the Daughters of the American Revolution, Deanna has traced her family history back to the Revolutionary War. She currently serves on the Arizona Historical Society Board of Directors.

INTRODUCTION

This edition of the Images of America series provides a glimpse into the town site of Parker's past through the photographic resources that were readily available as the book developed. This project is limited in scope; a diverse history still remains to be told.

The Mohave (Mojave), Chemehuevi, and other Native American tribes of the Colorado River and its tributaries offer a window into the area's pre-history. The earliest documentation also provides a resource for understanding each tribe's culture, language, and spirituality. The Colorado River Indian Tribes (CRIT) has its own unique story of how and why four different tribes—the Mohave, Chemehuevi, Navajo, and Hopi—were brought together as one. Since the 1940s, the Parker Valley has experienced tremendous agricultural development, evolving over the decades into an industry that uses the most modern farming technology available.

Beginning in the mid-1920s, 13 cities in California, known collectively as the Metropolitan Water District of Southern California, began seeking out an additional source of water to handle their projected growth. The result was the construction of Parker Dam and the Colorado River Aqueduct.

Parker was touched as a community when World War II took many young men and women from the safety and comfort of their homes and sent them to Europe and the far reaches of the Pacific to protect the freedom America holds dear. In the desert southwest, troops of Gen. George S. Patton performed endurance military training and top-secret experimentation in the development of night lighting for tanks. The training was carried out in the surrounding area of Parker—from Laughlin, Nevada, to the north; Bouse, Arizona, to the east; Yuma, Arizona, to the south; and Rice, California, to the west. Members of the Ancient and Honorable Order of E Clampus Vitus and those who served in the Arizona desert continue to make an annual pilgrimage of remembrance and fellowship to Bouse each February.

Pearl Harbor was attacked by Japan on December 7, 1941, a day Pres. Franklin D. Roosevelt proclaimed "will live in infamy." The ensuing fear, hysteria, and lack of trust for those of Japanese descent resulted in Executive Order No. 9066, which relocated and interned Japanese Americans with no regard to their citizenship. The three Poston internment camps located on the Colorado River Indian Reservation were similar to the others throughout the West.

In 1964, Operation Desert Strike brought nearly 100,000 army and air force soldiers and airmen to the Parker area for joint training maneuvers. A mock war was executed between the mythical Nezona and Calonia, with the POW facility being dubbed Camp Sun Stroke. Many of Parker's teenage girls were charmed by the attentions of these uniformed warriors, and for some marriage became a welcome reality. Said Tina Gorrell, who owned and operated the Parker Dairy Queen with her husband, Lloyd, for over three decades, "At the time, the teenage girls who worked at Dairy Queen were always on time to work, and the young soldiers were always willing to give up their R and R days to help wash the DQ windows or empty the trash." The results proved to be good for business.

Struggling for recognition as part of Yuma County, the people of northern Yuma County voted by initiative petition to form a new county. The initiative passed, and on January 1, 1983, Parker became the county seat for the newly formed LaPaz County. The county first experienced the separation from Yuma as what can best be compared to a messy divorce. Today LaPaz County continues to meet successes and challenges while looking into "a future unlimited."

This Images of America book will explore the settlers who first came to the town site of Parker, those who came in good faith to build a future for their families. Their belief was if a person was willing to work hard, the American Dream could be realized. Some 100 years have passed, and the community and its people are still striving for the same.

The original town site of Parker was surveyed between January 7 and March 31, 1909, by Capt. William Strover, examiner of surveys, under instructions from Hon. Commissioner Fred Dennett of the General Land Office (GLO) dated December 12, 1908. The town site encompasses 973.38 acres, laid out with all regular blocks 320 by 300 feet with 20-foot alleys. Block Nos. 6, 15, 24, 39, 46, 63, 72, 90, 106, 120, 135, 151, and 164 are 400 by 300 feet with 25-foot alleys. California Avenue is 112 feet wide, while Arizona Avenue is 124 feet wide. Block Nos. 101, 111, and 238 are reserved for schools and Block Nos. 140 and 146 for public buildings. Block Nos. 125, 130, 240, and 253 are reserved for public parks. All lots in regular blocks measure 50 by 150 feet, totaling 7,500 square feet. Irregular tracts, blocks, and lots are dimensioned in detail on the plat. Tract A, 33.16 acres, and Tract B, 7.31 acres, are reserved for the Arizona and California Railroad. Containing 6.58 acres in the southeastern part of the town site, Tract C is reserved for a cemetery. A Street NE (today's Hopi Avenue) is 70 feet wide, while all other streets are 100 feet wide. The plat map of the town site of Parker was recorded in Yuma County, Arizona, on October 27, 1910, in Plats Book 1, page 50. The Parker Town Council has made one revision to the plat map by Ordinance No. 45, dated March 16, 1956, regarding street names.

The town site began as a service center for railroad and mining interests and the eventual agricultural development on the Colorado River Indian Reservation. Over the passage of time, an appreciation for the river's recreational benefits developed, changing the services offered to adapt more to the needs of tourists, fishermen, hunters, and boat enthusiasts.

Parker has long experienced growing pains, wanting to maintain its small-town ambiance while at the same time recognizing the need for development. With no room for expansion within the town site, the U.S. Department of the Interior proposed a 21-section town site four miles east of the original site when the department issued the Lower Colorado River Land Use Plan in January 1964. Even with this recognition, no further attempts were initiated to address land expansion until 1980. The federal government drastically changed the way it was handling its resources as a result of the Federal Land Policy and Management Act (FLPMA) of 1976, which included some saving provisions. The proposed 21-section area was still in the Bureau of Land Management's active Land Use Plan. The Parker community created a committee to explore land growth options and reached the conclusion that the location designated in 1964 was no longer viable. Parker looked elsewhere, finally deciding on 13,000 acres of non-contiguous land 12 miles to the southeast. In 1990, the Town of Parker adopted a plan for Parker Annex, and by 1996, a significant amount of land within the core area of Parker Annex had been sold.

Every effort has been made to present an accurate documentation through oral interviews or written histories. However, occasionally errors or omissions occur and are subject to correction.

One

The Lure of the River
Ferryboats to Speedboats and Everything in Between

The lure of the Colorado River is for time immemorial. Native Americans have always revered the life-sustaining qualities of the Colorado River. According to the *Congressional Globe* of March 2, 1865, the first documented travel on the Colorado River was by trappers, beginning in 1826 with Sylvester Pattie and his son James of Kentucky. Father and son, along with a few spirited individuals, had been trapping on the Gila River, eventually making their way to the confluence with the Colorado. There they embarked their canoes on the muddy waters, drifting down to the Gulf of California.

Not long thereafter, the federal government determined the need to evaluate the navigability of the waterway. The first such exploration was carried out in 1857–1858 under the direction of 1st Lt. Joseph Christmas Ives, as ordered by secretary of war John B. Floyd. The Ives journey began at the mouth of the Colorado River and was completed upon reaching the end of Black Canyon. Ives's expedition from the south was followed by the more notable expeditions of Maj. John Wesley Powell during the years of 1869, 1870, 1871, and 1872. Powell began from the north, exploring 1,000 miles of the Colorado River and making the first recorded trip through the Grand Canyon.

Around the same time, a mountain man, trapper, and scout named Pauline Weaver was prospecting along the Colorado River in 1861–1862, discovering gold and setting off a gold rush near the river settlement of LaPaz. As settlers moved into the area, the river became a travel and commerce corridor where steamboats and ferryboats plied the river from Fort Yuma to Fort Mohave, transporting ore to distant smelters and bringing supplies and mail to otherwise unreachable destinations. When activities began to expand along the Colorado River, it was not long until the Colorado was used for recreational activities.

The earliest known winter visitors to the Parker area were Wyatt and Josie Earp. They dabbled in mining and fished from the banks of the Colorado River, enjoying the quiet beauty and splendor of their desert surroundings.

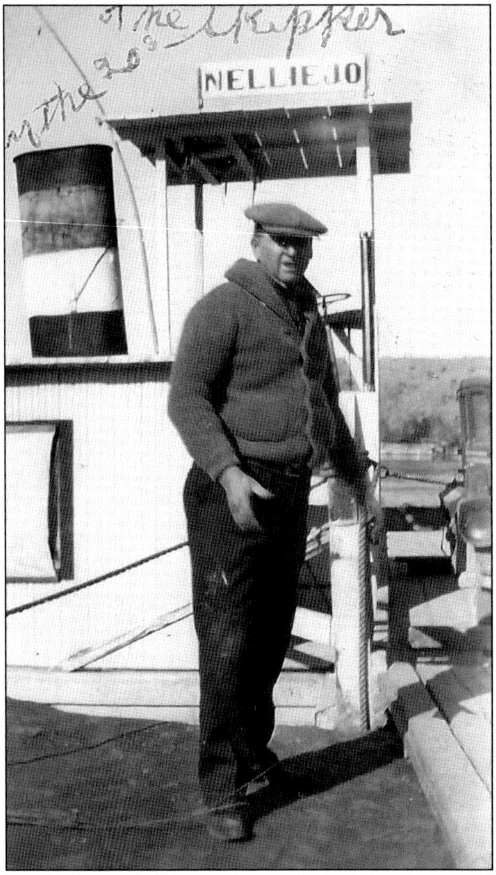

Joe Bush, pictured about 1920, was one of Parker's earliest pioneers and was affectionately referred to as "the Skipper" by his wife, Nellie. Prior to relocating to Parker in 1915 after purchasing part interest in the ferryboat *Iola*, Joe had worked as a builder of streetcar tracks. Upon completion of the Phoenix Street Railway, he had become a trolley inspector.

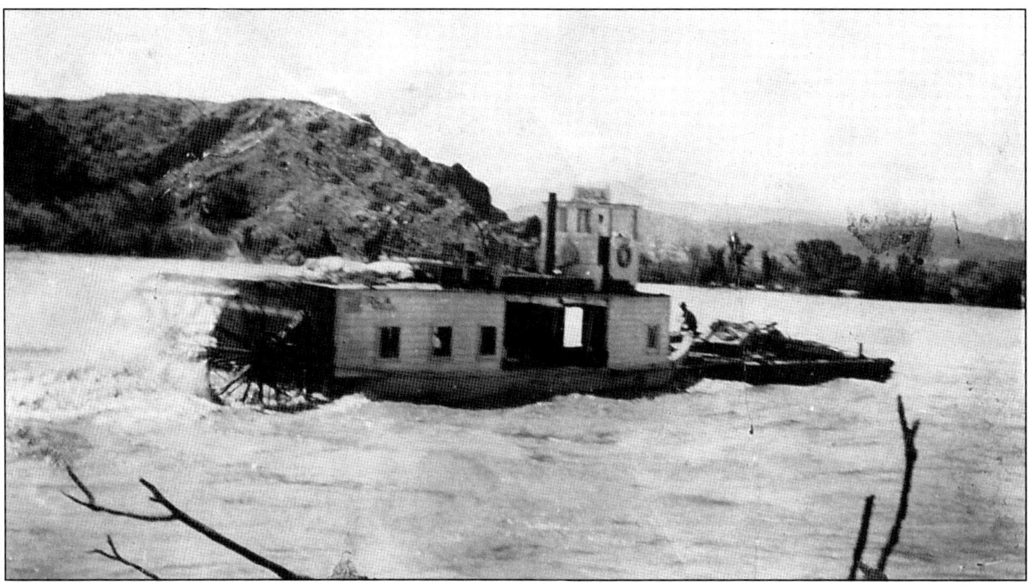

The *Iola* was one of the earlier ferryboats on the Colorado River that carried a variety of freight, including mining equipment and other supplies for the distant mining operations in the mountains near the river.

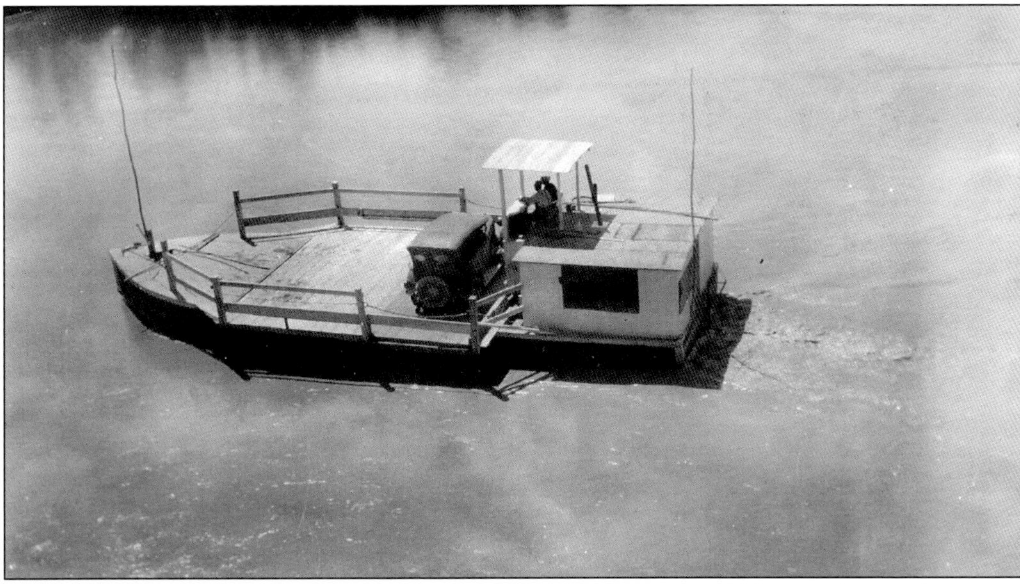

In this overhead view, a car is ferried on the river. Conditions could be treacherous because of the river's unpredictability. During early freighting, the Colorado River was also referred to as the Red River because of the thick mud silt carried with the water's flow.

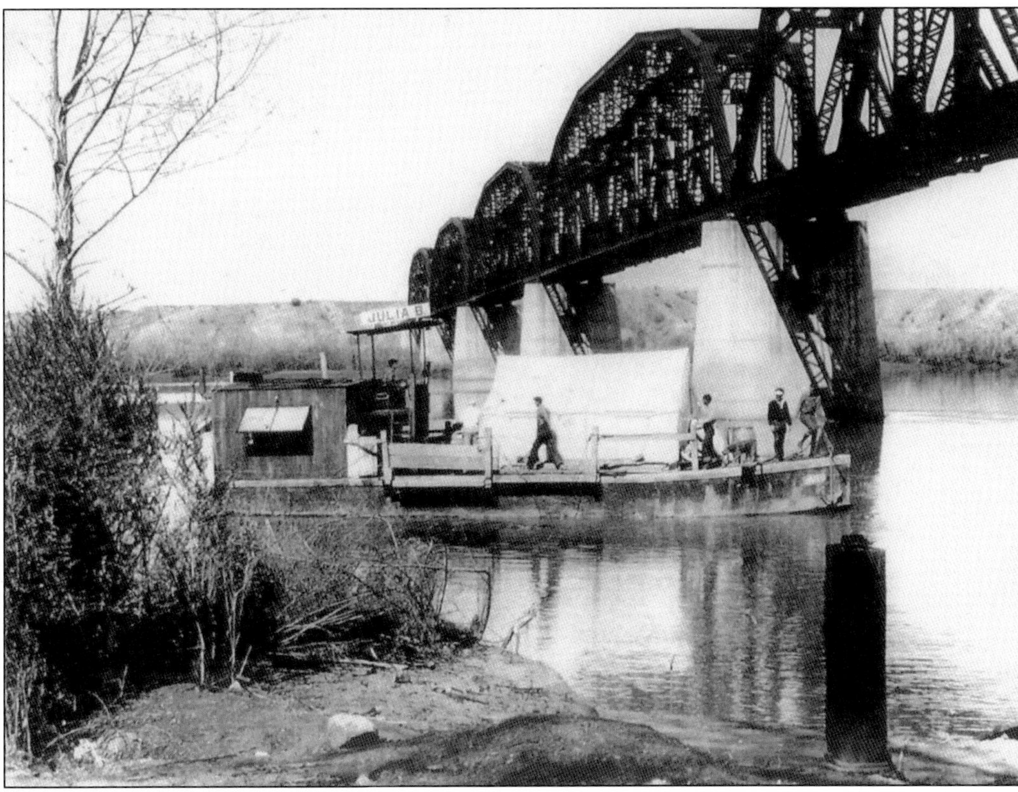

The *Julia B* passes under the Parker train bridge while transporting supplies. The pitched tent was used for privacy and shelter when the ferryboats had to be gone for an extended amount of time.

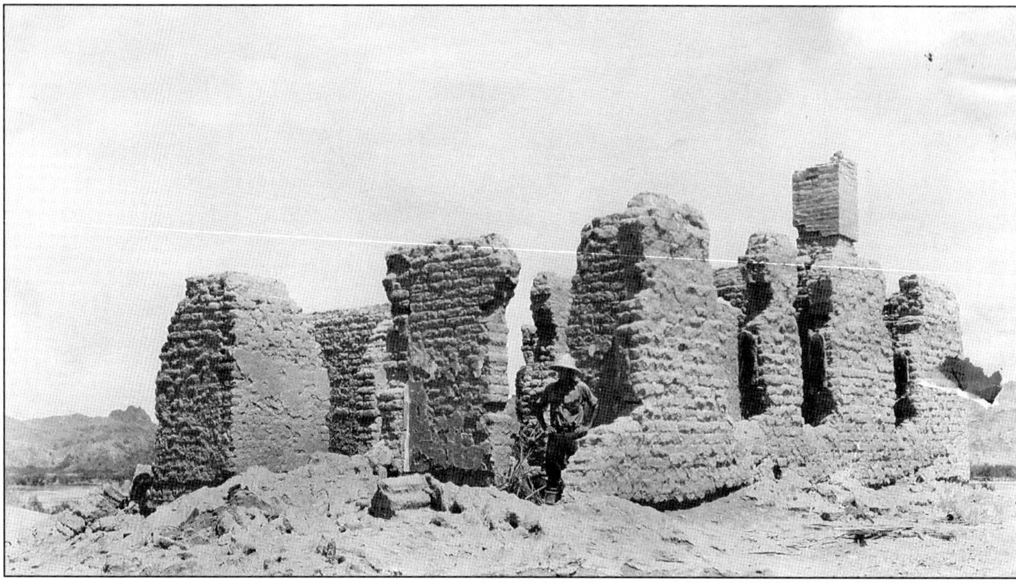

Because of its proximity to nearby mining operations, Aubrey Landing was considered an important shipping point. In 1864, the site was named to honor Francois Xavier Aubrey. Aubrey Landing, now under Lake Havasu, was located at the mouth of the Bill Williams River.

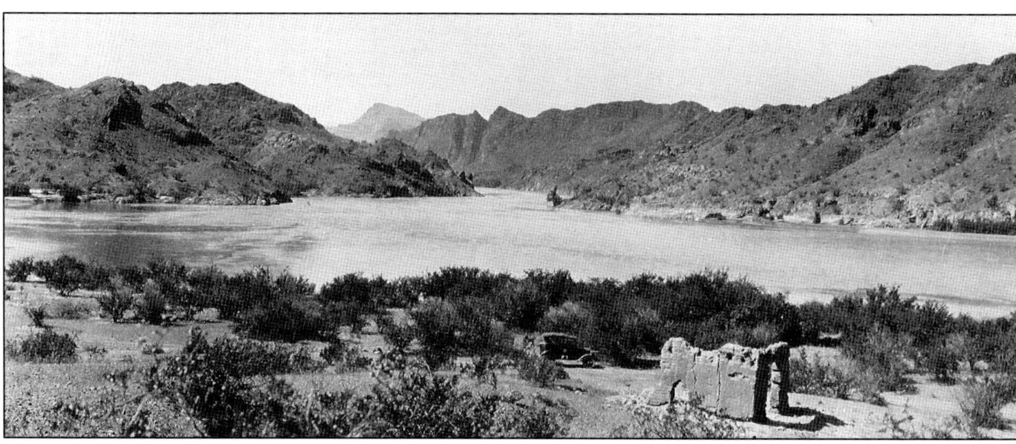

Aubrey Landing never did develop as a community. According to Will C. Barnes's *Arizona Place Names*, "By 1878, all that remained of Aubrey Landing [was] under one roof: the post office, saloon, and hotel. A ship's cabin had also been converted into a residence." By the 1920s, adobe remains could still be seen at the mouth of the Bill Williams River, an area providing a panoramic view of the future Parker Dam site.

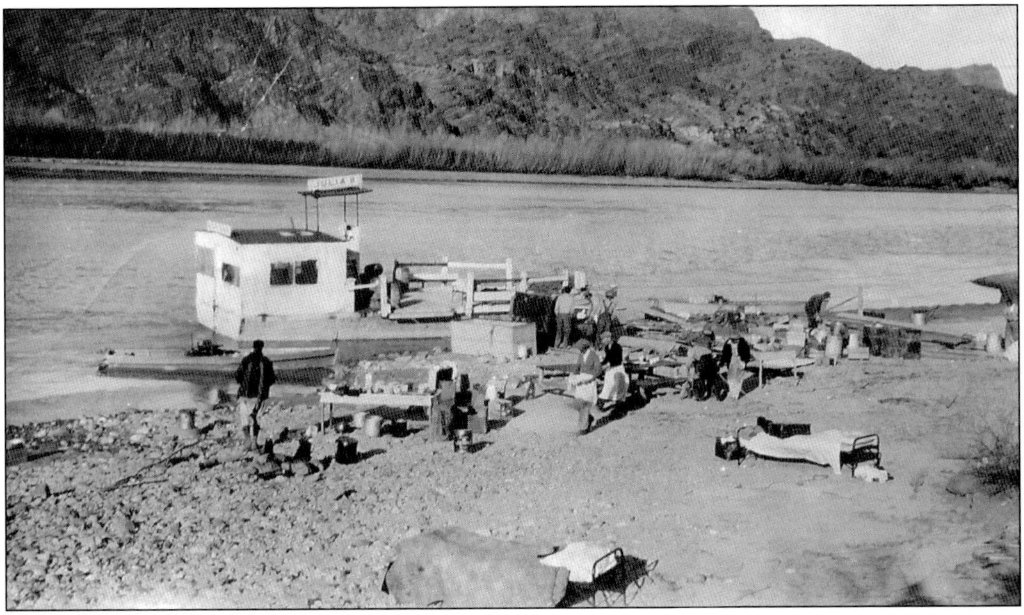

Aubrey Landing was located at the mouth of the Bill Williams River, where ferryboats similar to the *Julia B* could dock to transfer supplies or rest for the night under the stars.

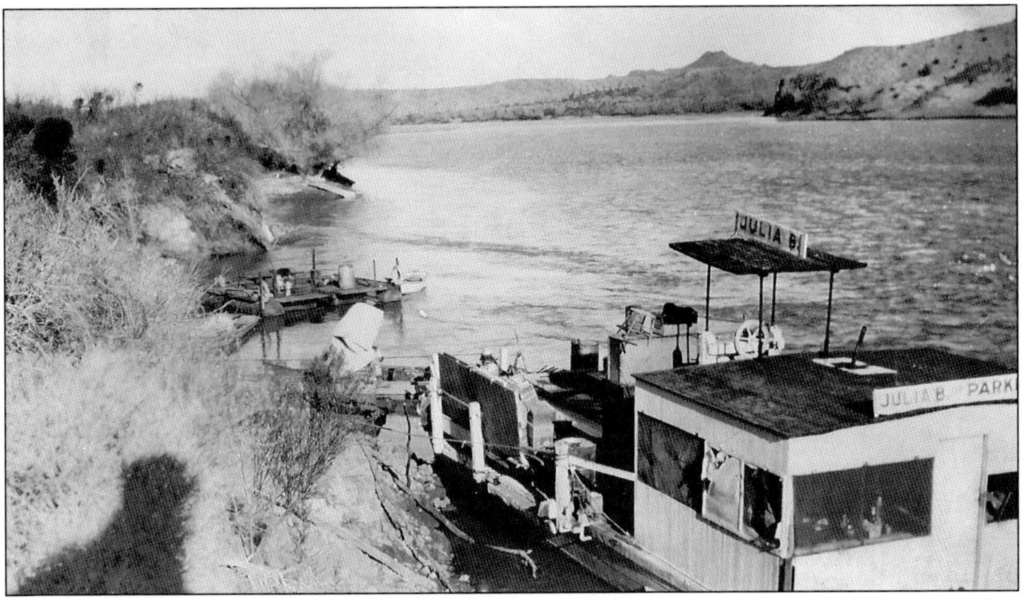

The *Julia B* would tie down at a number of landings along its route. These sites were somewhat predetermined by the location of the washes that ran directly into the river. Miners found the washes allowed for easier travel, especially when a wagon was loaded down with ore.

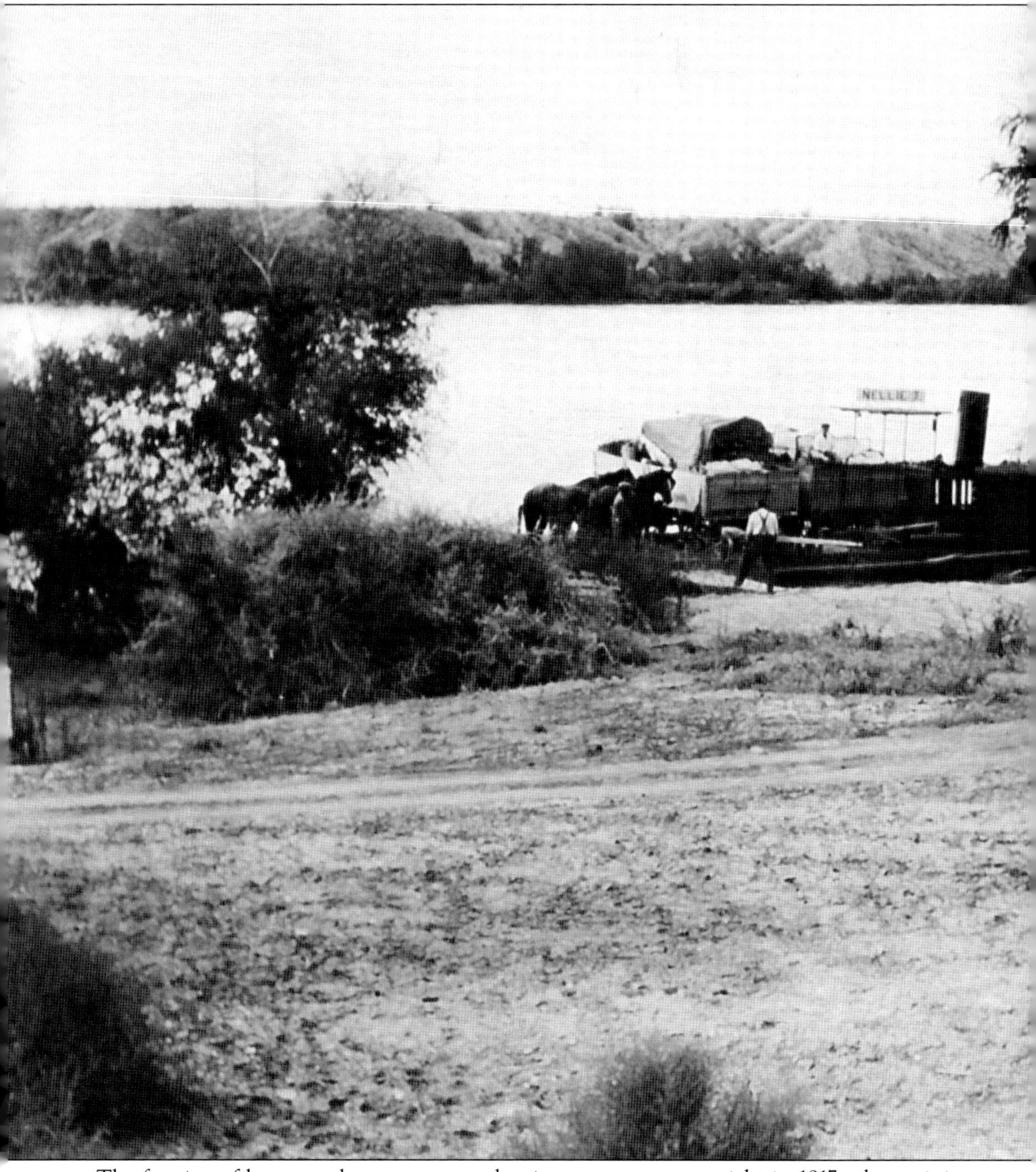

The ferrying of horses and wagons across the river was a common sight in 1917, when mining in the area was at its peak. Horses made travel much easier for prospectors, as the animals gave them the ability to look for ore at more distant locations. This ferry landing is situated not too

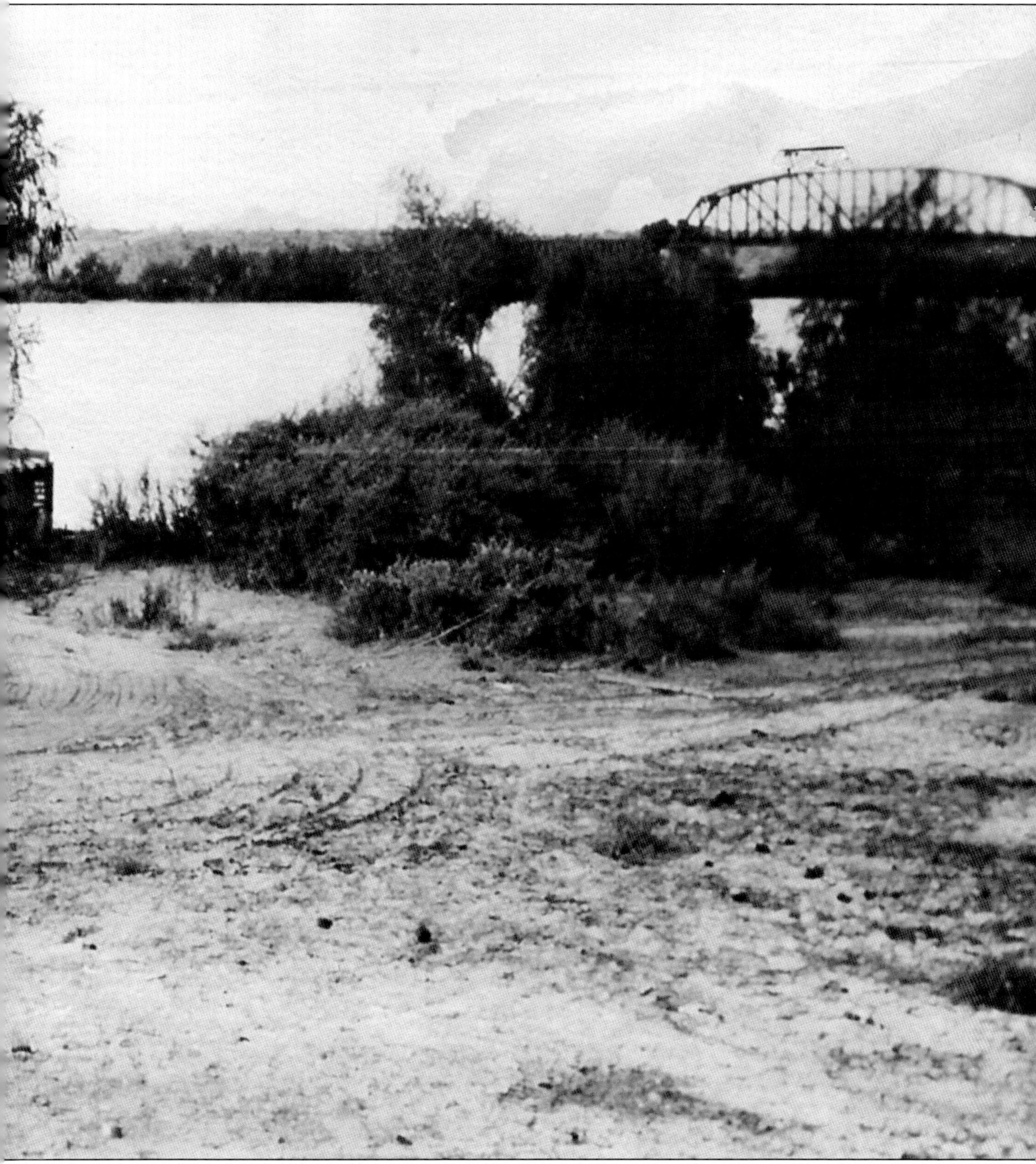

far from the Parker Train Bridge. Folklore tells of Wyatt Earp occasionally riding his horse across the train bridge rather than waiting for the first available ferry.

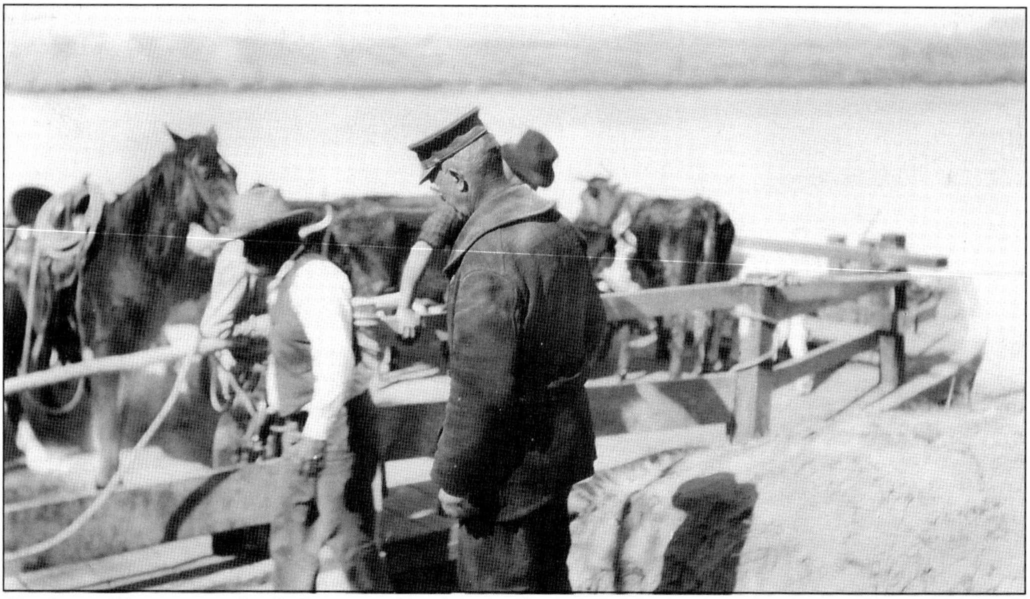

Cattle and horses are loaded onto a ferryboat, which provided a faster means of transportation for Parker-area ranchers in the early 1900s.

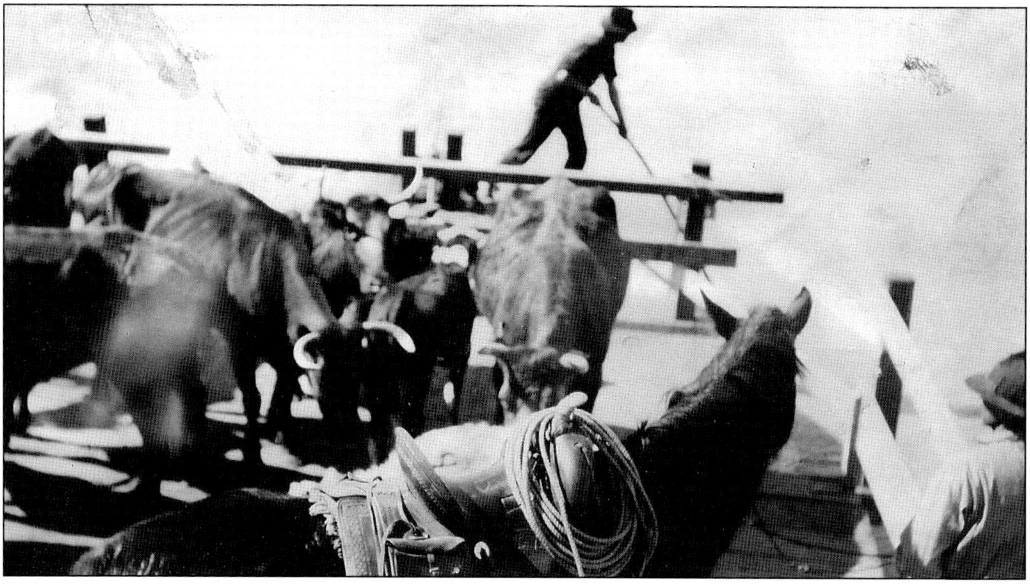

When the movement of the river was rough, ferrying cattle and horses occasionally presented some challenges. A number of ranches were located north of Parker along the riverbank, including the Graham family ranch, situated where the Moovalya Keys Development is today. Sharing a story, A. E. "Bud" Graham told of how when the river was low, ranchers had to make regular daily checks on their cattle. Riding their horses along the river's edge, ranchers looked for cattle that had become stuck in the deep mud silt. If these cattle were not lassoed and pulled to safe ground, buzzards would swoop down, tormenting them and then pecking out their eyes.

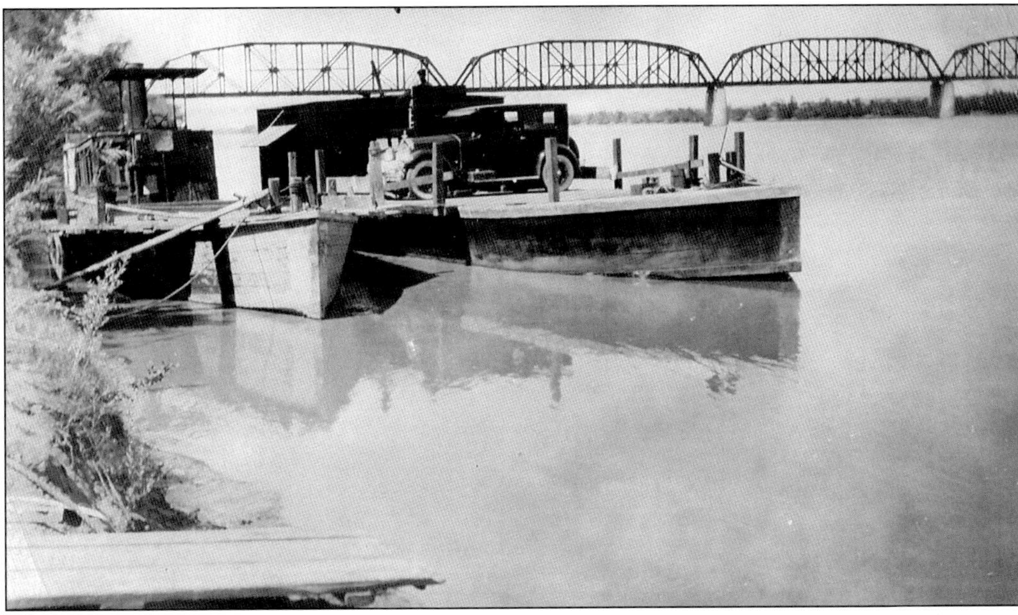

With the Parker Train Bridge as a backdrop, ferryboats are docked at one of Parker's landing sites. A car is transported on one of the ferryboats.

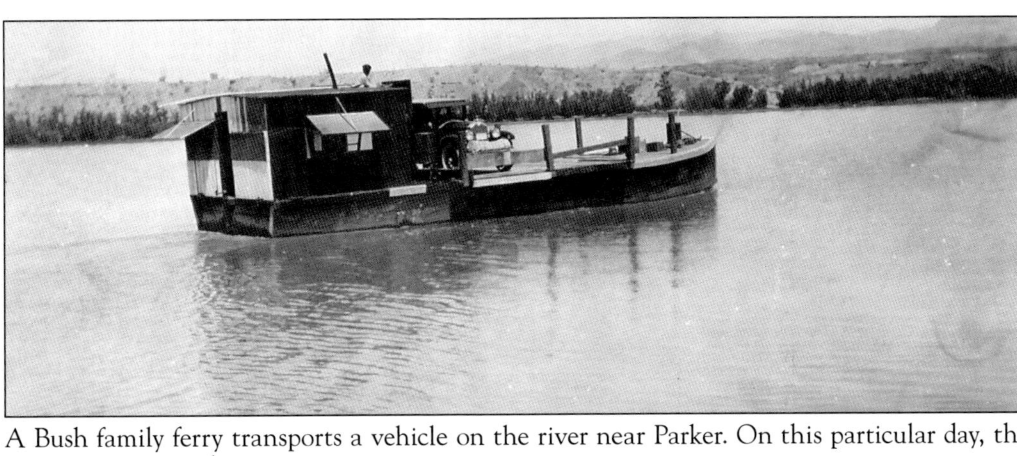

A Bush family ferry transports a vehicle on the river near Parker. On this particular day, the water was as smooth as ice.

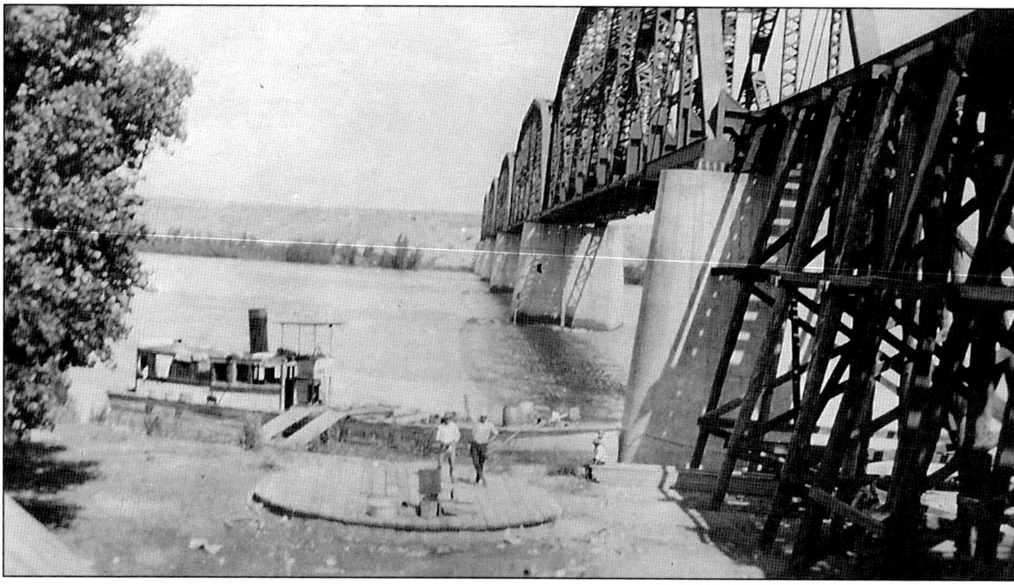

The *Nellie T* is seen at the base of the Parker Railroad Bridge in 1917, prepared to load wagons or vehicles, as evidenced by the loading ramps set in place.

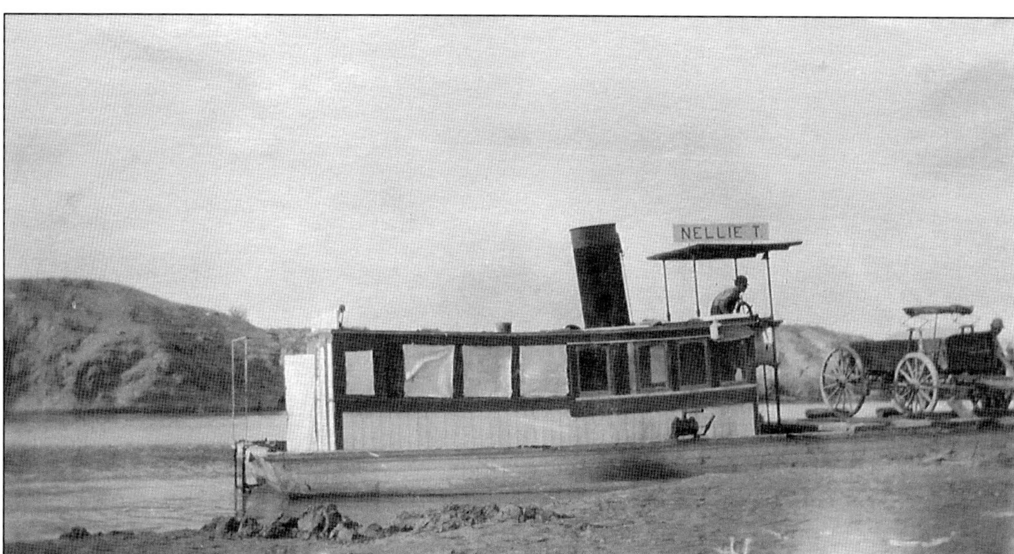

In 1917, the *Nellie T* ferries horses and wagons up the river.

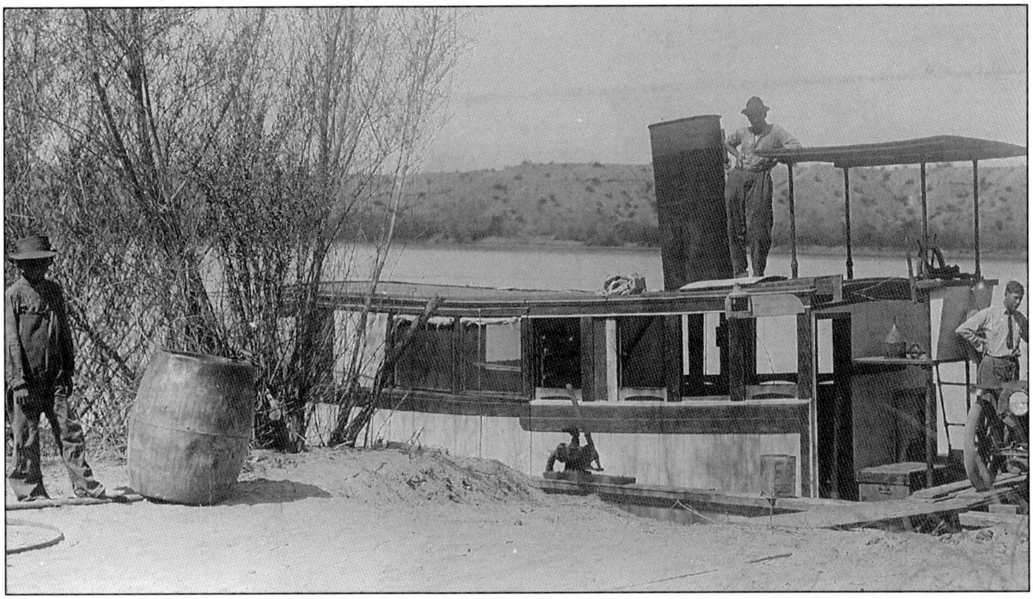

Workers experience a lull in activities prior to unloading the vehicle and disembarking from the ferry docked at the Parker landing site.

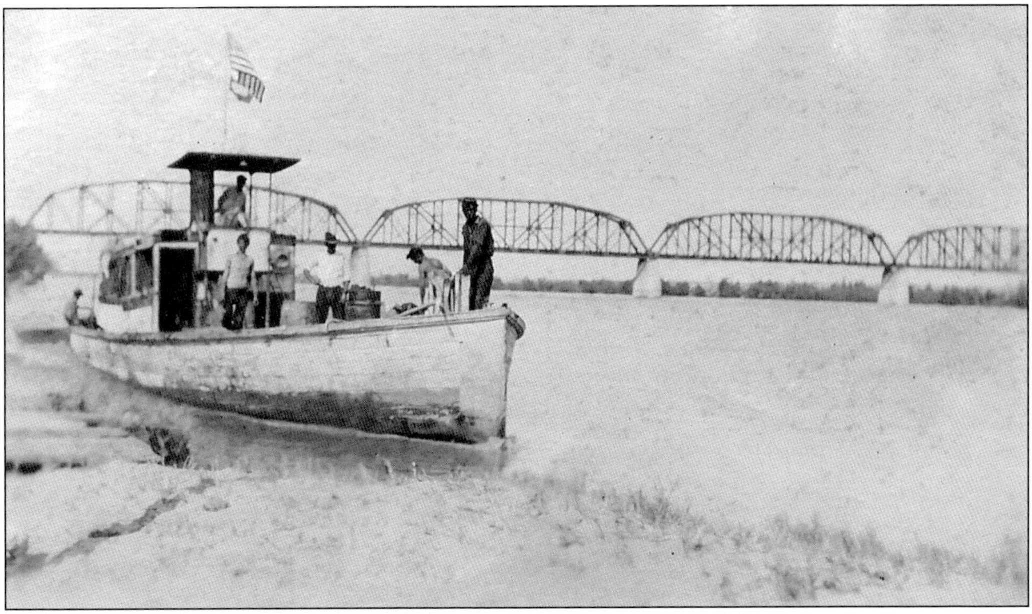

Flying the American flag, a fully loaded ferryboat pulls into one of the Parker landing sites.

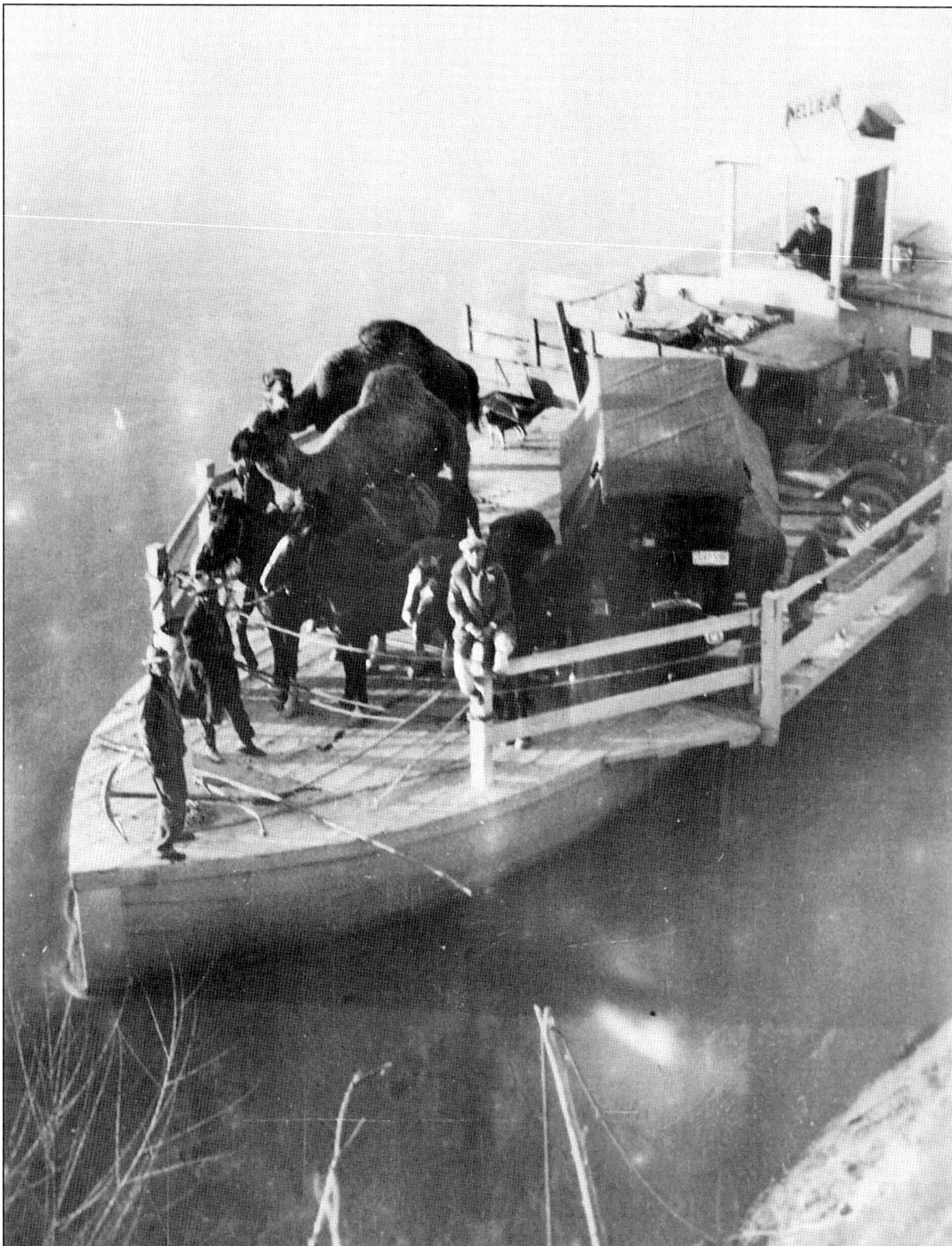

In 1924, the *Nellie Jo* was given a unique opportunity: ferrying camels used for a circus. Circus animals were also commonly transported across the country by train. Camels were not uncommon for the area, as they had been used by the U.S. military in the years 1857 to 1860 under the authority of Congress for Lt. E. F. Beale's expedition to locate road routes. The animals were well known for their stamina, ability to travel great distances without water, and strength for carrying heavy loads. Hadji Ali "Hi Jolly," who was Lieutenant Beale's camel driver during the expedition, is buried in the community of Quartzsite, Arizona, located in LaPaz County.

Jack and Nellie Hertwick, the young couple shown here, were married in Parker in 1933.

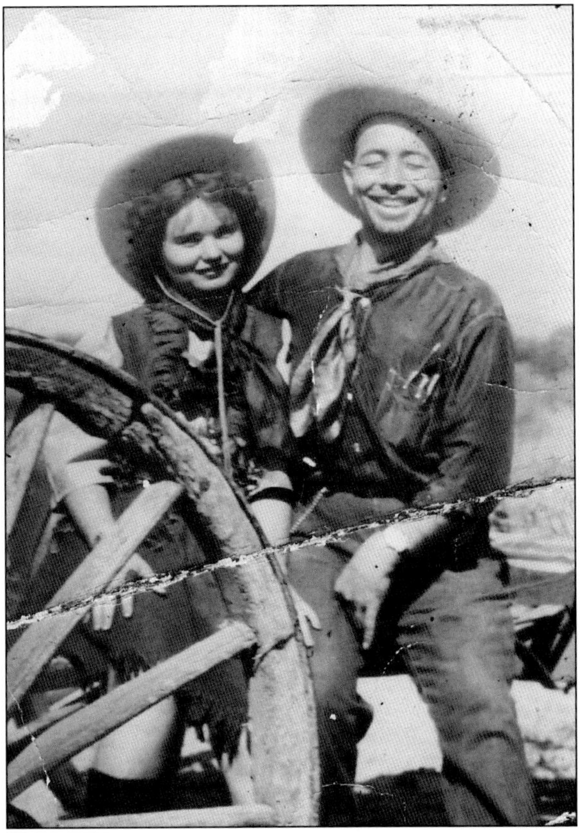

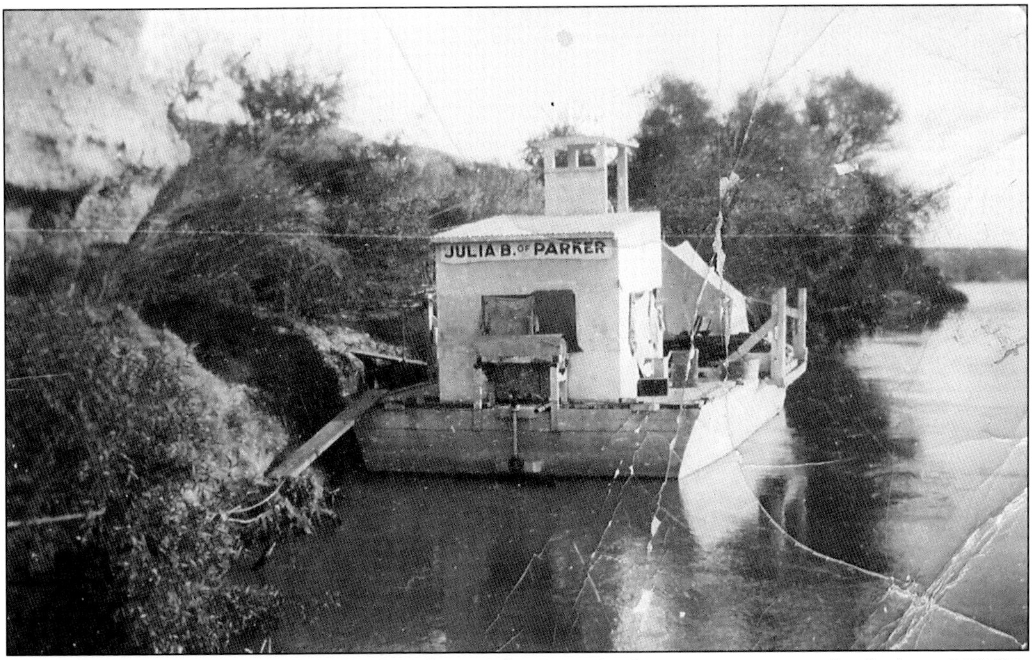

Joe and Nellie Bush provided the ferryboat *Julia B* as the honeymoon suite for Jack and Nellie Hertwick on their wedding day.

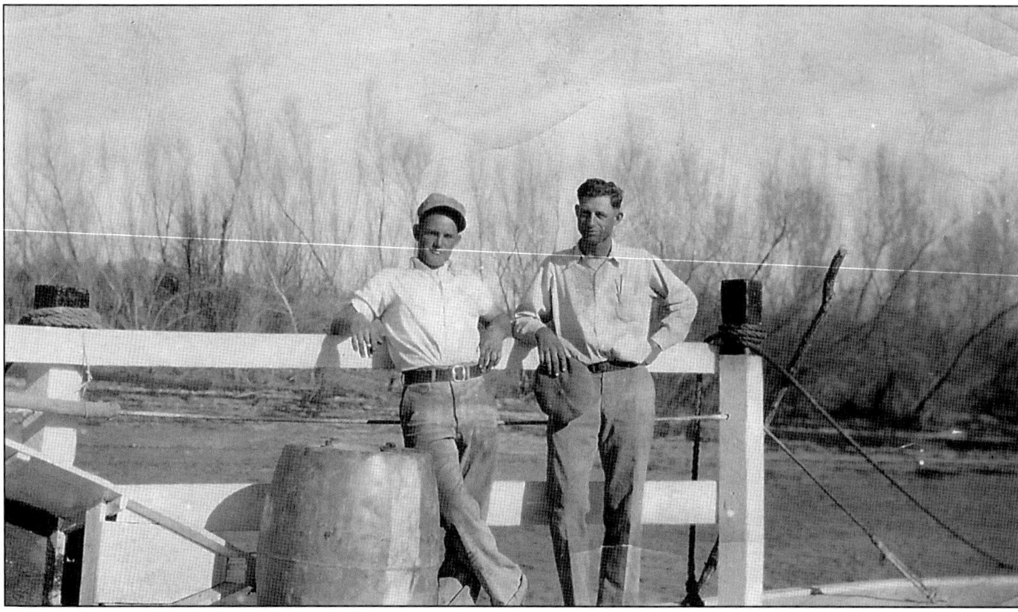

Mr. Walters (left) and Alfred Preston both worked on the Metropolitan Water District road survey crew during the late 1920s and early 1930s. Here the two are posing on a Bush ferryboat. Preston had previously worked for the Bushes as a ferryboat pilot.

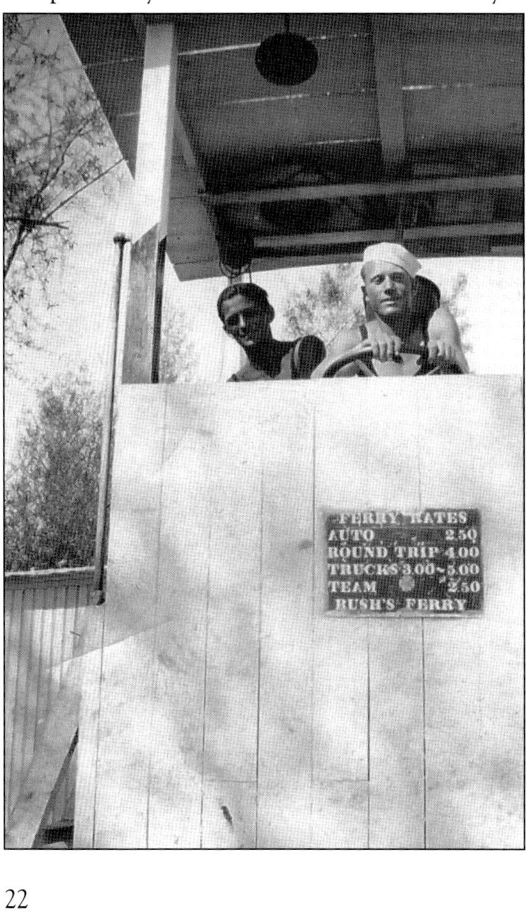

Gale Dean (left) and Tom Kinder are shown at the helm of a Bush ferryboat. The ferry rates are posted as "Auto 2.50—Round trip 4.00—Trucks 3.00 to 5.00—Team [of Horses] 2.50."

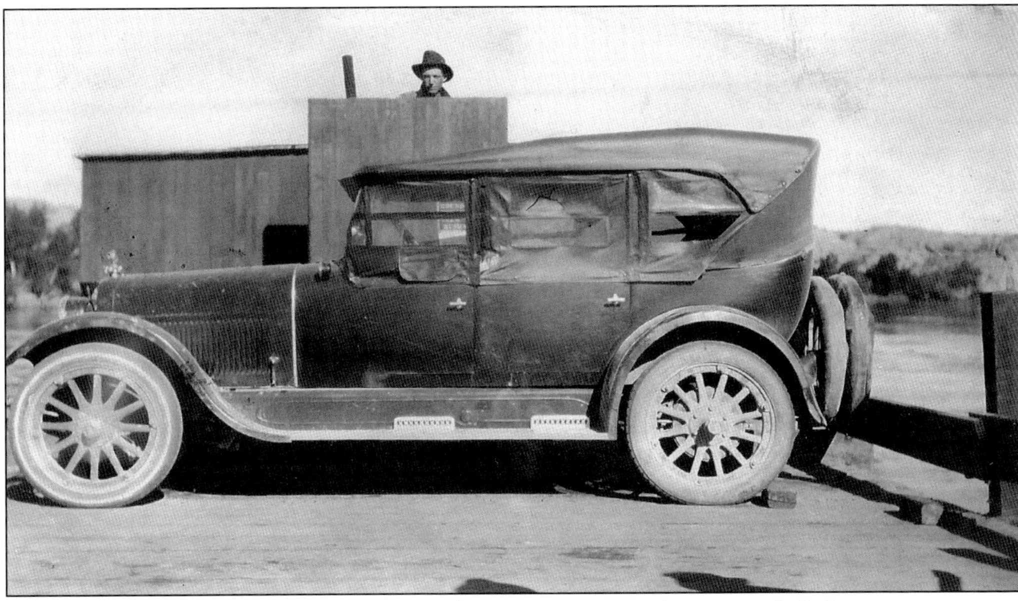
An unidentified pilot ferries a car across the river, a routine done on a daily basis.

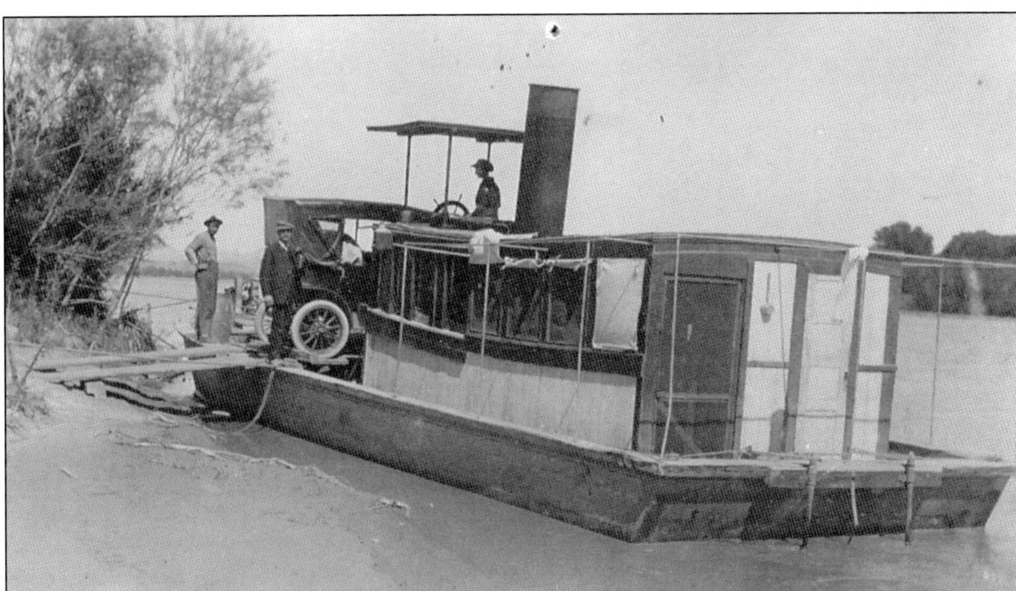
Nellie Bush stands at the helm as a vehicle is loaded onto the ferryboat—just another day of business for the Bush ferryboat fleet.

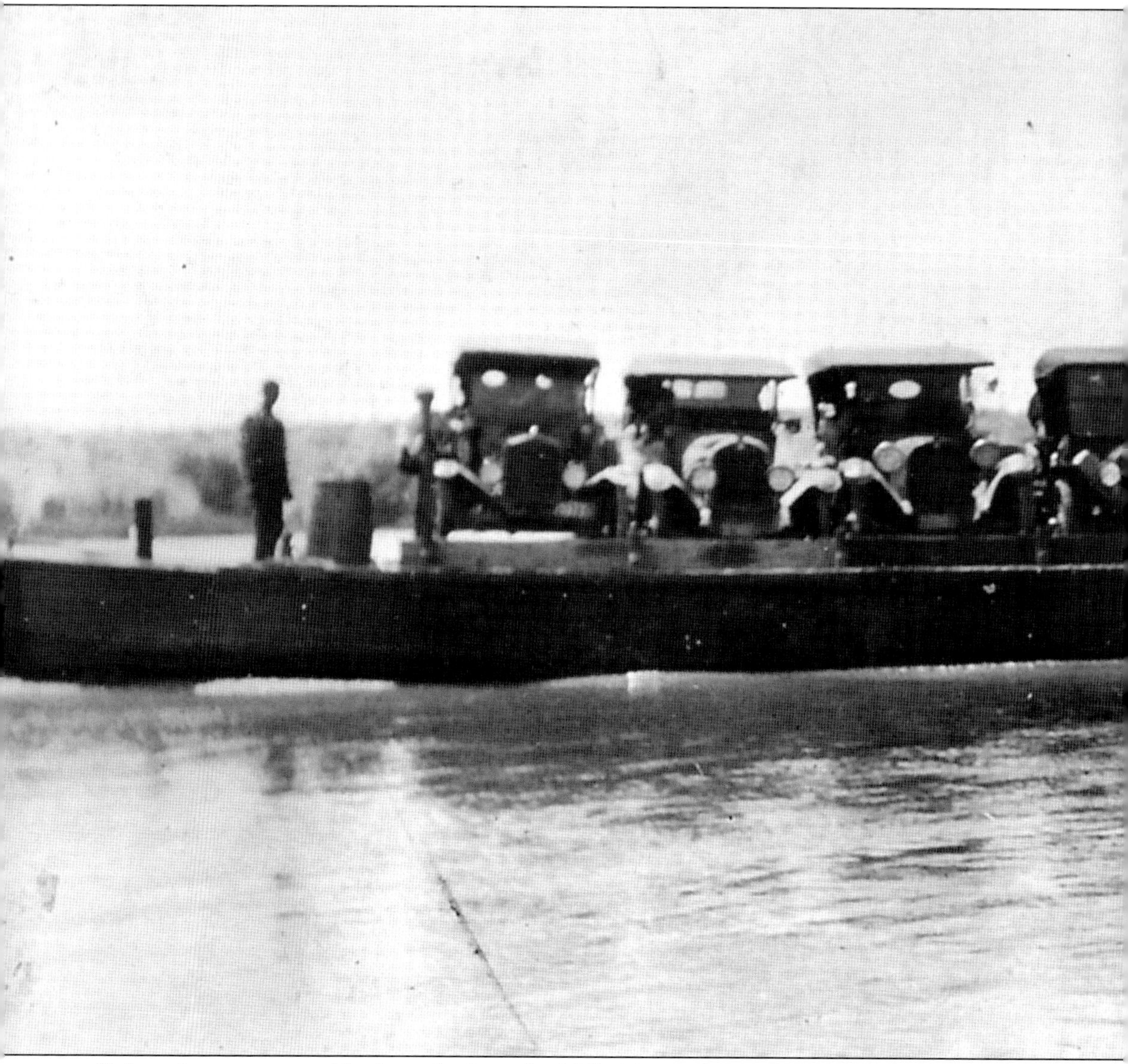

Before the pontoon and highway bridges, the *Nellie T* was almost the size of a barge, plying the river with a full load of automobiles. The Colorado River prior to the construction of the dams

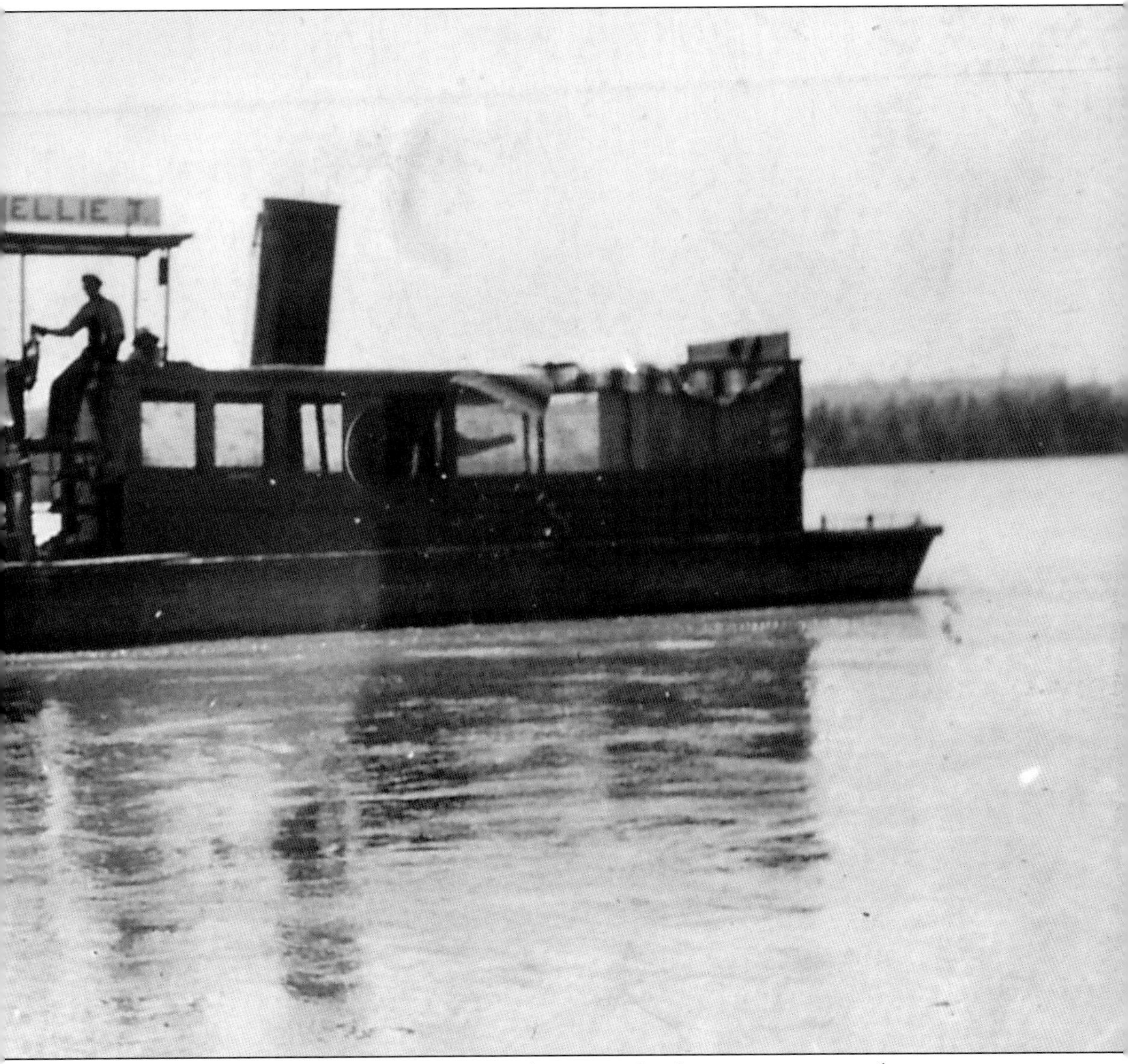

had a reputation for unpredictability, but on this particular day, it appears smooth.

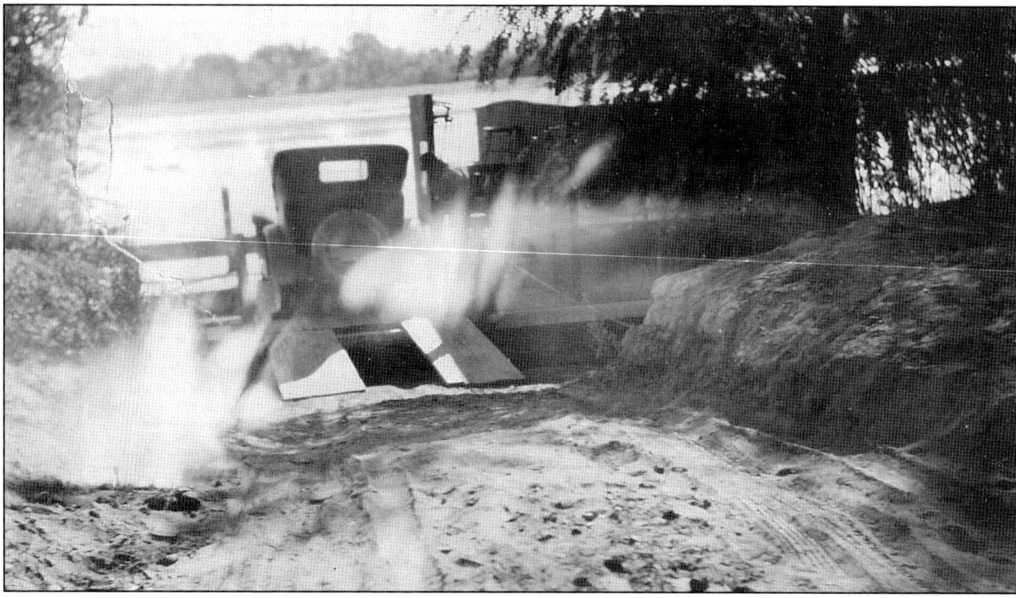

The sun shining through the sand dust creates an almost mystical appearance as a car is loaded onto a ferryboat for transport at the Parker landing site.

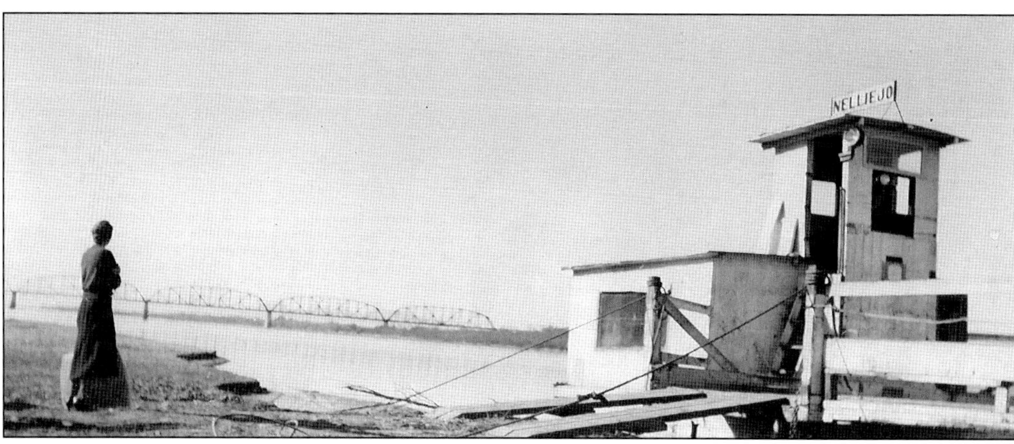

Joe Bush arrived in Parker on May 15, 1915. His wife, Nellie, arrived six months later. Nellie Bush learned an early lesson about the river when her beloved Joe did not return home the day of her arrival to Parker for the first time. The river could be unpredictable, so it was not unusual for Nellie to keep vigil while scanning the distance, waiting for Joe's return home.

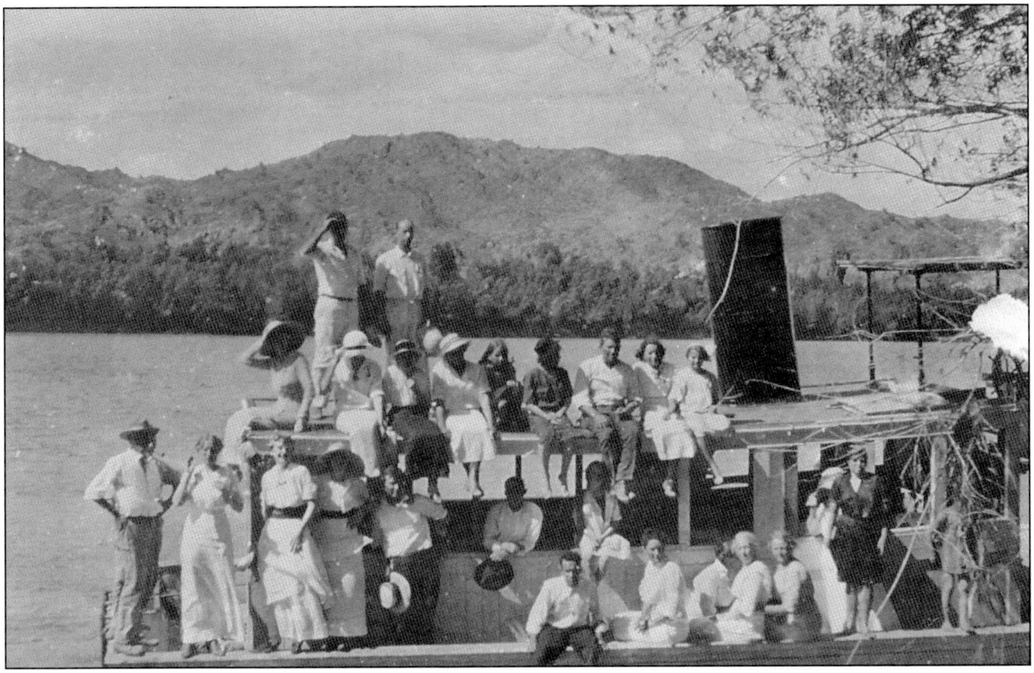

The Terry family and relatives pose as they board the ferry for a leisurely ride on the river.

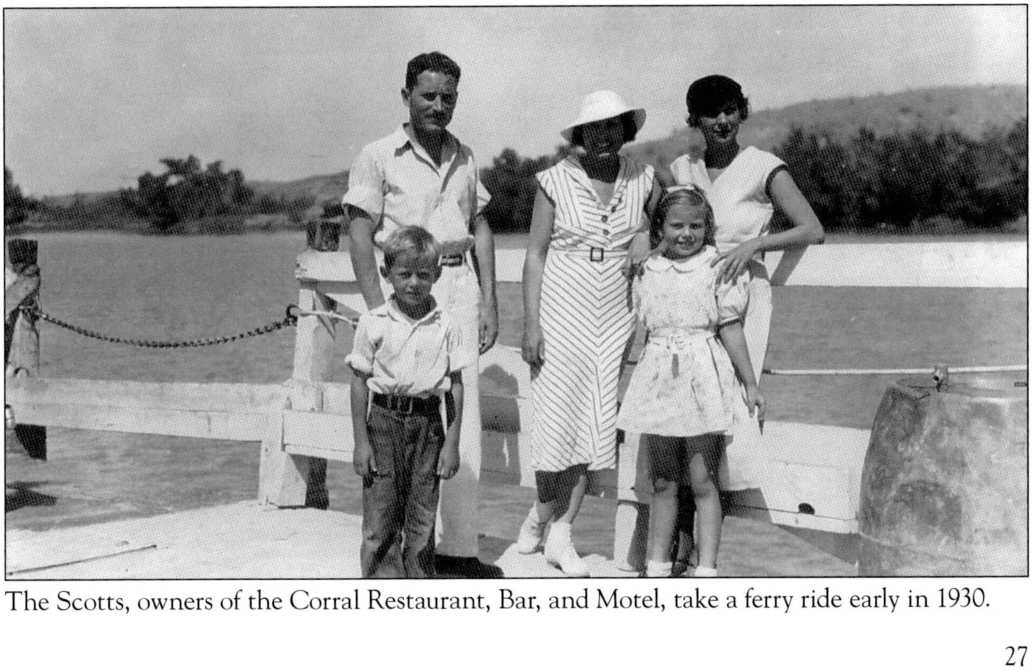

The Scotts, owners of the Corral Restaurant, Bar, and Motel, take a ferry ride early in 1930.

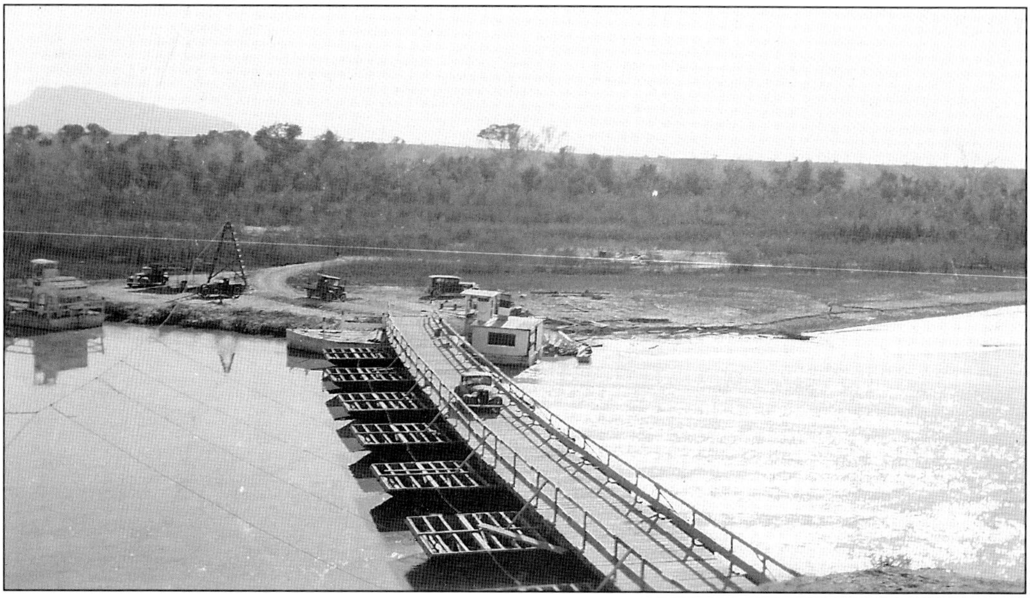

Joe and Nellie Bush ran their ferry service from May 1915 to 1937. In 1934, they constructed the pontoon bridge across the Colorado River and operated it until it was washed out by flooding in February 1937.

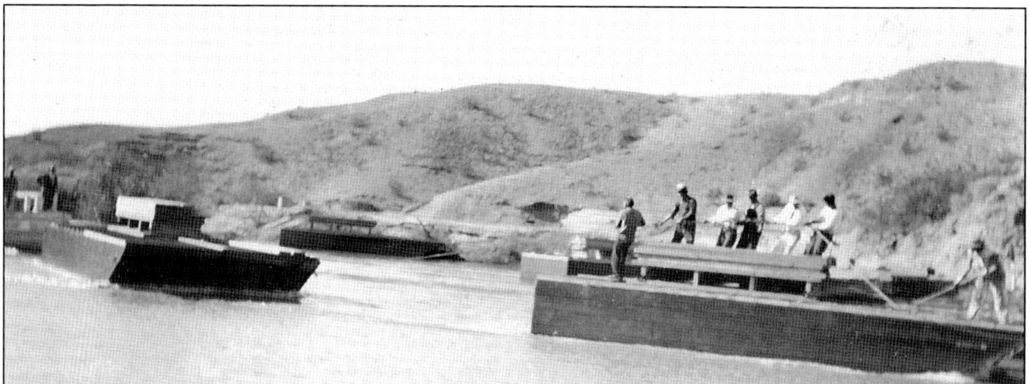

Work crews are moving pontoons into place for Bush's new pontoon bridge in 1934.

From left to right, A. C., Adam, and Marshall McVey take time to show the day's catch of carp following their fishing outing at the Lost Lake Slough in 1938.

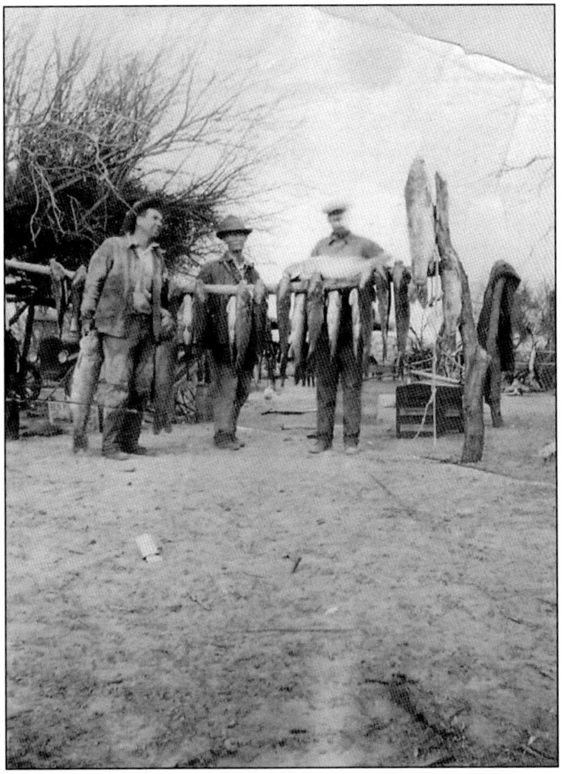

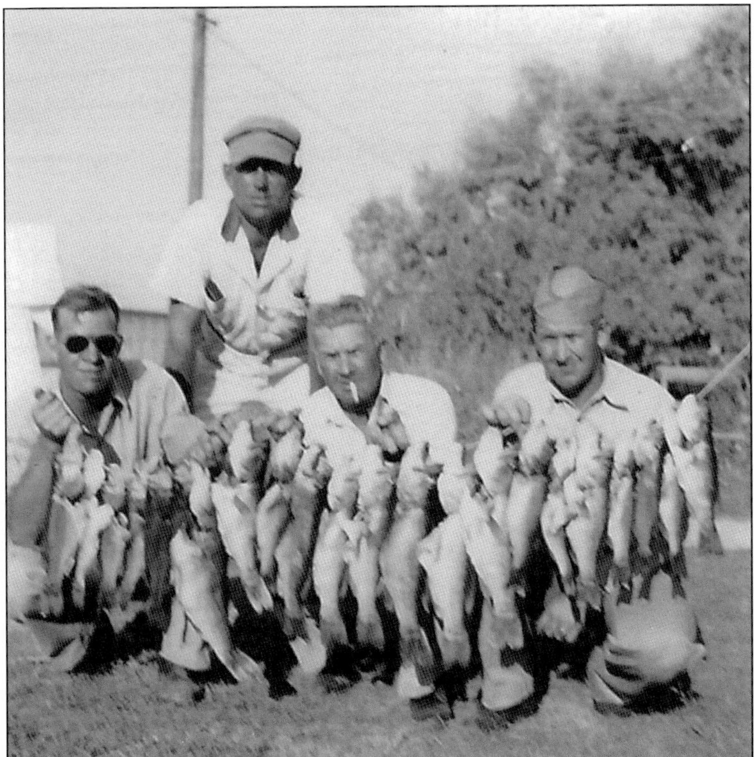

In this 1944 photograph, Johnny Johnson stands second from left with unidentified friends, showing the results of a good fishing day on the banks of the Colorado River.

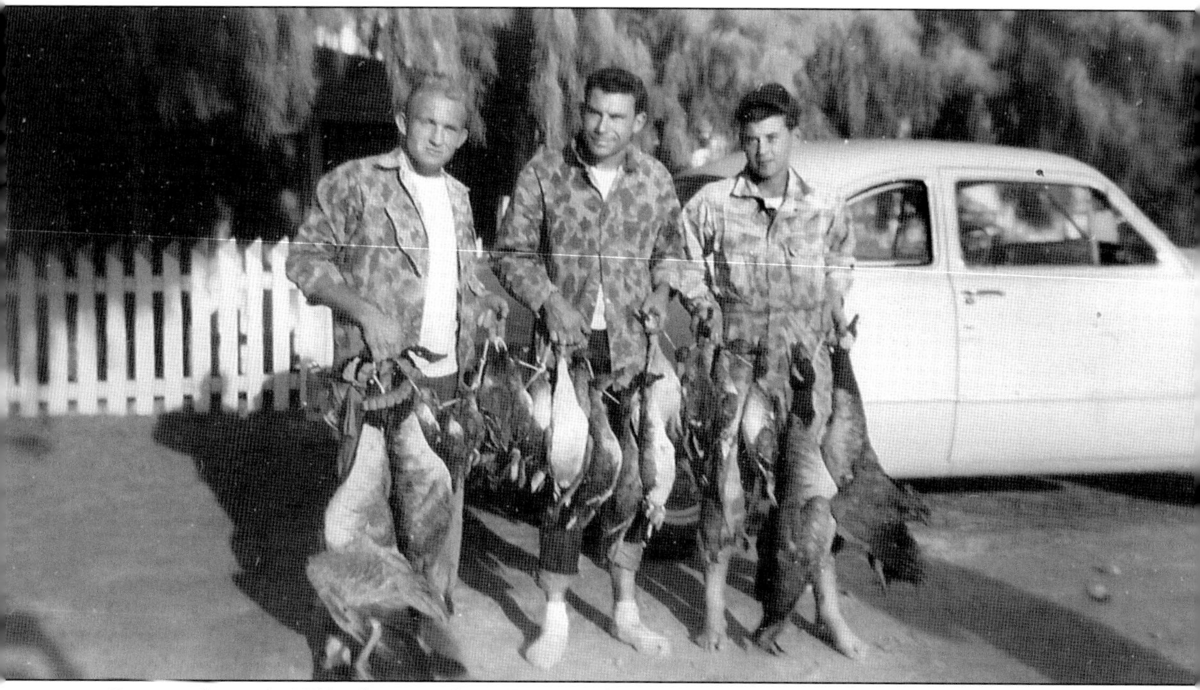

Seen in this early-1950s photograph are Raymond Patrick (left), Bobby Joe Gnau (center), and George Hendrix following a successful duck and geese hunt along the banks of the Colorado River.

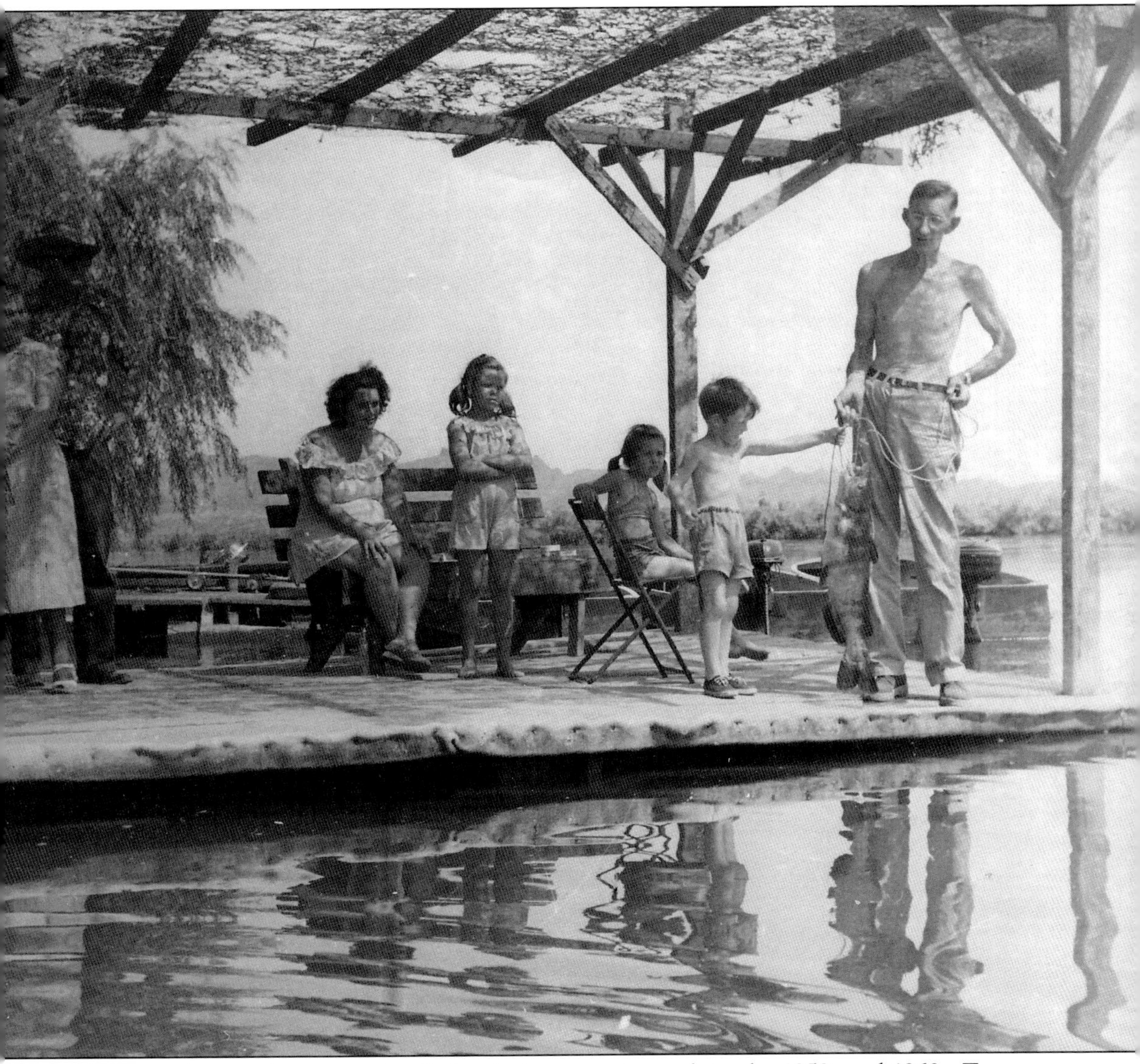

Fishing in the area known as the Parker Strip was at its peak in the 1950s and 1960s. Tommy Kinder's Camp, located on the California side of the river, was one of many campgrounds where good fishing was to be expected.

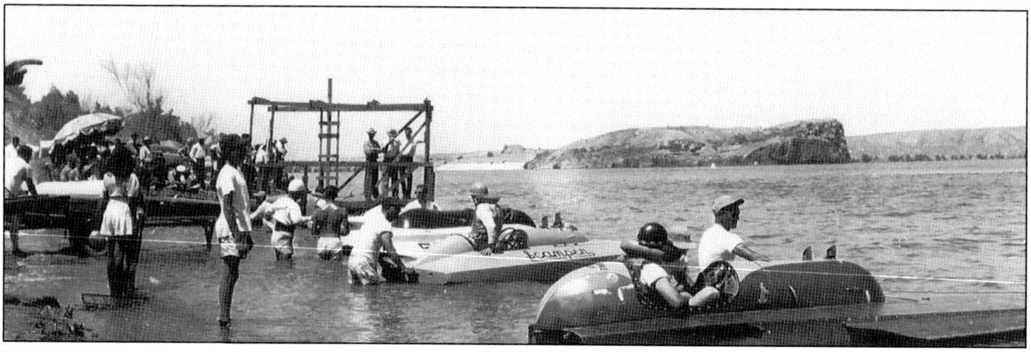

In 1948, several years prior to the clearing and development of the beachfront for Enduro racing, the first May Regatta was held in a small area with a natural clearing.

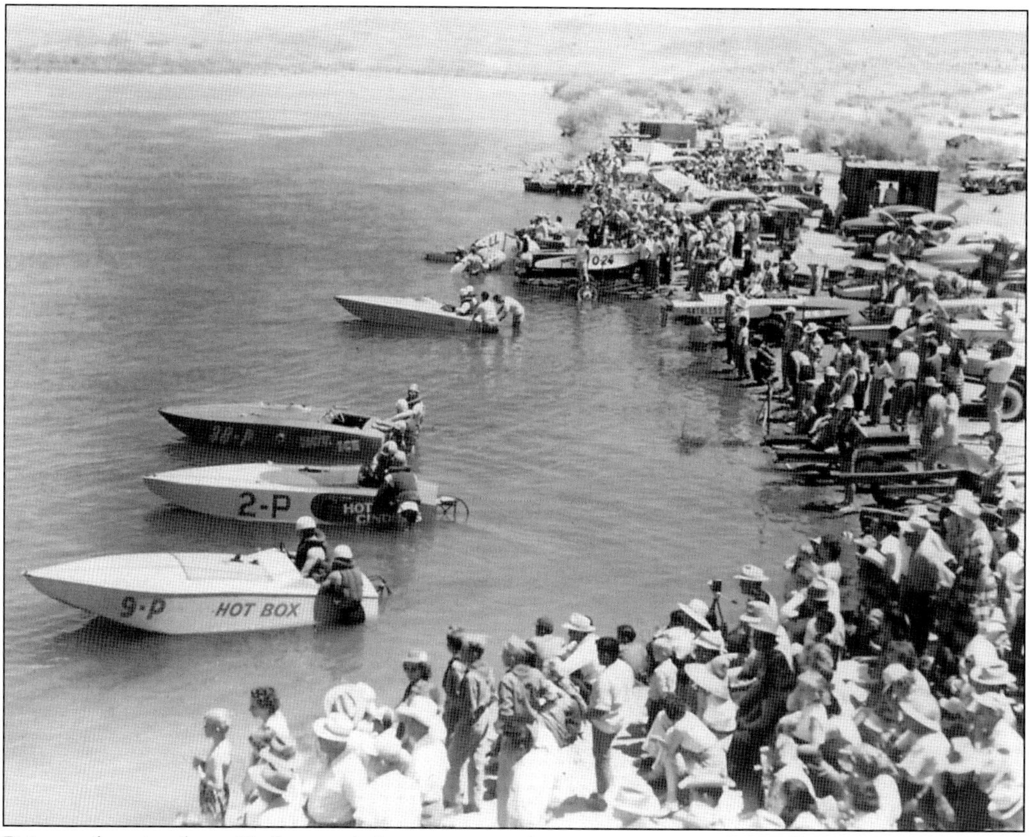

Prior to the nine-hour Enduro-style boat races, earlier races were much smaller in scale—in terms of both participants and spectators.

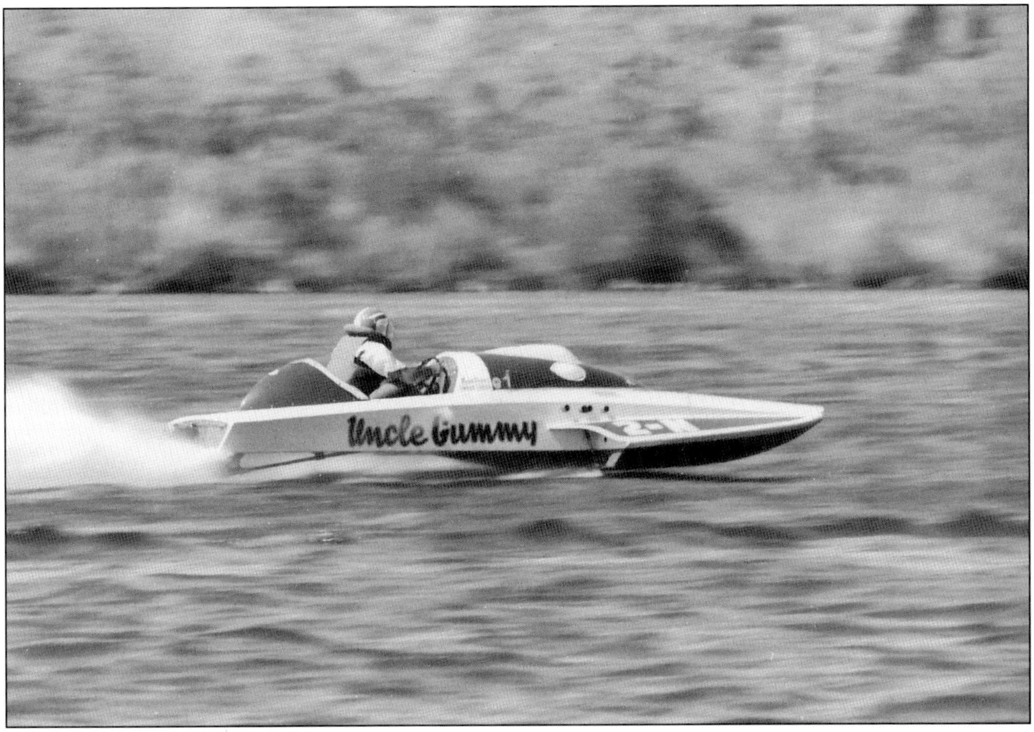

In the early 1960s, Marion Beaver races *Uncle Gummy* on the Colorado River. Beaver was a member of the Southern California Speed Boat Club (SCSC), the American Power Boat Association (APBA), and the Parker Boat and Ski Club. His vision was realized when boat racing became a common event in Parker, bolstering the economic benefits brought about by increased tourism.

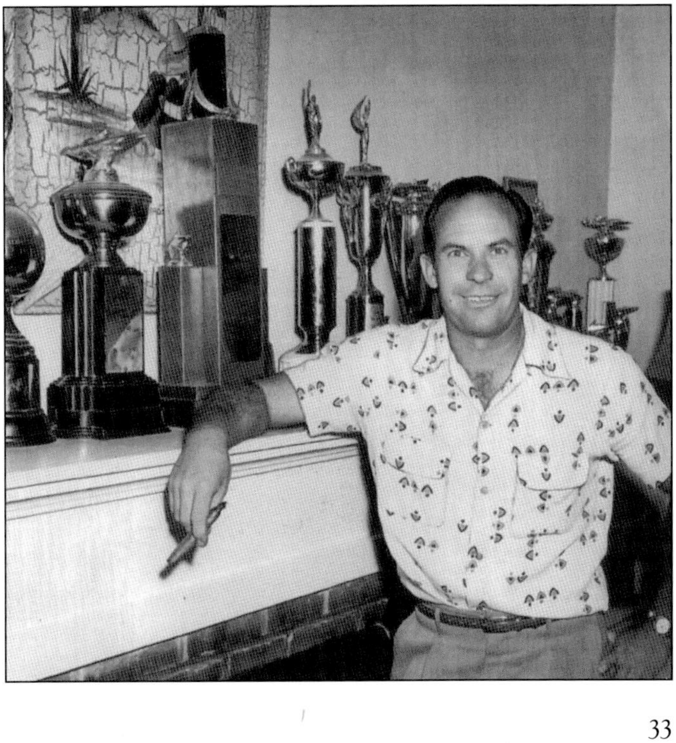

Marion Beaver stands in the trophy room showcasing his many boat-racing accomplishments, including Pacific One Design Hydroplane (PODH) National Champion in 1952–1958; PODH National High Points in 1953, 1954, and 1956; E Boat National Champion in 1955; 225 Hydroplane National Champion in 1959, 1960, and 1962–1964; 225 Hydroplane National High Points in 1959; and eight world speed records. His PODH records stand today. Beaver belonged to the GULF 100 MPH Club and was inducted into the GULF Marine Racing Hall of Fame in 1965. He was also placed on the APBA Honor Squadron in 1968.

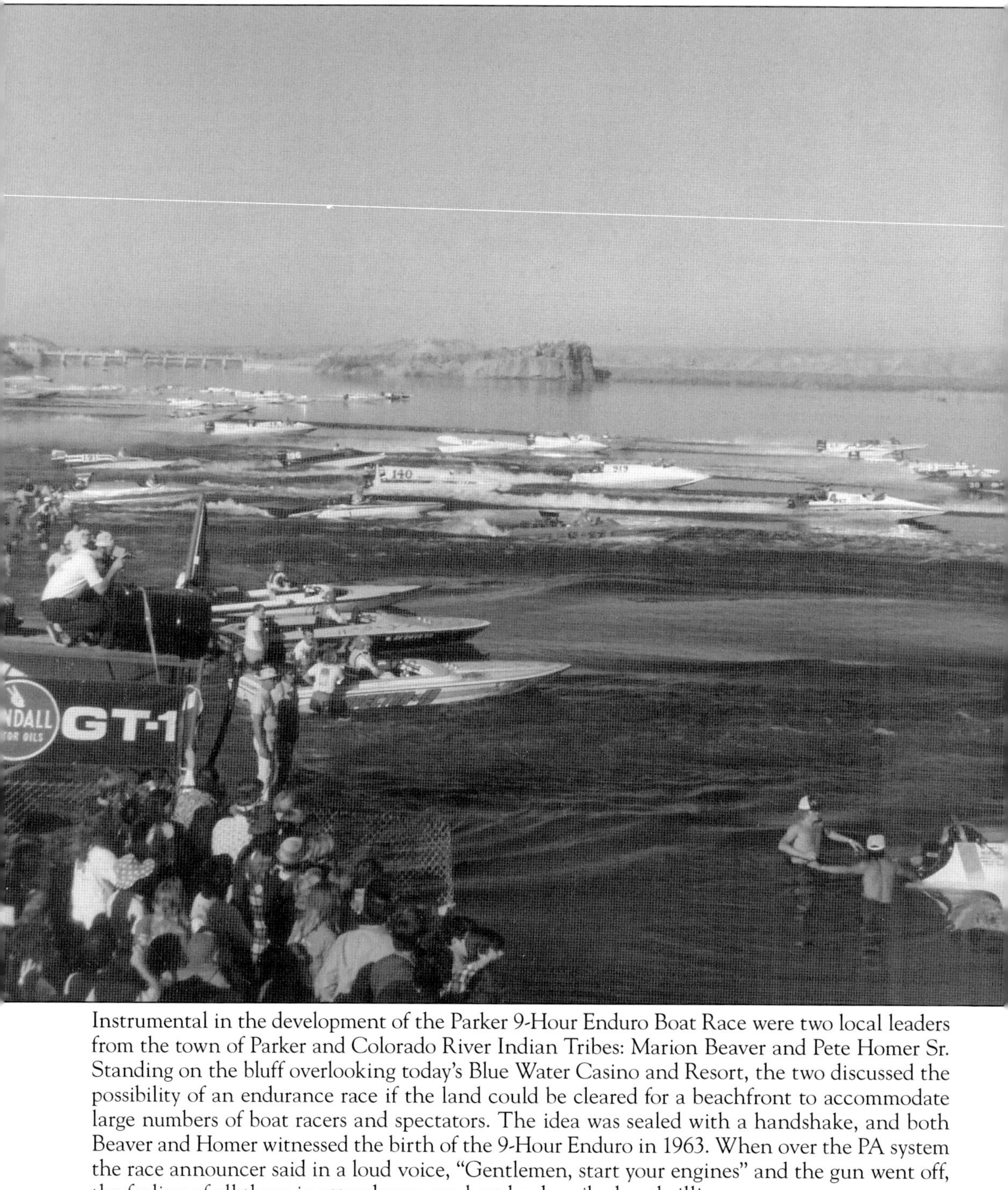

Instrumental in the development of the Parker 9-Hour Enduro Boat Race were two local leaders from the town of Parker and Colorado River Indian Tribes: Marion Beaver and Pete Homer Sr. Standing on the bluff overlooking today's Blue Water Casino and Resort, the two discussed the possibility of an endurance race if the land could be cleared for a beachfront to accommodate large numbers of boat racers and spectators. The idea was sealed with a handshake, and both Beaver and Homer witnessed the birth of the 9-Hour Enduro in 1963. When over the PA system the race announcer said in a loud voice, "Gentlemen, start your engines" and the gun went off, the feeling of all those in attendance can best be described as thrilling.

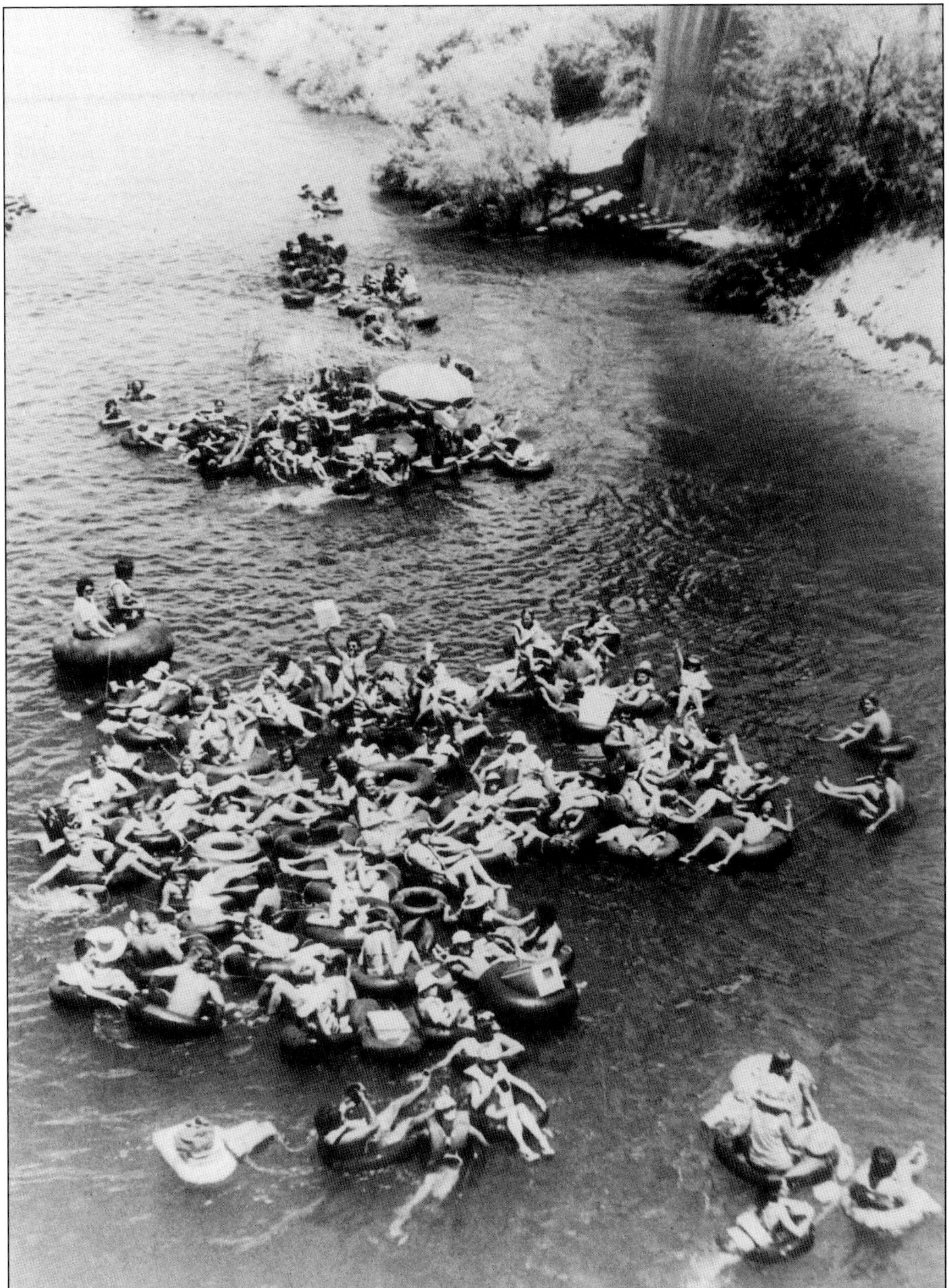

The first inner-tube float was organized by the Parker Area Chamber of Commerce in the early 1970s. Some of the best ideas are drafted on a paper napkin. It is unknown if this was how the event was developed, but one thing is for sure: the inner-tube float was a great idea however it was conceived.

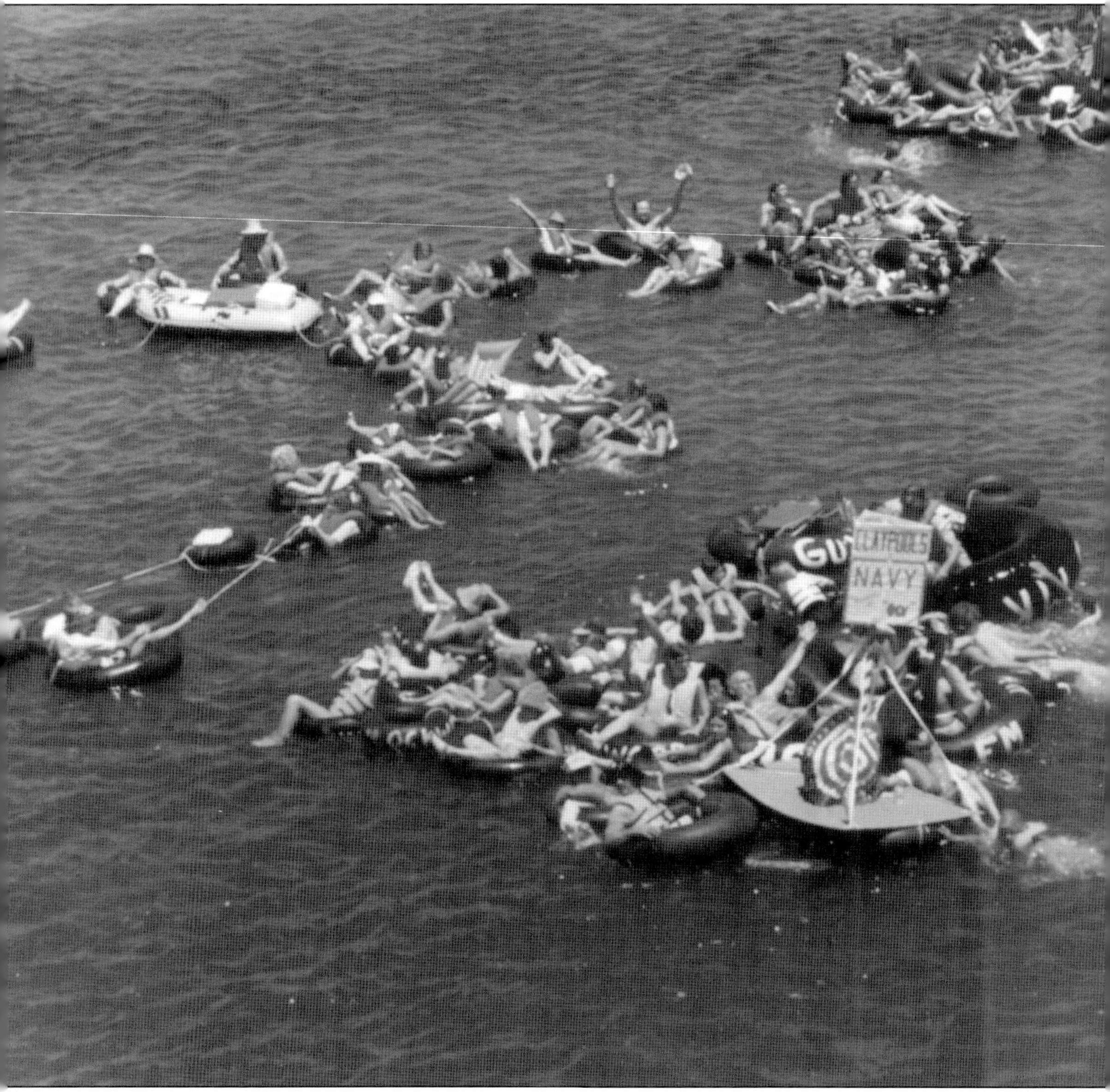

Mostly local folks entered the early-1970s inner-tube floats. Managed by Wally Davis, Claypool's Market entered its employees under the name "Claypool's Navy."

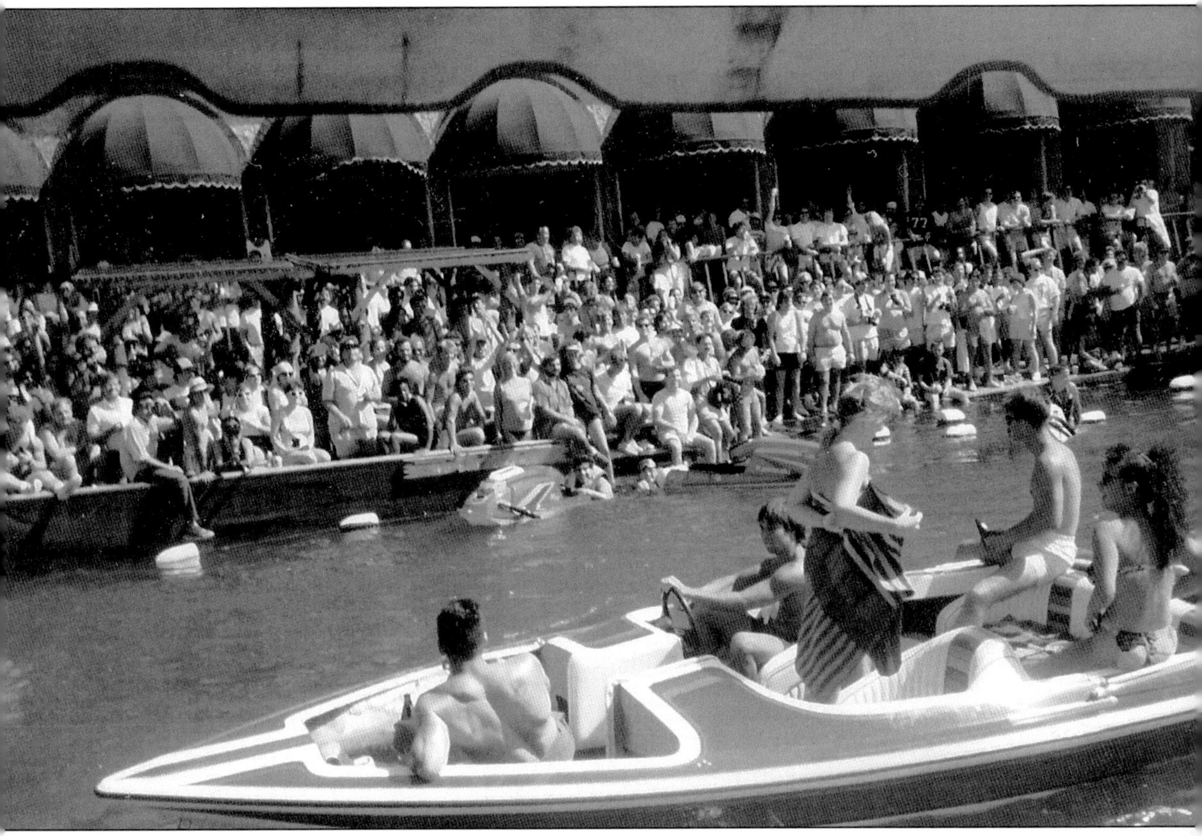

For more than 30 years beginning in the 1970s, "getting crazy" at Sundance on the river was a regular event. It was tough work for the sheriff's boat patrol to manage a bunch of women flashing the crowds standing on the dock. If flashing was not enough, then the wet T-shirt contest was a must. When Sundance closed, a piece of Parker's more interesting history went with it.

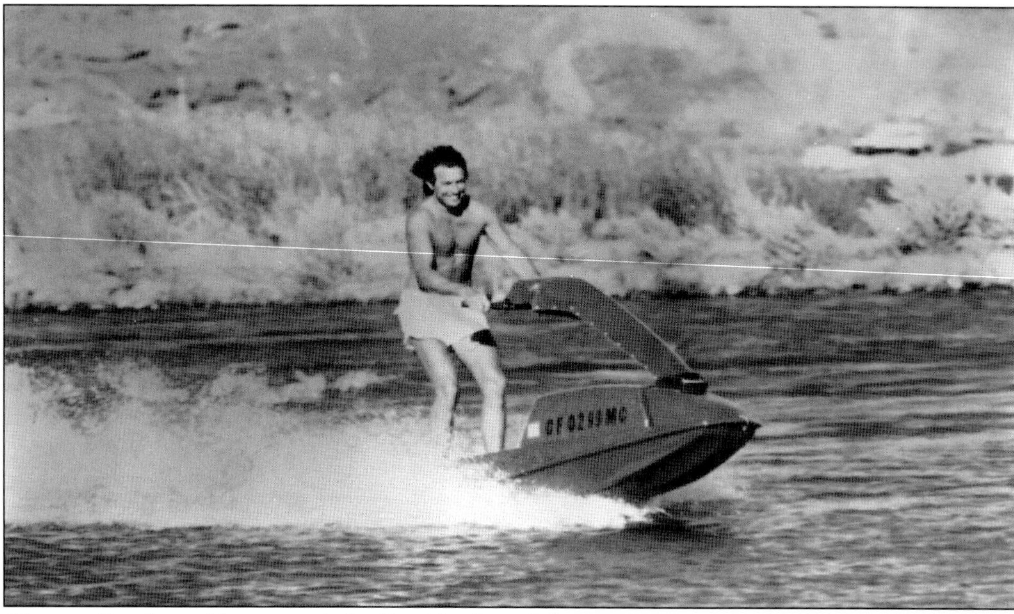

Clayton Jacobson II invented the Jet Ski. In a July 2006 *Boating Business* article written by John Heselwood, Jacobson stated, "I used to race and build motorcycles and was a member of the Matchless Racing Team back in the late 1950's and early 1960's. After a day of taking a few spills I said to my buddy, there has to be a better way than this." Testing and adjustments for this invention were performed by Jacobson on the Parker Strip portion of the Colorado River. In 1971, Jacobson sold his patent and prototype to Kawasaki.

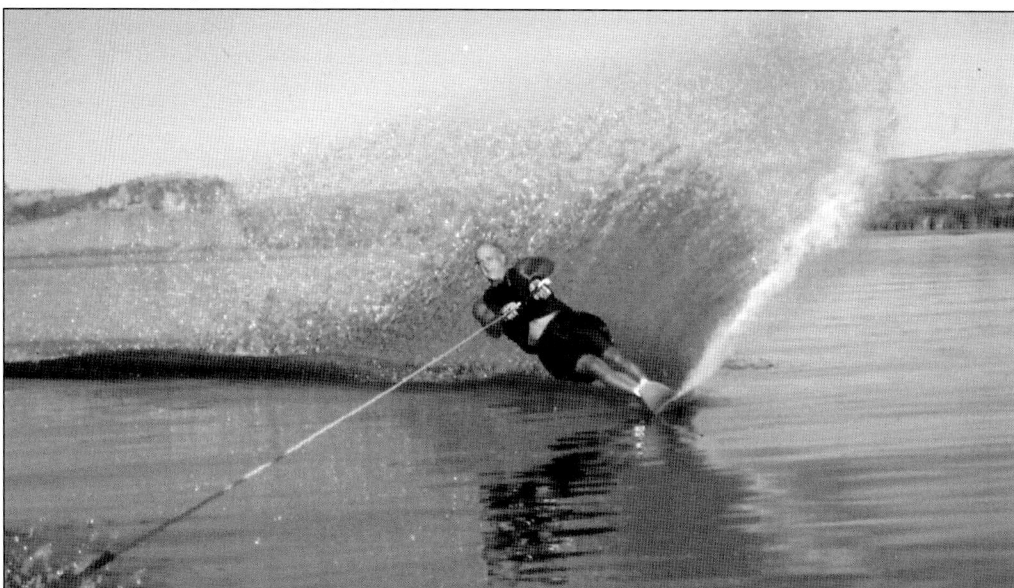

After learning to ski at 11 years old, Mike Mack moved to the river in 1977. Mack has taught people from all over the world to water-ski and worked with several magazines to promote the Parker area. The six-time world champion in hydrofoil has been sponsored by Body Glove, served as team rider for Quicksilver, and received a 1989 award from the Arizona Special Olympics for his 14 years as a water-ski instructor for handicapped children.

Two

Next Stop
Now Entering Parker

The 1800s were a time of significant westward expansion for the federal government. By the 1850s, five major surveys had been completed in the search for suitable routes to finish the transcontinental railroad. In 1875 and again in 1899, Congress granted railroads the right-of-way through public lands and Native American reservations. Nearing the end of the 19th century, the rail lines were all but finished.

According to Donald Duke in *Santa Fe: The Railroad Gateway to the American West*, "Edward Ripley, president of the Santa Fe, Prescott, and Phoenix Railroad, believed there was significant amount of traffic to justify the building of a cutoff between Los Angeles and Phoenix. Ripley sent surveyors out into the field to locate an appropriate route between Cadiz and Phoenix for a bypass. The route showing the most promise (because of the lack of mountain grades) included one costly portion spanning a bridge across the Colorado River at Parker. The opening of the Phoenix-California cutoff not only completed Santa Fe's basic system, but gave the road a strong strategic position in the Southwest. On July 1, 1910, the first freight train made use of the completed bypass with the last of passenger service being discontinued in the spring of 1953."

By March 1908, having already been granted right-of-way, the Arizona and California Railway Company was granted additional land for station grounds and terminal facilities. In less than two months, Congress authorized the town site of Parker to be reserved and set apart. The federal government intended the town site as housing for employees of the railroad company, which had already begun using the location as a division point. By 1918, funds arising from the sale of town lots were needed for the continued construction of a pumping plant and irrigation project on the reservation.

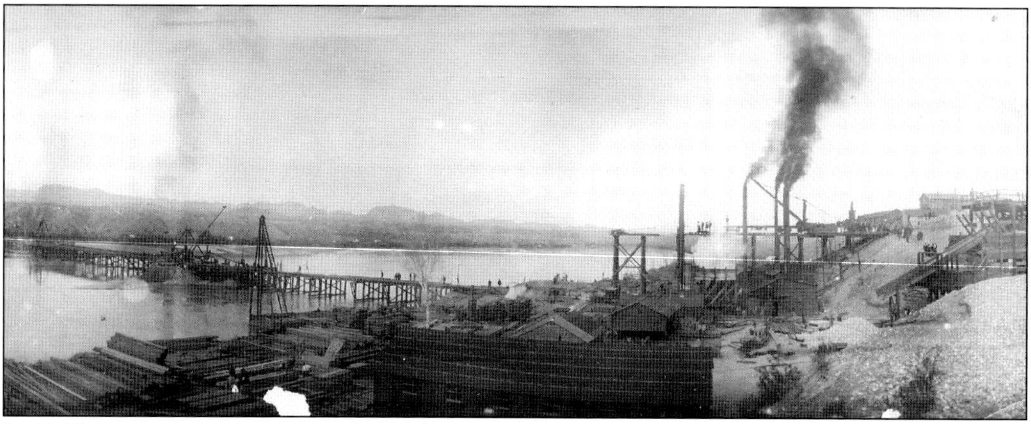

In 1907, construction began on the Parker Train Bridge, which was labeled "the Million Dollar Bridge." The dedication of the completed Colorado River span occurred on July 10, 1910.

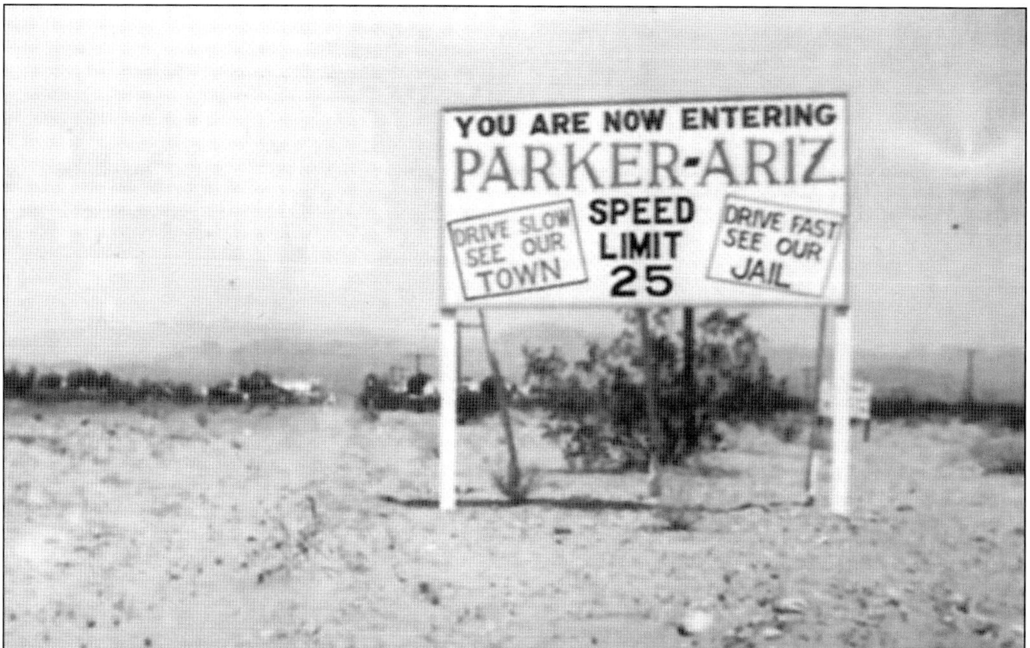

There is a bit of humor to be seen in this 1930s speed-limit sign posted at the entrance to Parker. Did cars or runaway horses actually go 25 miles per hour?

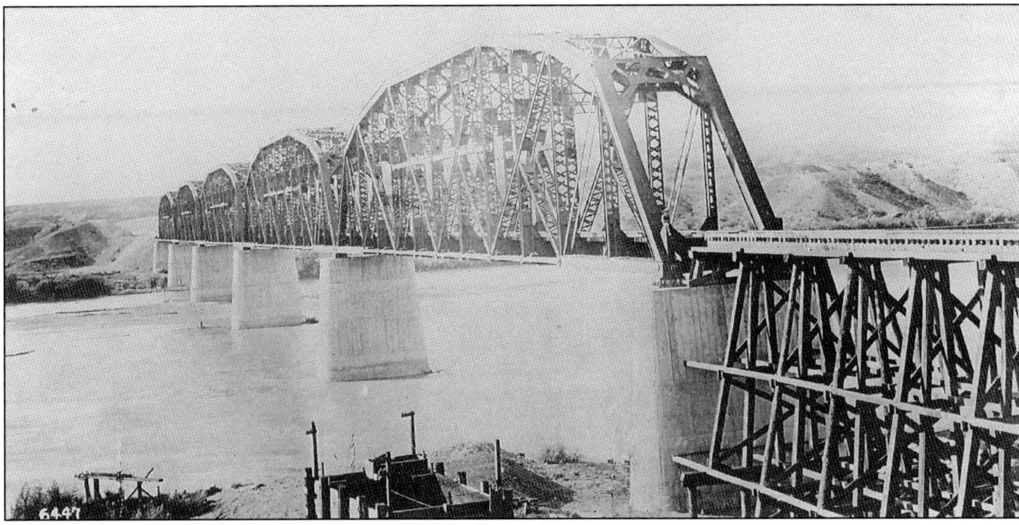

Under the Parker Train Bridge, the river looks to be at a low level in 1916.

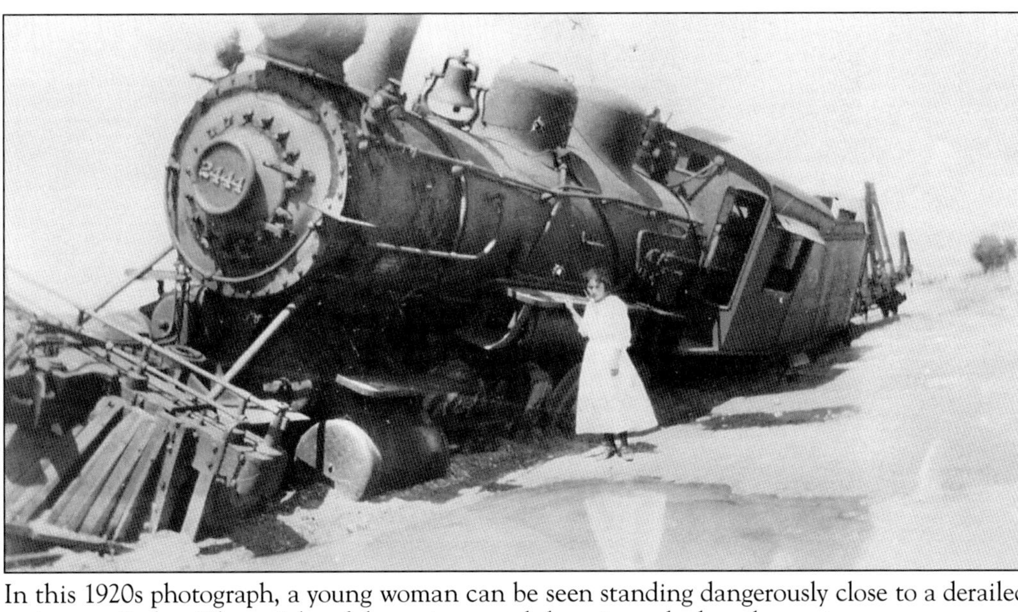

In this 1920s photograph, a young woman can be seen standing dangerously close to a derailed train near Parker. The weight of the train caused the rain-soaked tracks to give way.

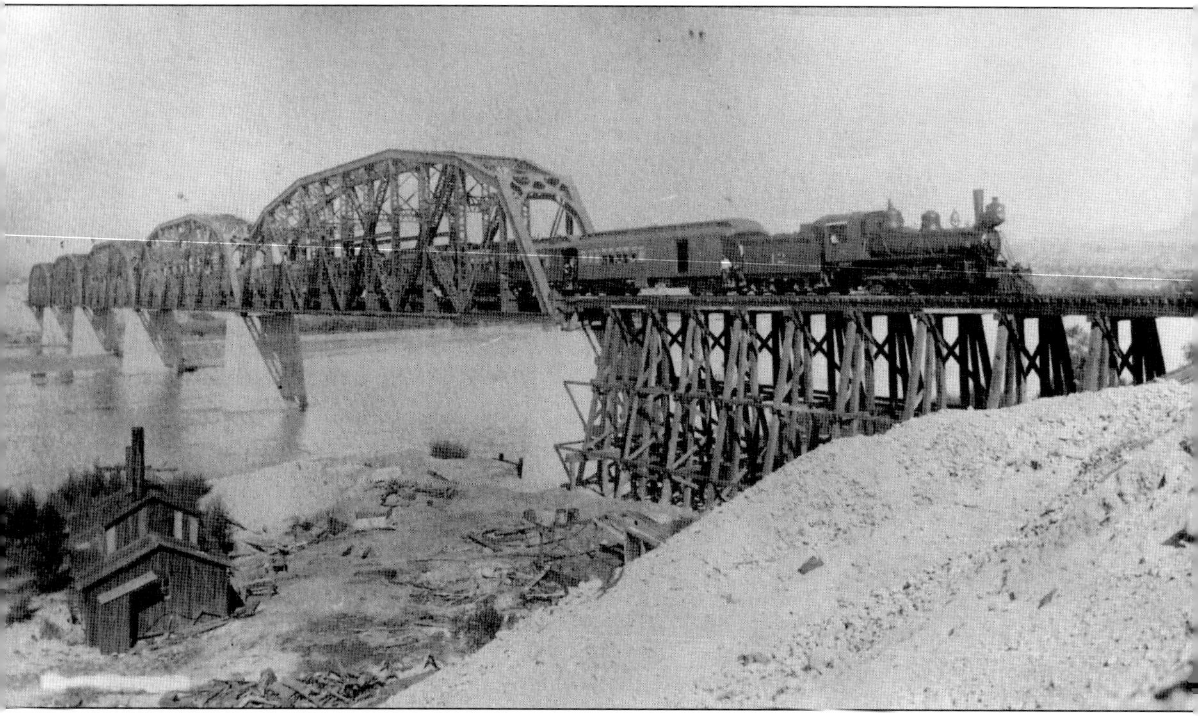

Following the construction of the Parker Train Bridge, the first passenger train reportedly crossed on July 1, 1910. As pictured, remnants from the construction of the bridge continued to be used for ferry business.

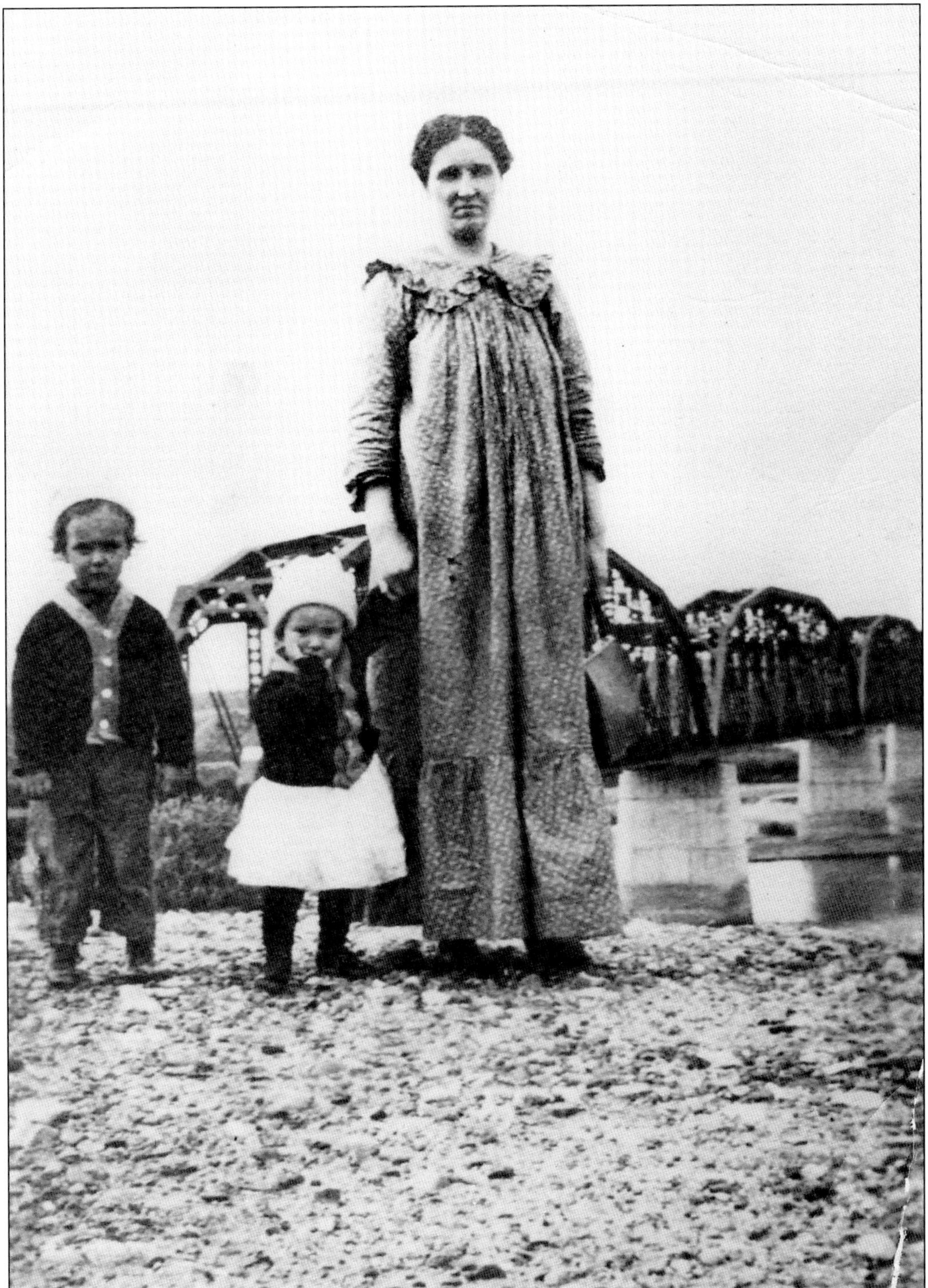

Early settlers in Parker were either employed by the Arizona California Railroad or seeking their fortune from mining in the surrounding hills. Here, from left to right, Barney, Pearl, and Jenny Fugatt stand on the mesa near the Parker Train Bridge around 1911.

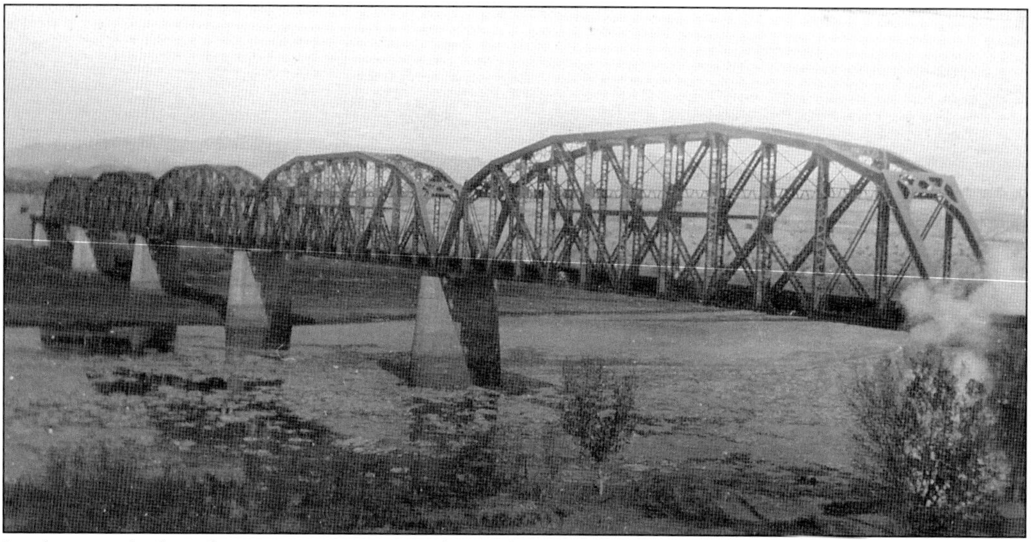

In the time before dam construction on the Colorado River, spring melt from the mountains in Wyoming is still visible as snow flows under the Parker Train Bridge.

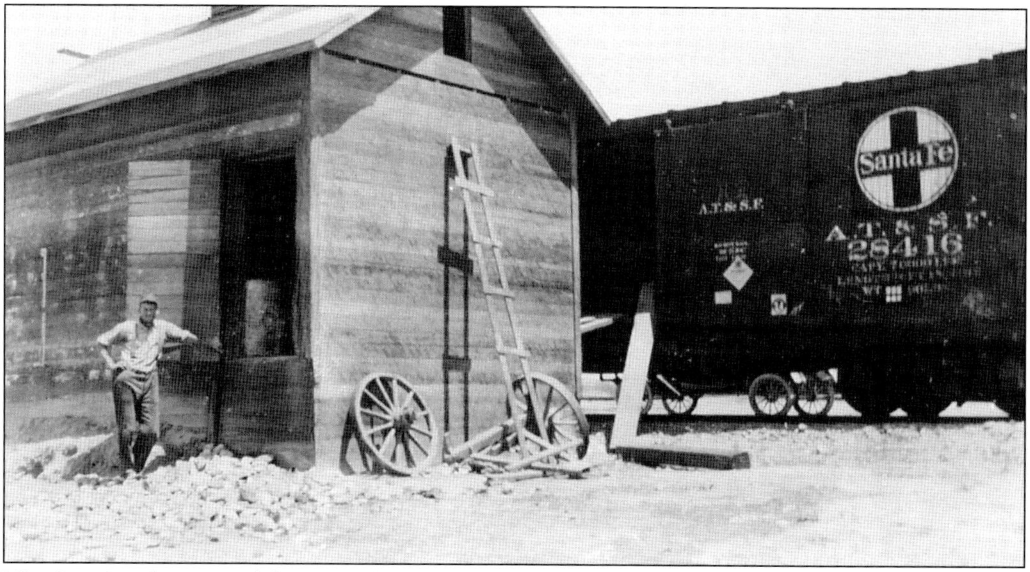

The first freight car to deliver gasoline, loaded with barrels, arrived in Parker in July 1916.

Berkeley M. Fuqua, pictured about 1930, was known with respect and affection as "Daddy Fuqua." According to Nellie Bush in an unpublished manuscript, "He was a slender man, who was well groomed. Daddy Fuqua had the quiet kind of gallantry that Texans sometimes have."

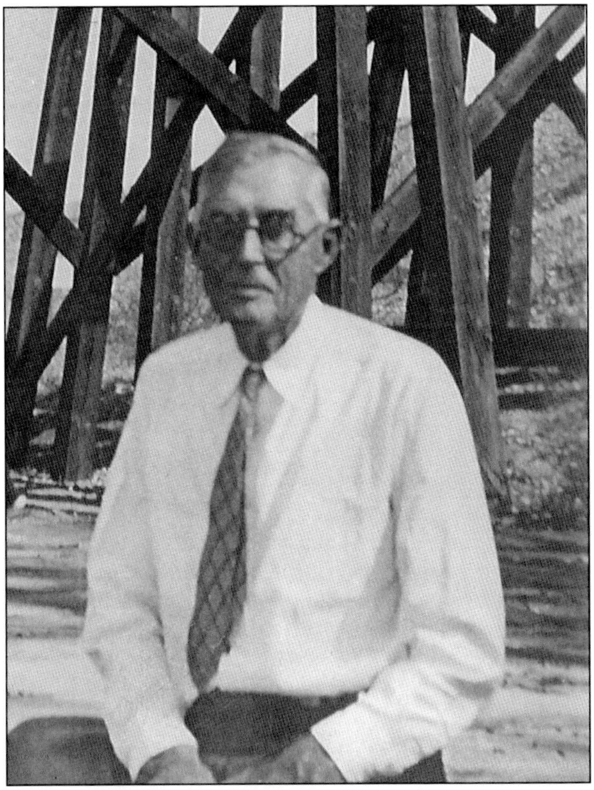

The children of Berkeley M. Fuqua are seen below at a family gathering in 1965. From left to right are Carrie King, Ellen Dick, Mabel Smith, Ruth Fuqua, James Granville ("Gran"), and Senee Creighton.

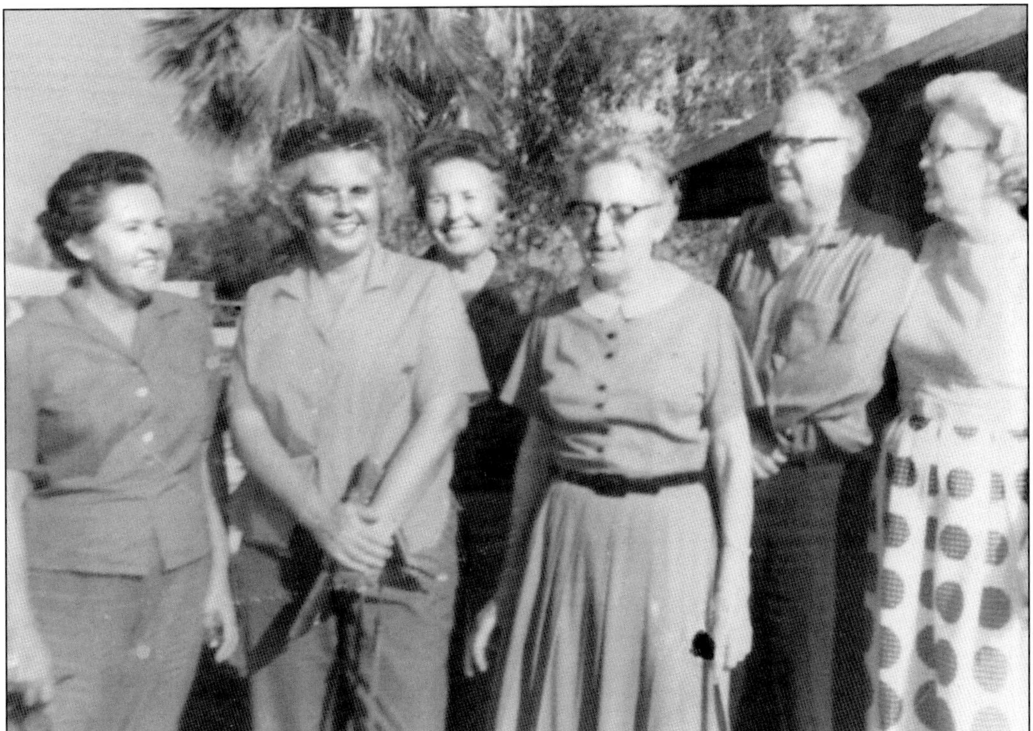

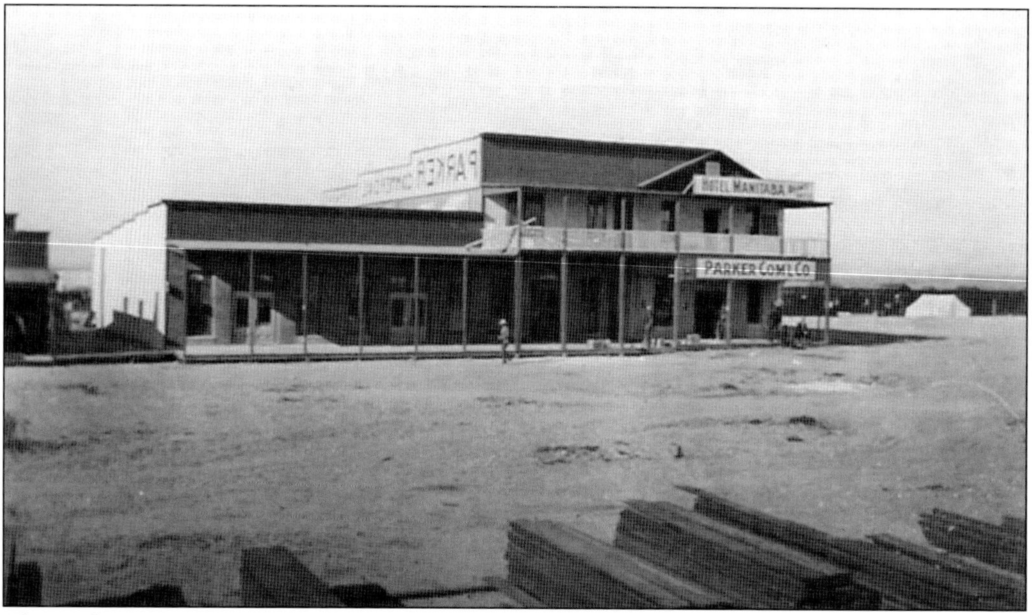

The Parker Commercial Company, shown around 1910, was established in 1905 and operated until 1965. Berkeley M. Fuqua ran the company from the time of his arrival in Parker in 1914 until his death in 1938, at which time his children assumed the responsibility.

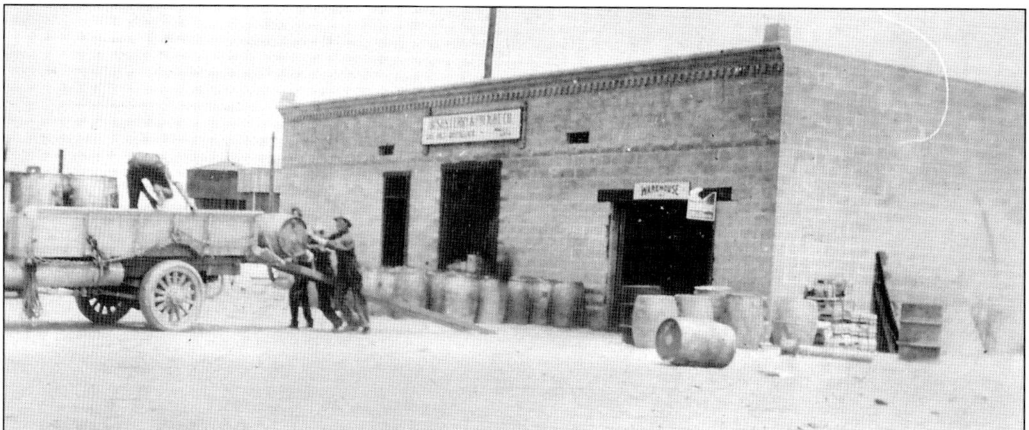

Barrels are being transferred from the warehouse of the Bush Freight and Ferry Company, near Parker Depot, and loaded into a truck in 1917.

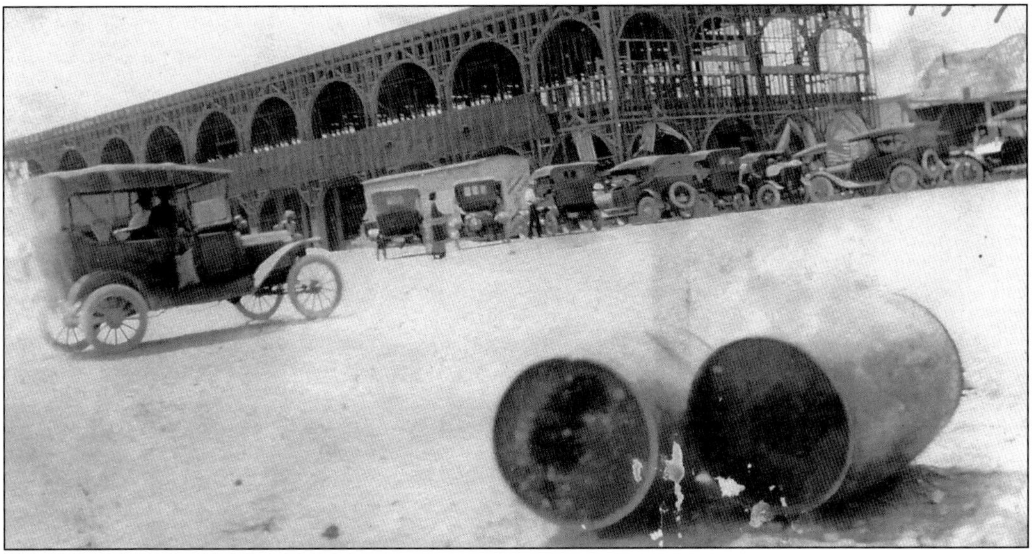

An entrepreneur named Guy Marsh began construction of the Grandview Hotel in 1916, only to find himself without the necessary financial capital to complete the project. Having gone into foreclosure, the property was purchased and construction completed by Joe and Nellie Bush. This 1917 image reveals an early stage of the hotel's construction.

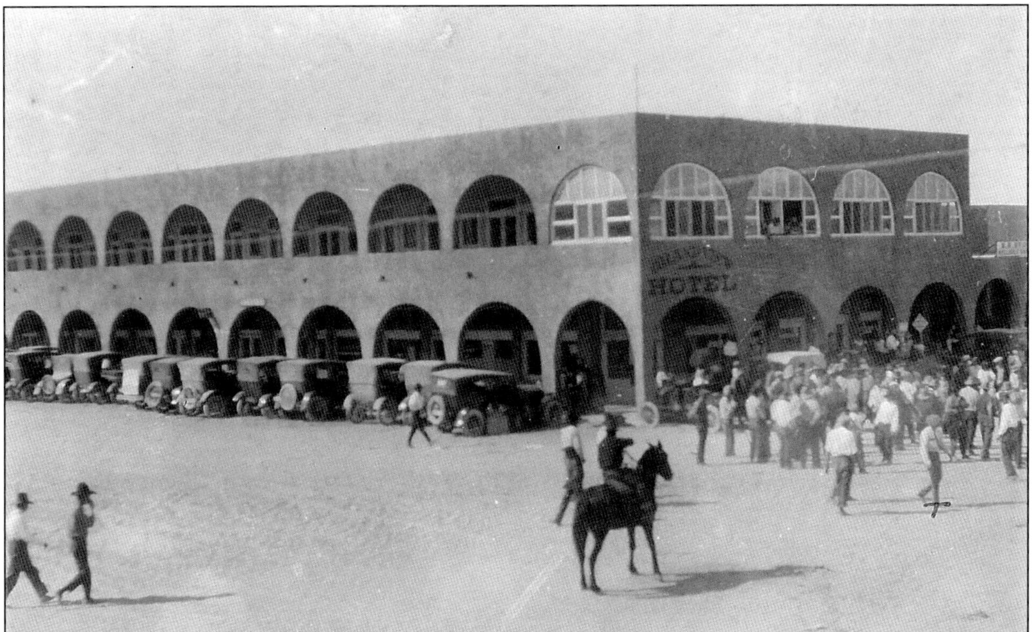

This 1925 street scene shows the completed Grandview Hotel, which was quite grand and opulent for a small desert town where roads were still virtually nonexistent and most travelers arrived via train.

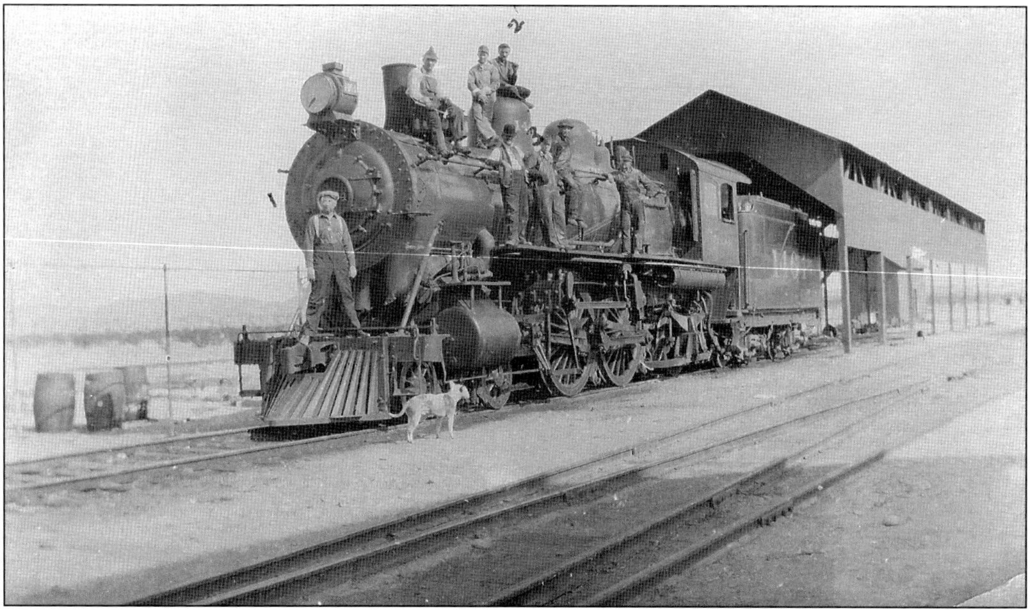

Atchison, Topeka, and Santa Fe Railway engine No. 1461 pulls away from the service stall at the Parker depot while a dog wanders past. Standing on the front of the engine is Al Green; Baker and Lester White are two of the additional crew. The others are not identified.

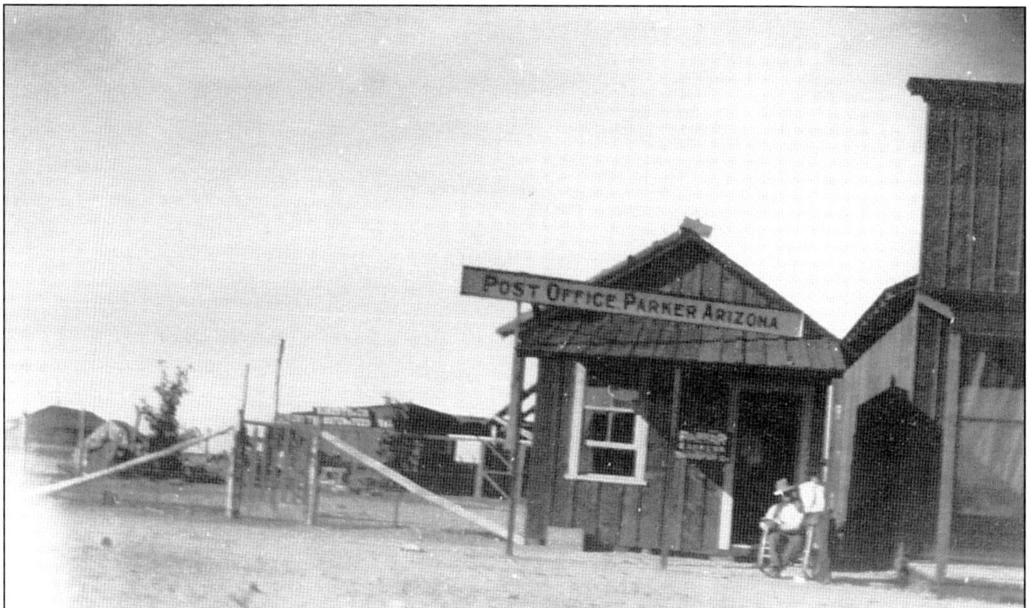

The first post office was established in 1871 at the Parker Indian Agency, which was named in honor of Gen. Ely Parker, appointed commissioner of Indian affairs by Pres. Ulysses S. Grant. In 1907, the Parker Post Office was relocated within the town site, where it would be nearer the activities of commerce. The post office is seen here in 1915.

Three

A Prospector's Dream
There is Ore in Them There Hills

While prospecting in arroyos along the Colorado River in 1861–1862, Pauline Weaver made the discovery of gold that would create a rush near the river settlement of LaPaz. It did not take long for mining districts to start popping up in the surrounding area.

Using the Colorado River as a transportation route, prospectors could easily explore and locate previously untapped veins of ore. In the Parker area, a few names come to mind instantly: Wyatt Earp's Happy Days Mines, Billy Mack Mines, Empire Mines, and Rio Vista Mines. Most notably, the Clara Consolidated Gold and Copper Mining Company was located at Swansea, also home to the only smelting plant for any significant distance. Over its lifetime, the Clara Consolidated produced 27 million pounds of copper. Additional ores mined and shipped from Parker included silver and magnesium.

By the beginning of World War II, much of the area's placer mining and dry washing (sifting) had disappeared. The Cyprus Copperstone Mining Corporation was the last to perform active gold mining, ending in the mid-1990s. At the time, the Cyprus operations were the most modern in the world.

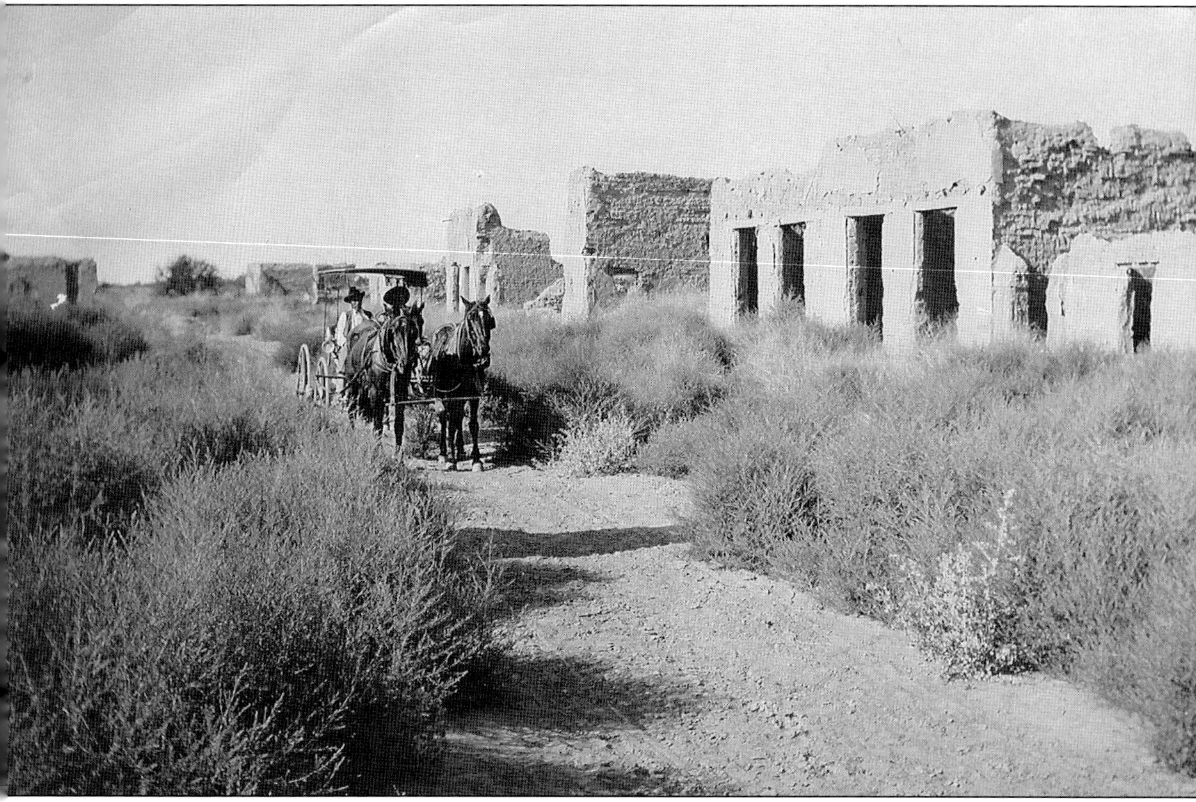

The discovery of gold on January 12, 1862, in the Arroyo de la Tenaja by a party of prospectors led by Pauline Weaver caused a mining town to quickly develop. According to Will C. Barnes's *Arizona Place Names*, "The town of LaPaz was named to honor the Feast of our Lady of Peace, which had always been celebrated on the same day as the gold discovery. By 1909, LaPaz was little more than some old adobe structures long since abandoned. The town's history was short lived, beginning in 1862 and ending by 1875 after the course of the Colorado River changed, leaving LaPaz high and dry without any river frontage."

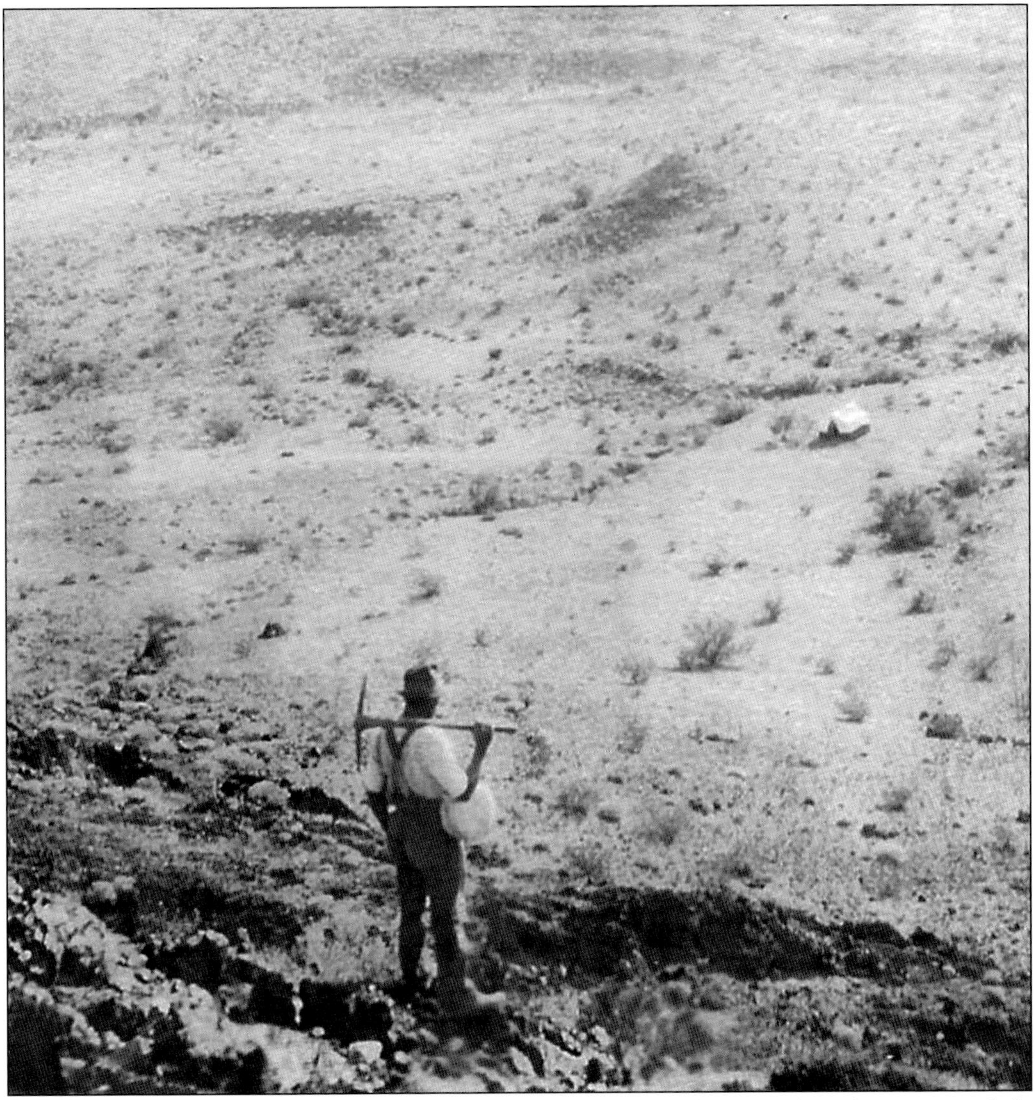

Early prospector Claude Fugatt, arriving in the Parker area about 1915, strikes a pose while looking back toward his camp. He carries the necessary supplies for mining: a pick and a water canteen.

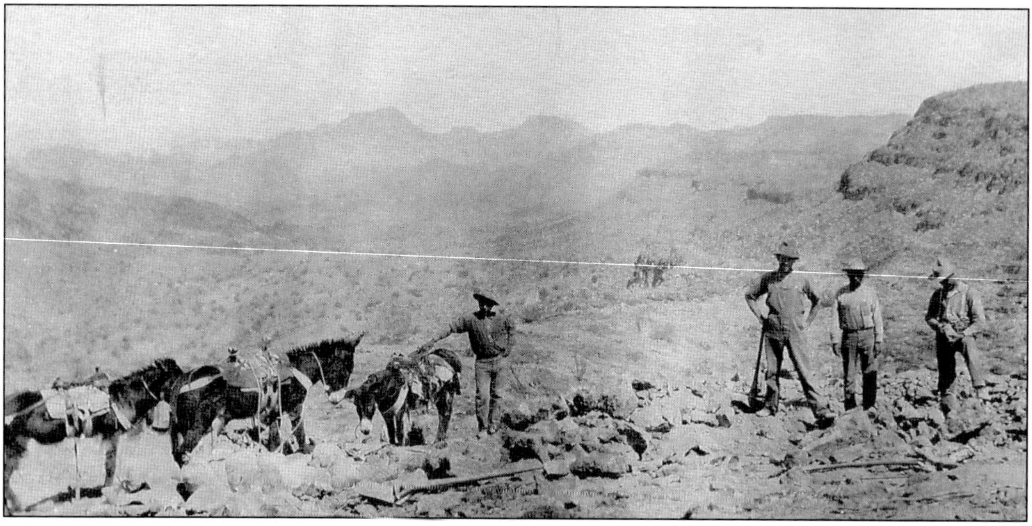

Around 1915, in the surrounding hills near Cienega Springs, the Fugatt men prospect for ore. With them are their shovels and several mules, which can be used for carrying supplies and—if good fortune strikes—hauling the weight of ore bags.

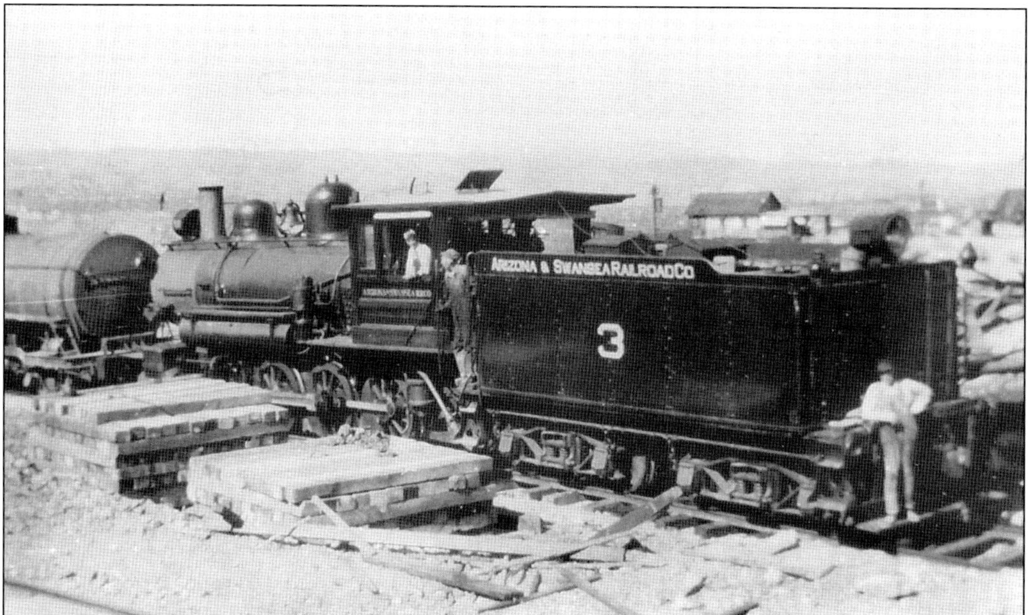

As seen in this 1928 photograph, the Arizona and Swansea Railroad Company ran a train that could carry ore to the junction at Bouse. The engineer was Sam Cunningham.

After arriving at the Empire Mine, this wagon and horses are temporarily left unattended. Next to the rock outcrop are the tent cabins that were common housing at area mining camps.

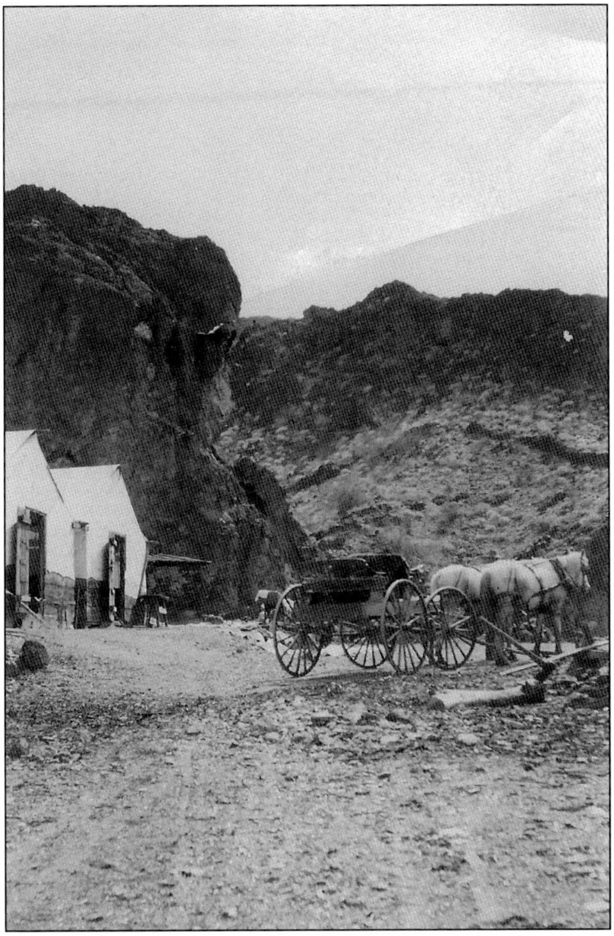

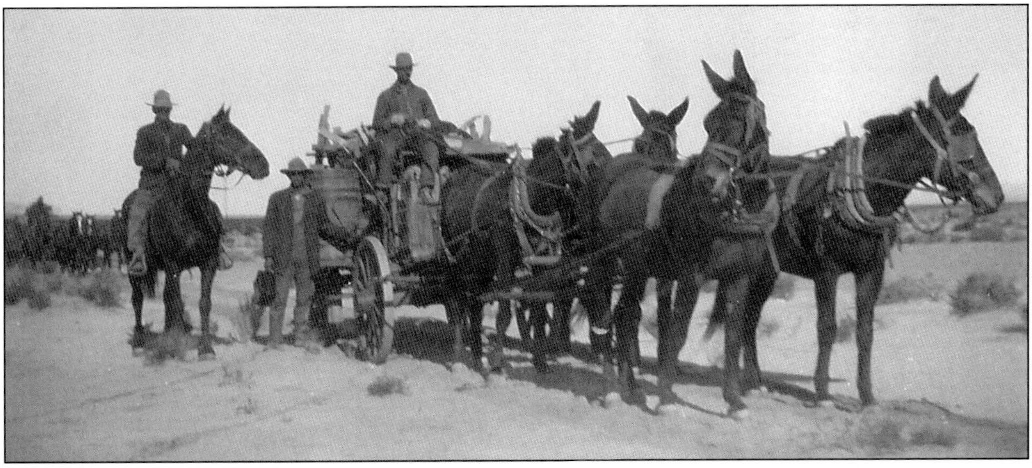

After days of prospecting and mining ore in the surrounding hills of Parker, the Terry men return home on horseback in 1909. Some of the men are also driving wagons with their teams of horses.

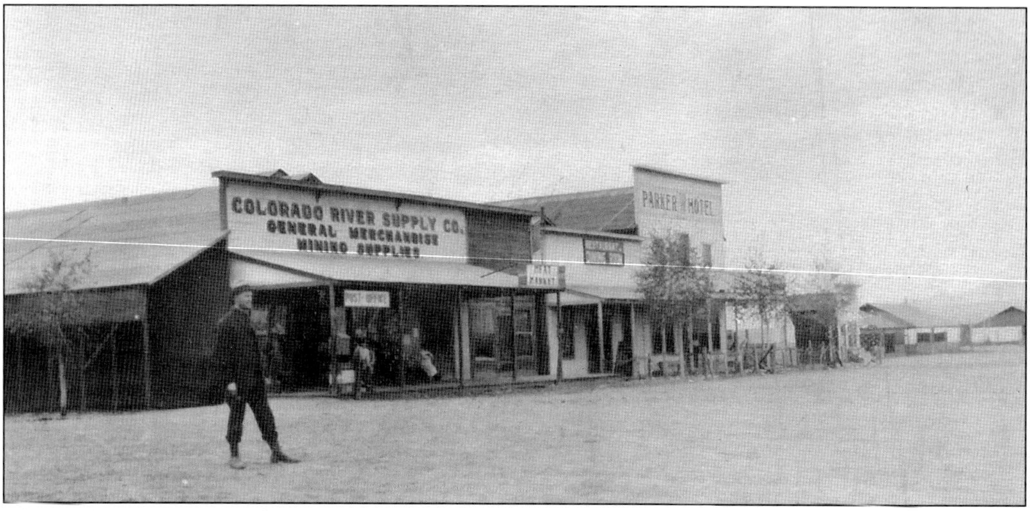

This early street scene, depicting Front Street in Parker, was photographed by W. E. Beck. The Parker Hotel and the Colorado River Supply Company offered general merchandise and mining supplies to customers.

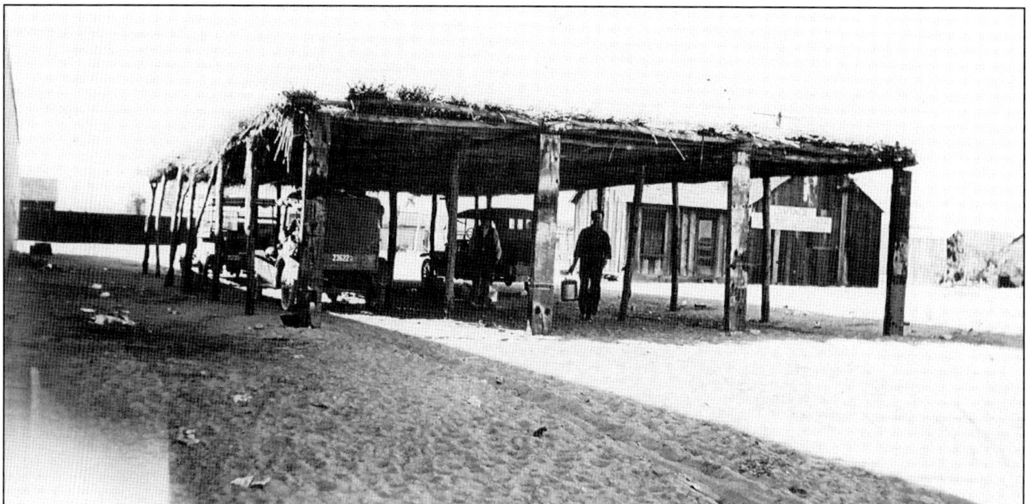

This early Parker ramada was used as protection against the searing effects of the desert sun.

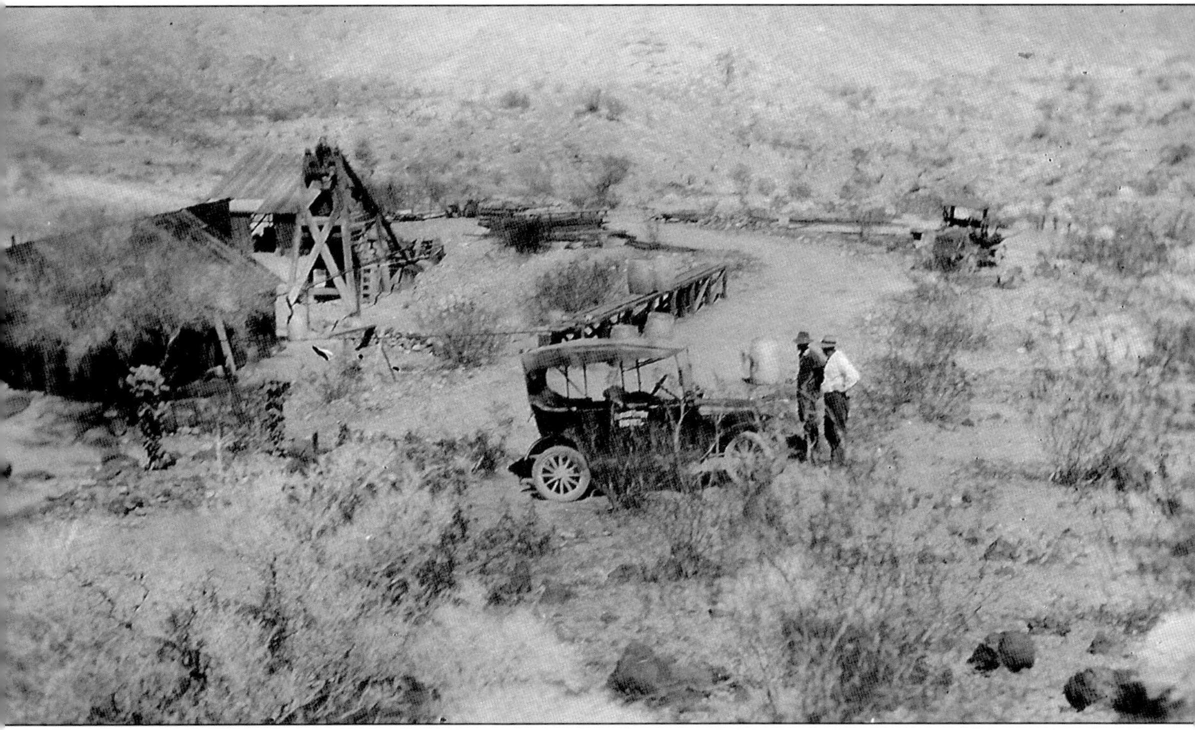

These two gentlemen appear to be discussing the automobile near the Copper Basin Mine in 1917.

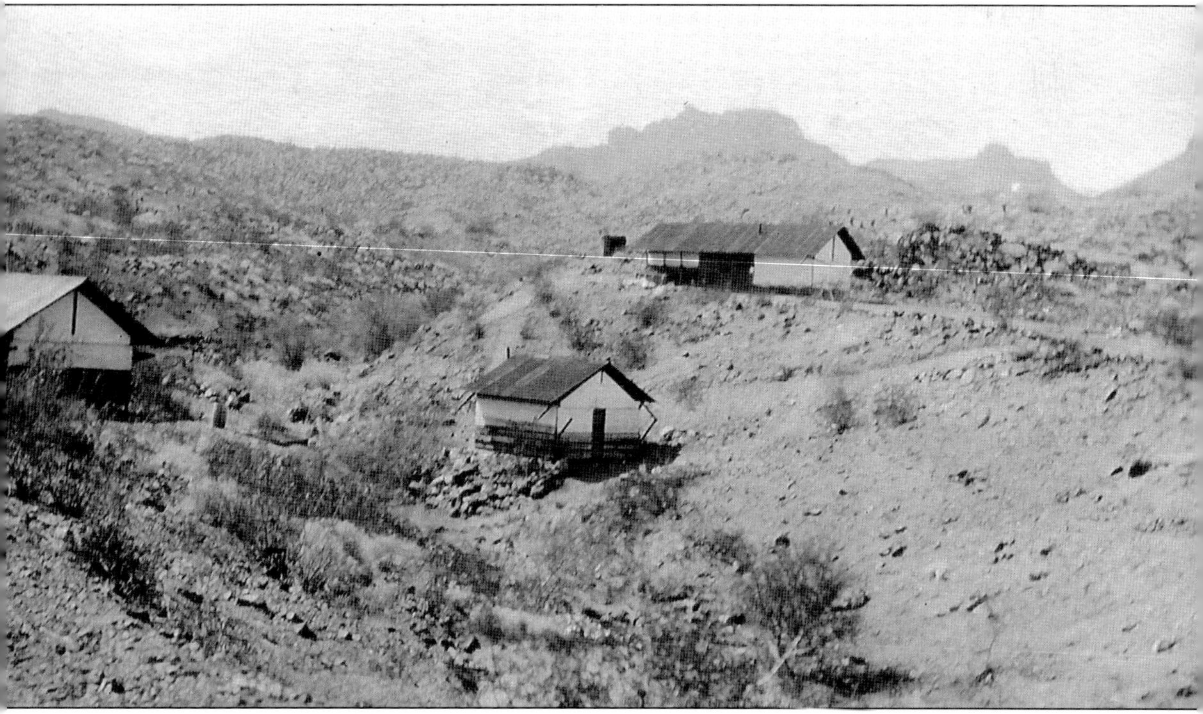

Tent cabins were sprinkled throughout the desert landscape, as seen at the Copper Basin Mine in 1917.

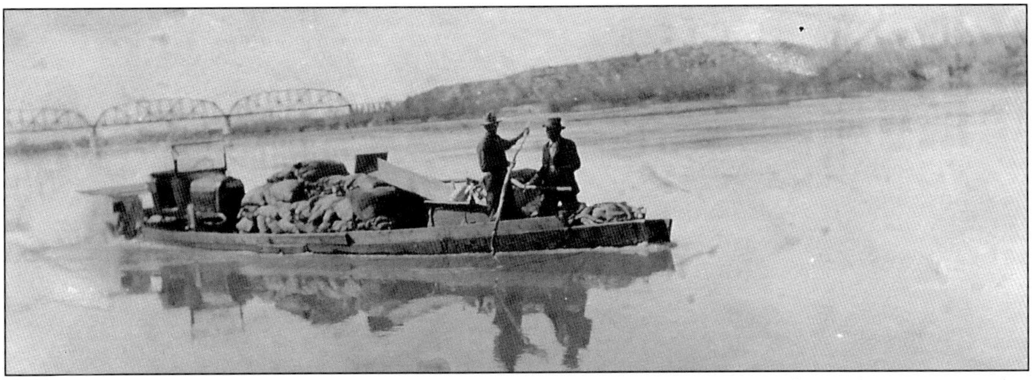

Bud Norton returns to the Parker landing with a full load of ore in 1917. The Parker Train Bridge is visible in the background. His ferry also transports a vehicle—probably the more modern way of traveling to a distant mine site.

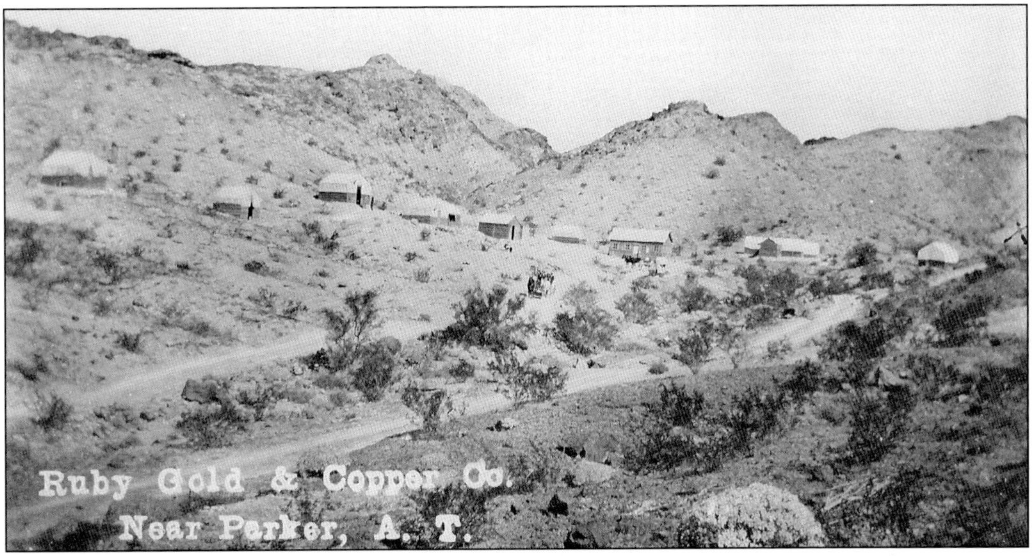

This panoramic postcard scene shows the Ruby Gold and Copper Company near Parker sometime before 1912, as the reference to "A.T." (Arizona Territory) would indicate.

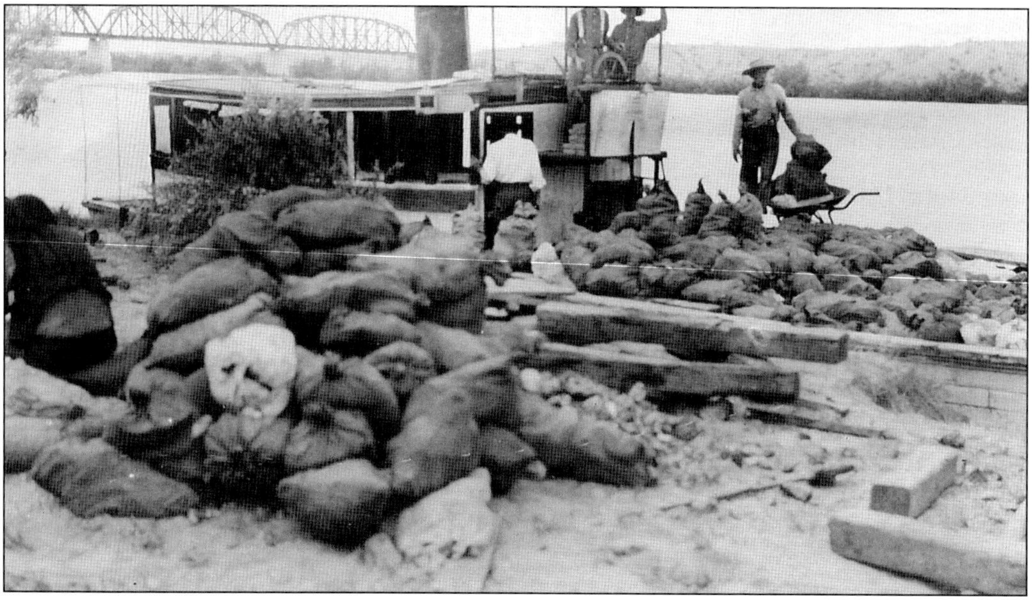

The Parker Train Bridge is a landmark showing the location of ore being loaded onto one of the Bush ferries at the Parker landing in 1917.

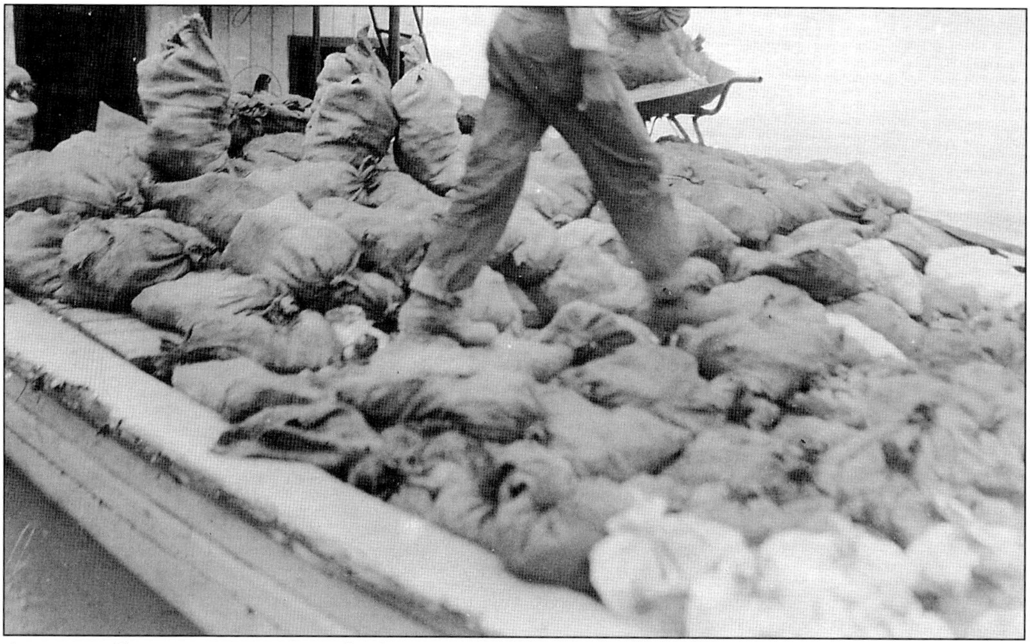

A man walks across to arrange the loaded ore for transport via a Bush ferry in 1917.

Four

The Road Traveled
Couldn't Get Lost—Only One Set of Ruts to Follow

Joe and Nellie Bush relocated to Parker in 1915. Joe had been working as a trolley inspector for the Phoenix Street Railway Company but, following the trolley drivers strike, decided to set off for Parker, where he had bought part interest in the ferryboat *Iola*. While Joe took care of the couple's increasing business operations—the water company, electric utility, hotel, and ferry service—Nellie taught elementary school in Parker for several years. Very much a partner with Joe in the business, Nellie soon realized the value gained by having roads leading to Parker. She states in *The Life Story of Nellie Bush*, "People wanted cars, wanted to tour the country at their own pace, not just look from the windows of a passing train. But they didn't want to get lost, or run without water or gasoline. It wasn't a crazy idea, it was a good idea."

Nellie was persistent. The couple had purchased a Model T Ford without a top or a windshield for $25, and Nellie gathered together all the boxes and stray boards she could find. These she painted into signs, directing the public from the east and west to cross the river at Parker. After loading the signs into the Ford, Nellie, along with the help of an old prospector, set out across the desert on an advertising campaign. When they arrived at favorable locations, the prospector dug the post holes while Nellie placed the arrow to point in the proper direction. They placed signs at all points of mining roads.

With the construction of Parker Dam, Nellie received some unanticipated help from the Metropolitan Water District of Southern California (MWD), which was limited to transporting supplies and equipment solely by train. Seeing the potential need, MWD began surveying and building roads from Los Angeles to the Parker area to facilitate its construction project.

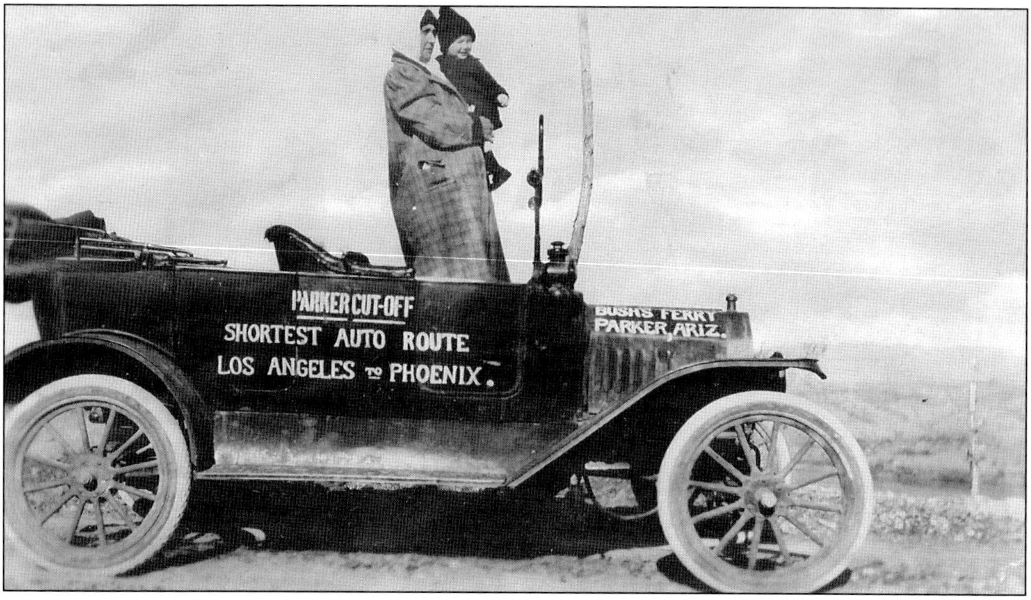

Mary Trent, the mother of Nellie Bush, holds her grandson Wesley Bush in 1917. They both gaze into the distance, standing in Joe and Nellie's Ford, which advertises the Parker Cut-off as the shortest automobile route from Los Angeles to Phoenix.

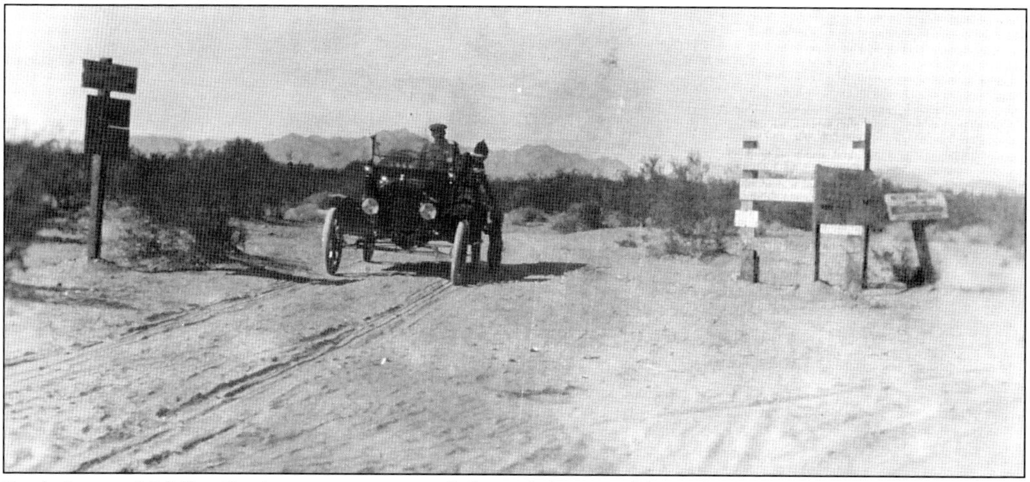

Both Joe and Nellie Bush were convinced that if they could mark the dirt roads with signs for directions and distance to services, travelers would be more likely to venture out into the unknown of the desert. Nellie coined the phrase "couldn't get lost—only one set of ruts to follow." It was appropriate for the circumstances.

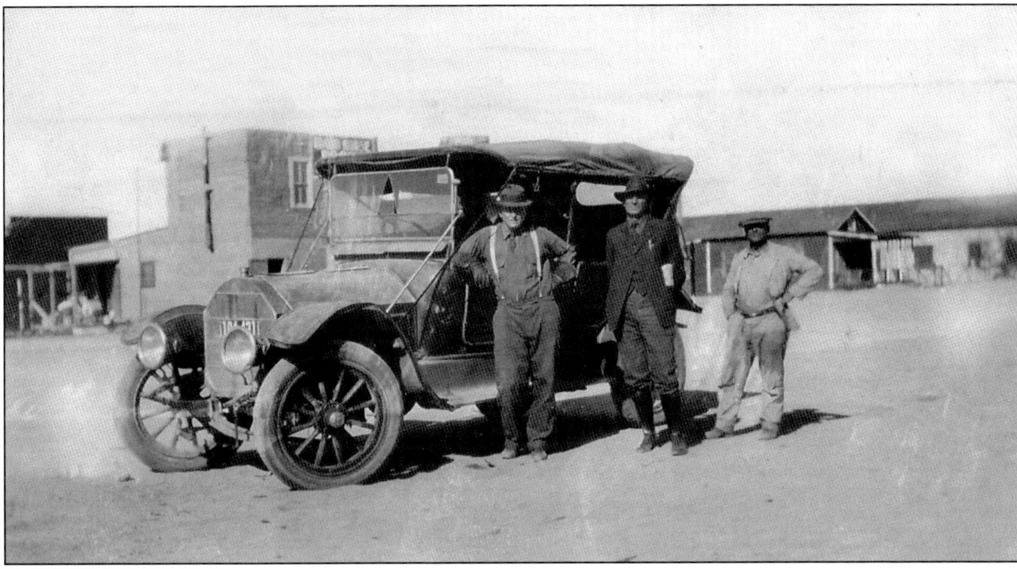

Joe Bush, left, wearing suspenders, leans on the vehicle. The other two gentlemen are unidentified. The image's notation indicates the men arrived in Parker from Phoenix, where they had been placing directional arrows. Joe wrote candidly, "It was a fast trip only taking three and a half days in 1917."

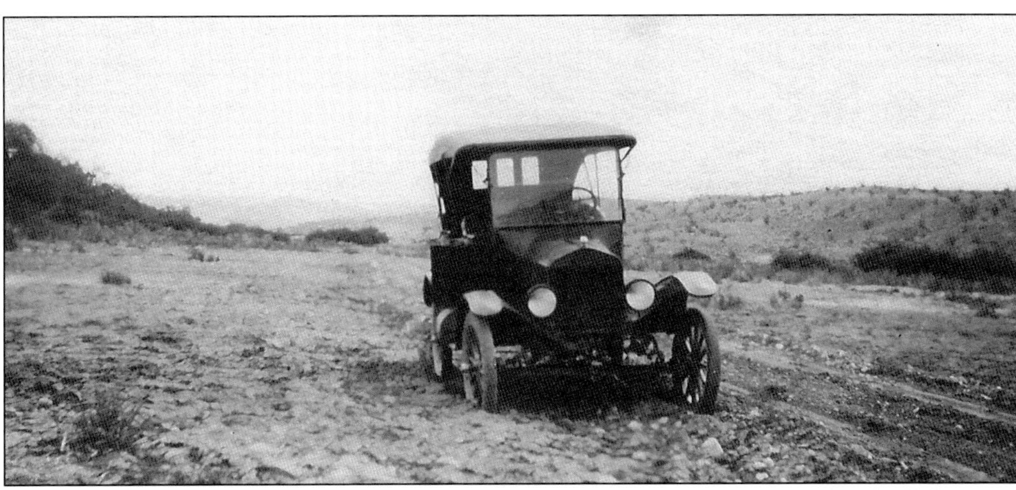

John Roberts's car is stuck in a sand trap in the 1920s. It looks like he ventured off the more-traveled, hard-packed road just enough to cause trouble.

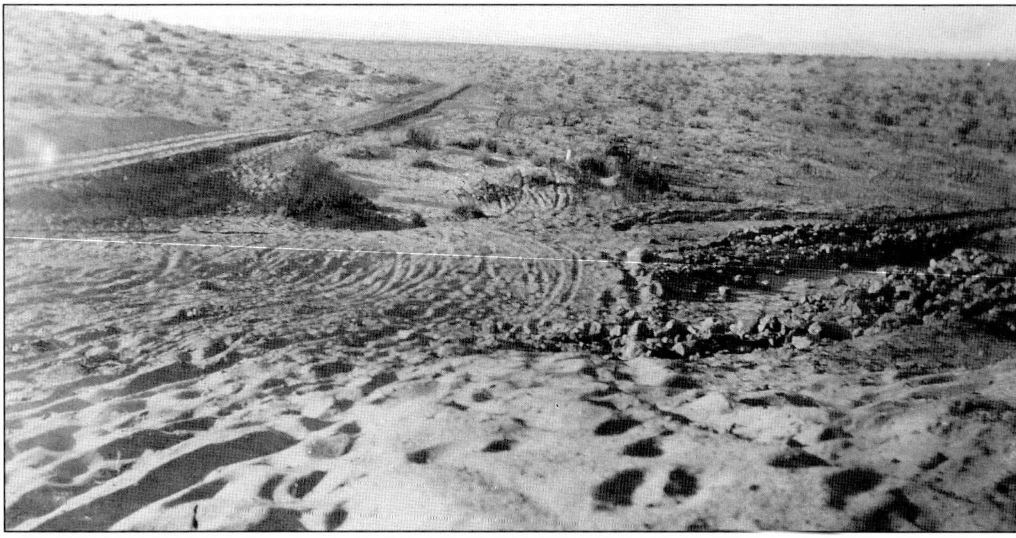

The notation for this 1918 photograph mentions road grading through the sand dunes near Parker. Most of the desert surrounding Parker is actually sand dunes; to this day, sand can be seen when the wind is blowing. Many of the early homes built in town used oleander plants for a wind block because they were able to grow fast and dense.

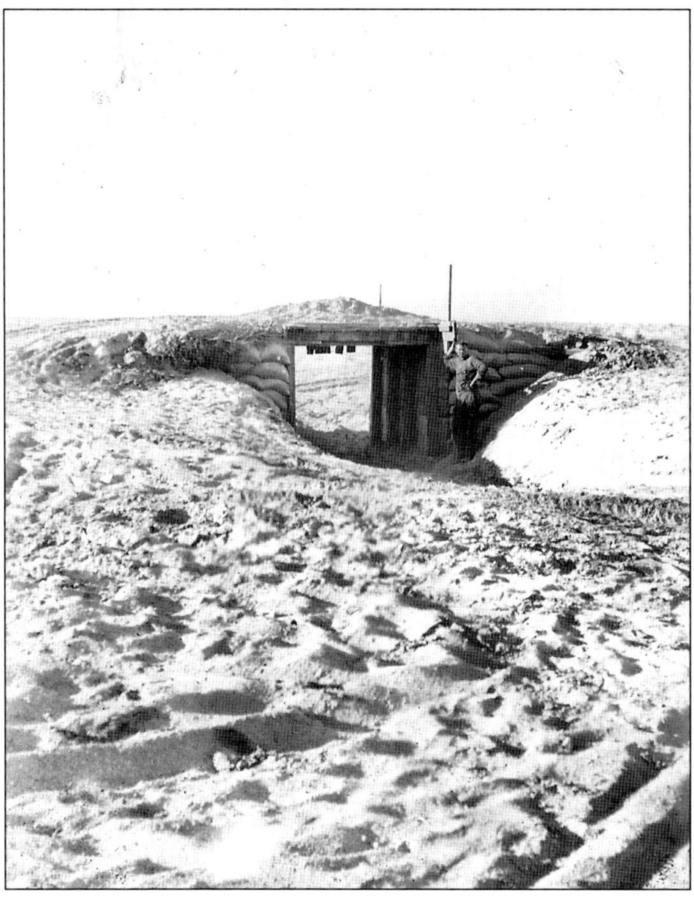

Joe Bush stands by a loading trap, a device used for packing road materials on a wagon, between Parker and Wenden in 1918. The Bushes' entrepreneurial spirit generated the business travelers brought, but the couple also played a significant role in the development of Arizona's rural roads.

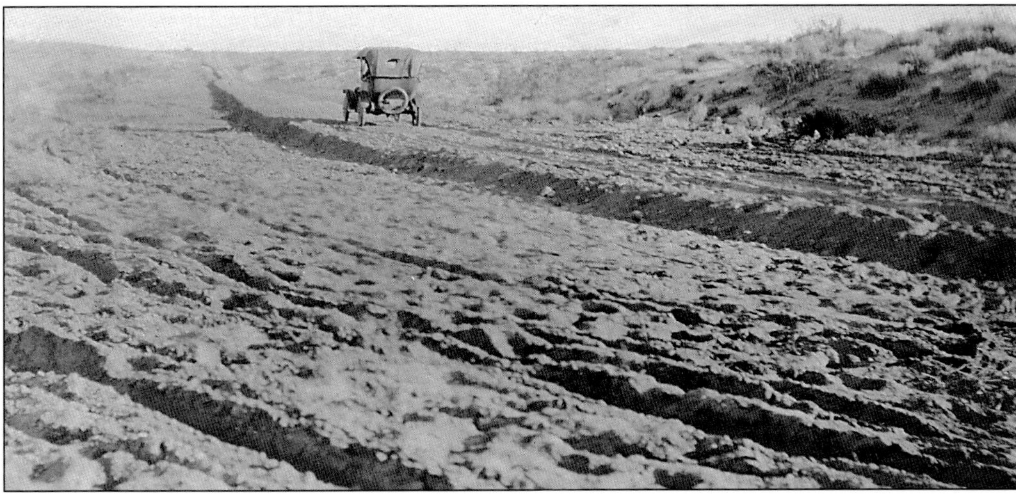

The road was finished through the sand near Parker in 1918. The materials used for the roadwork were all hauled by a wagon with a team of horses. The Bushes' labor and commitment to building roads cannot be matched.

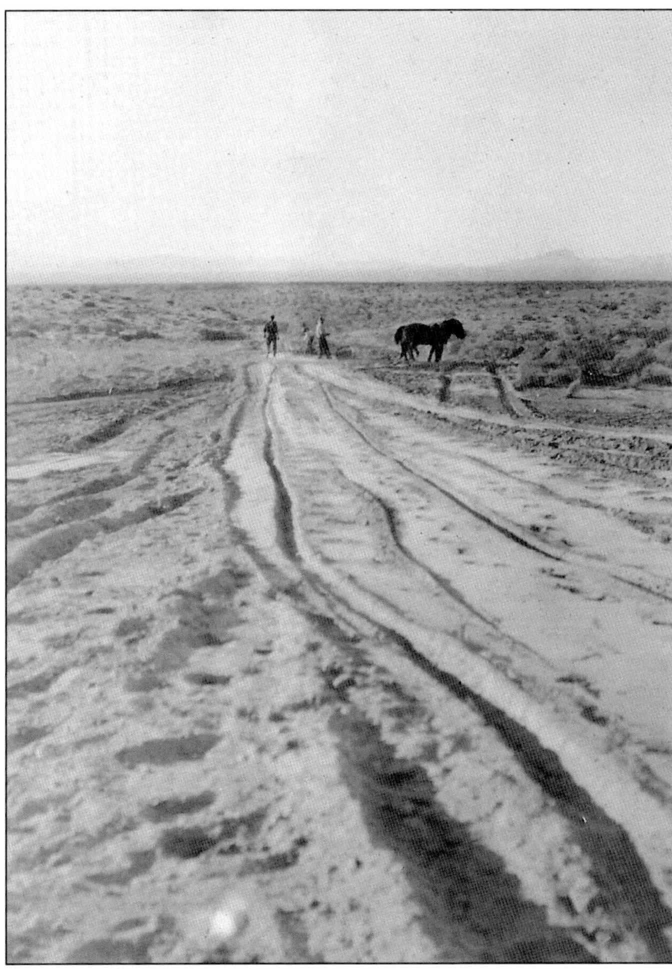

It looks like nothing but sand as far as the eye can see, yet Joe and Nellie Bush persevered. They are shown here during the process of road construction on the Yuma County Highway near Parker in 1918.

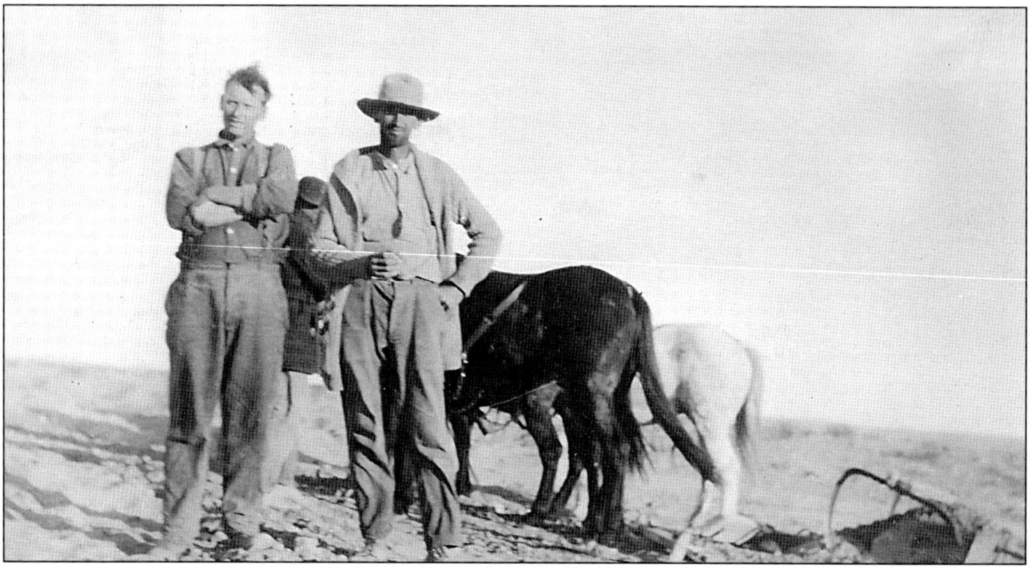

Joe Bush (left) and Tom Banks, pictured in 1918, served as the volunteer road crew between Parker and Bouse.

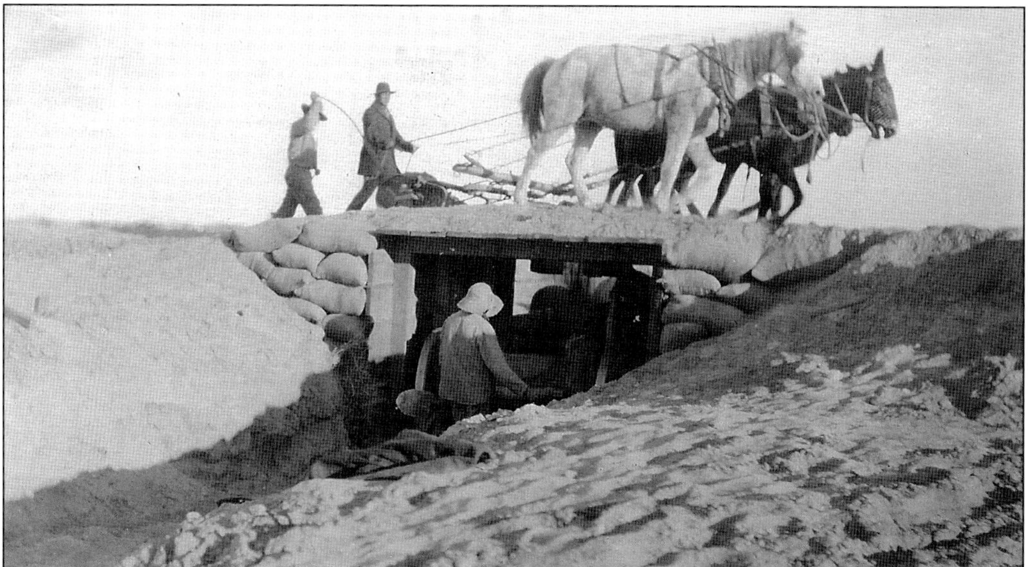

Some five miles east of Parker, a wagon backs up under the trap as dirt is loaded in 1918. A team of two horses helps with the process.

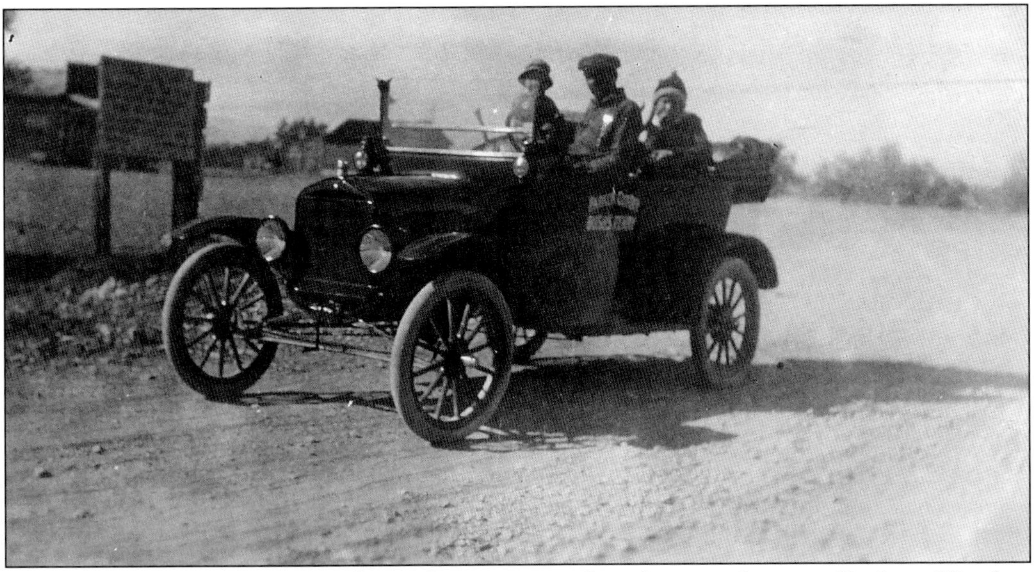

Driving their vehicle, Joe and Nellie Bush continue to place directional signs to Buckeye, Wenden, and Parker. The signs also indicate where to locate the better water wells for drinking.

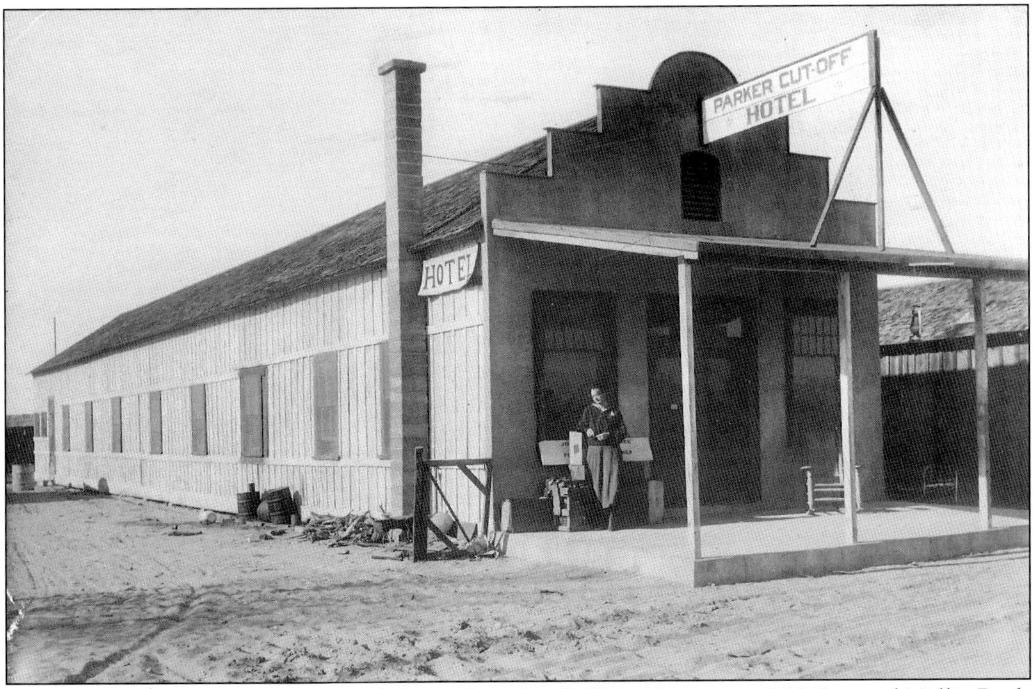

Nellie Bush stands on the porch of the Parker Cut-Off Hotel prior to 1916. Joe and Nellie Bush opened their second hotel, the Grandview Hotel, a two-story structure that became recognized as a Parker landmark, in 1916.

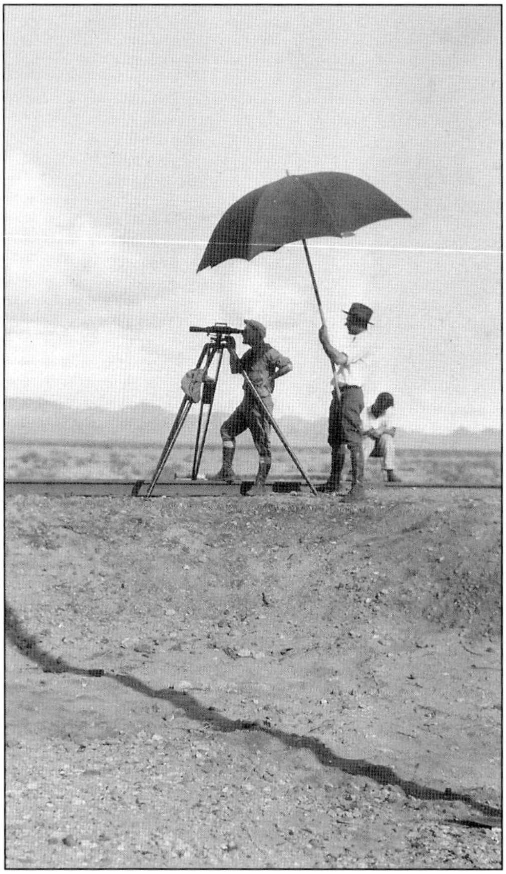

Standing on railroad tracks, the Metropolitan Water District survey crew finds that using an umbrella helps make enough shade to temper the searing heat of the desert sun.

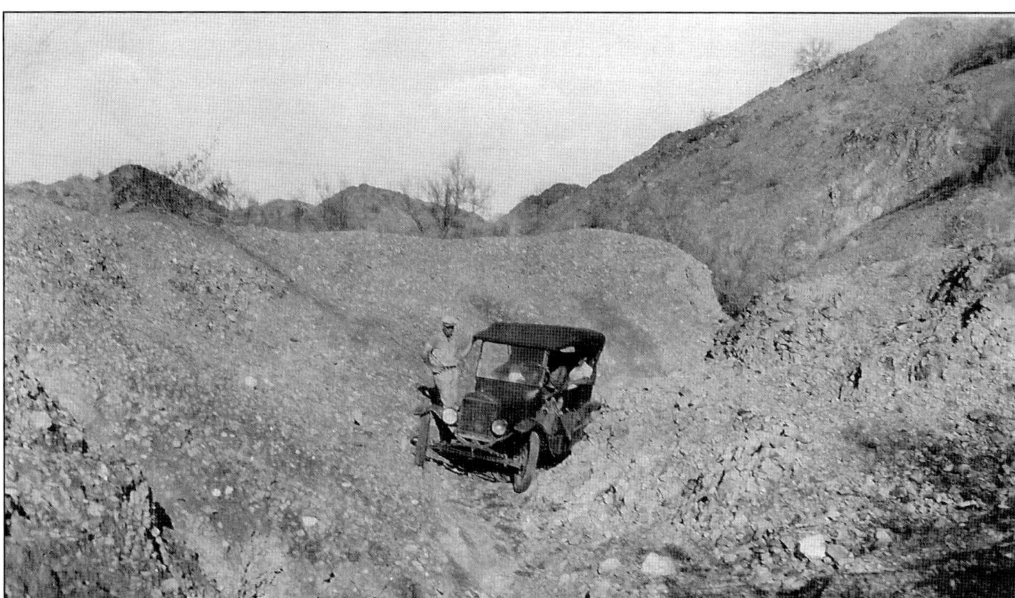

No route was too rugged, as evidenced by this survey crew making its way through a ravine. For these guys, it appears to be all in a day's work in the Southwest.

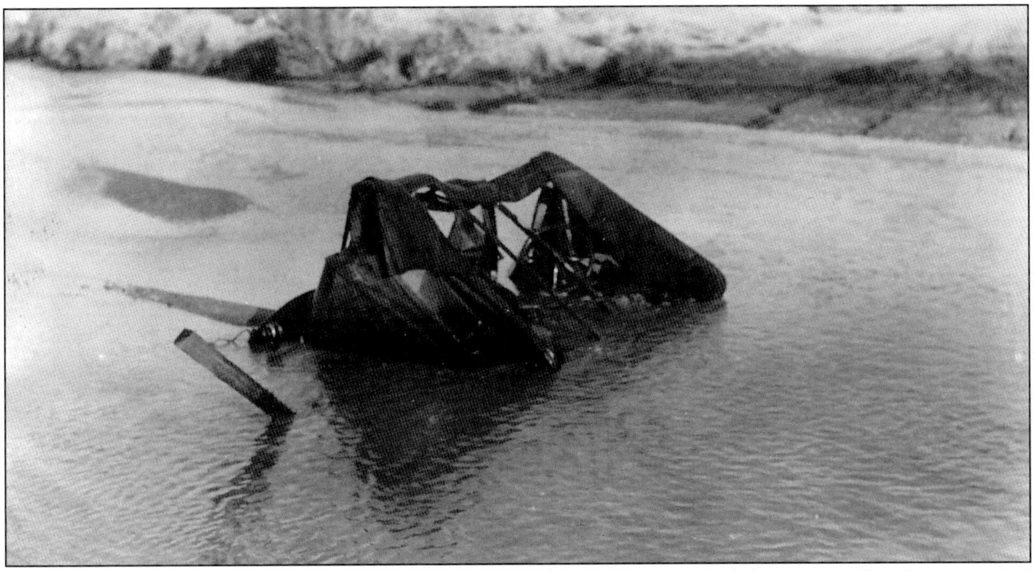

Desert flash floods, such as this one in 1930, can be dangerous and damaging for the powerful force of moving water they can generate.

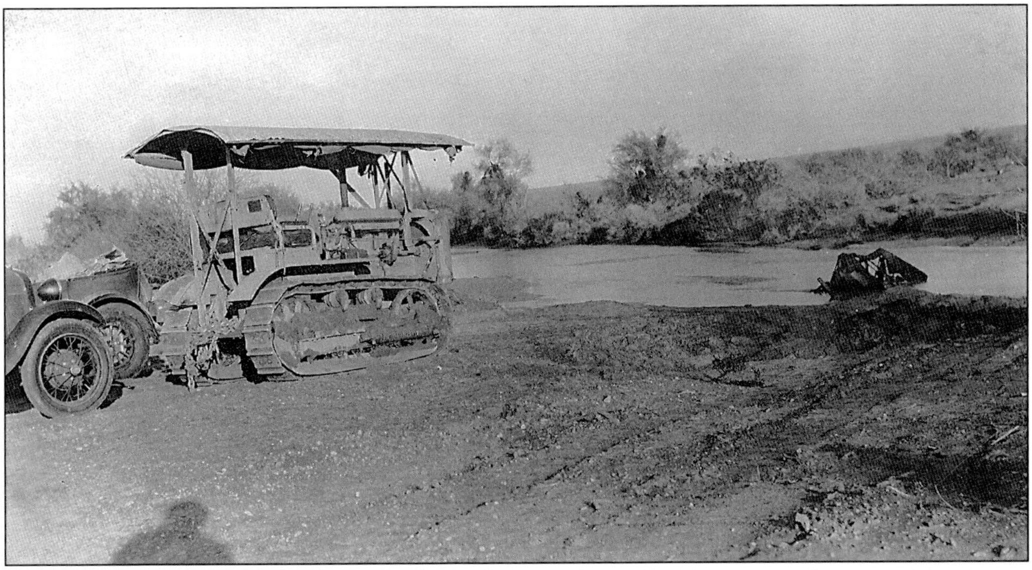

With the use of a tractor, this vehicle is about to be pulled from a wash created by desert flash floods.

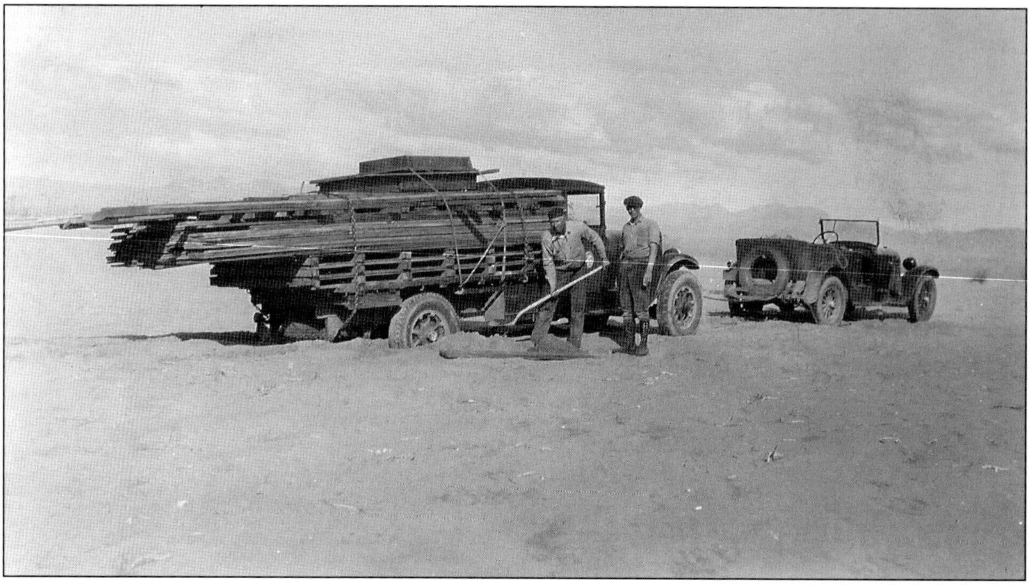

These two fellows have found themselves buried up to the axles and are probably not particularly happy about the photo opportunity. Their truck looks to be loaded down quite heavily, contributing to the difficulty they are having releasing from the sand trap. Experienced, they are using the two necessary tools—a shovel and a board—when the option of being pulled out will not work.

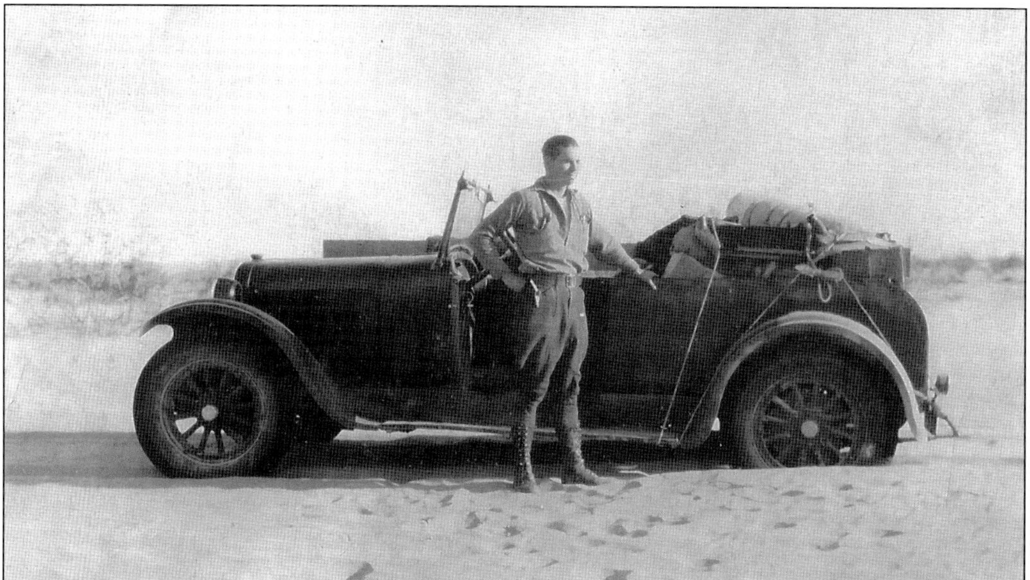

A man waits for help to arrive during early-day desert travel near Parker.

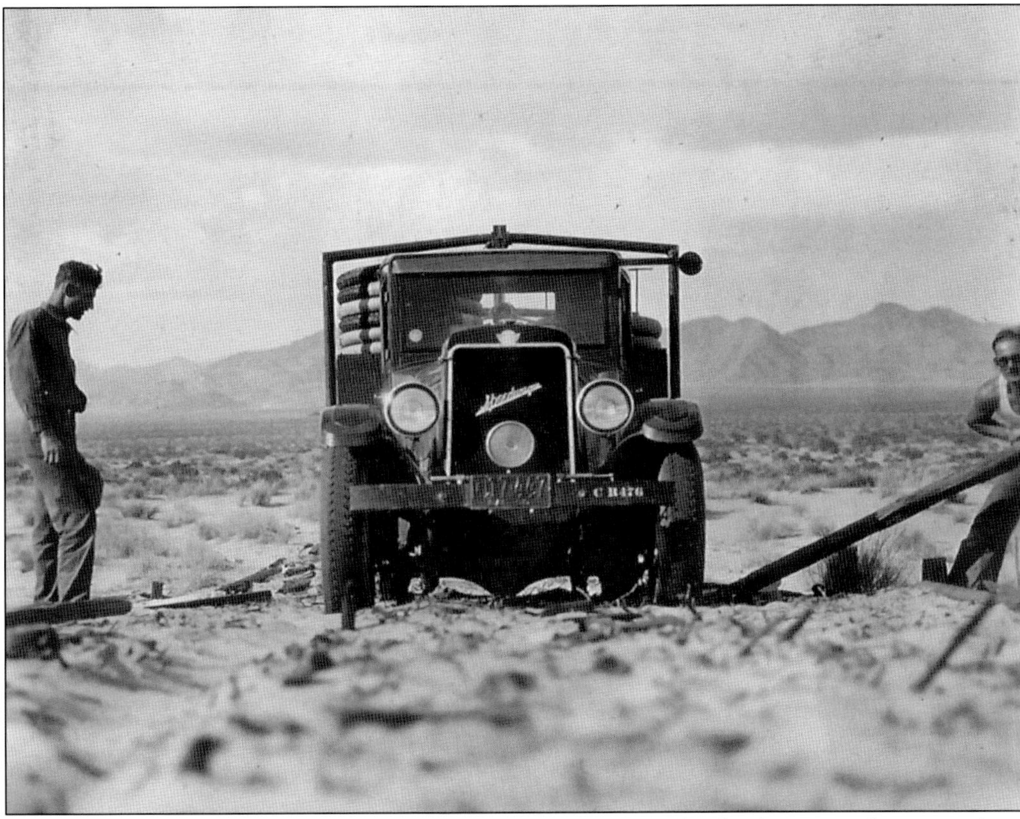

With nothing but sand for miles around and mountains in the far distance, these men have become stuck in the desert sand. Not to be discouraged, they seem to take the work of digging out in stride.

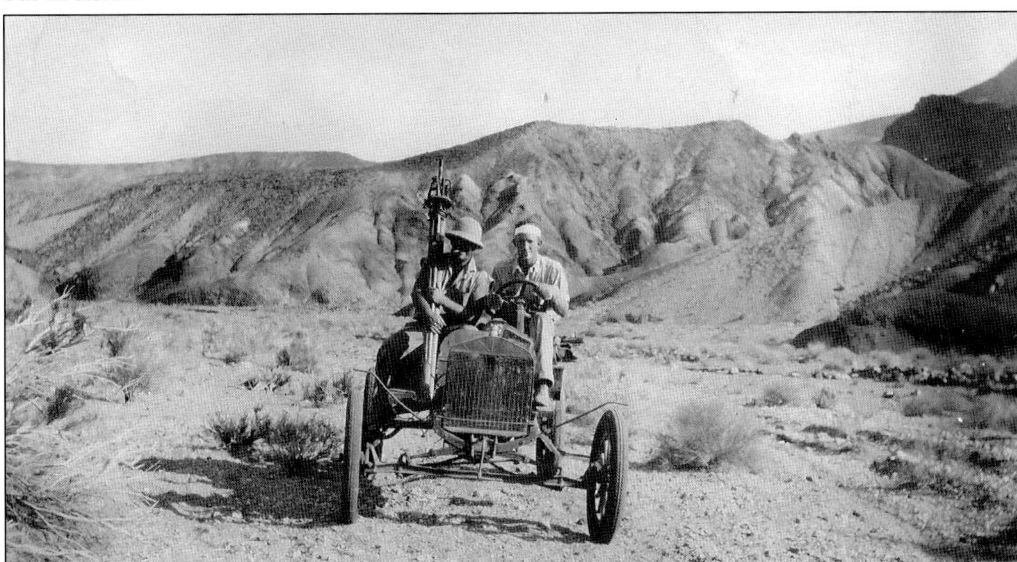

The Metropolitan Water District survey crew discovers some high ground to set up equipment where they will be safe from getting stuck.

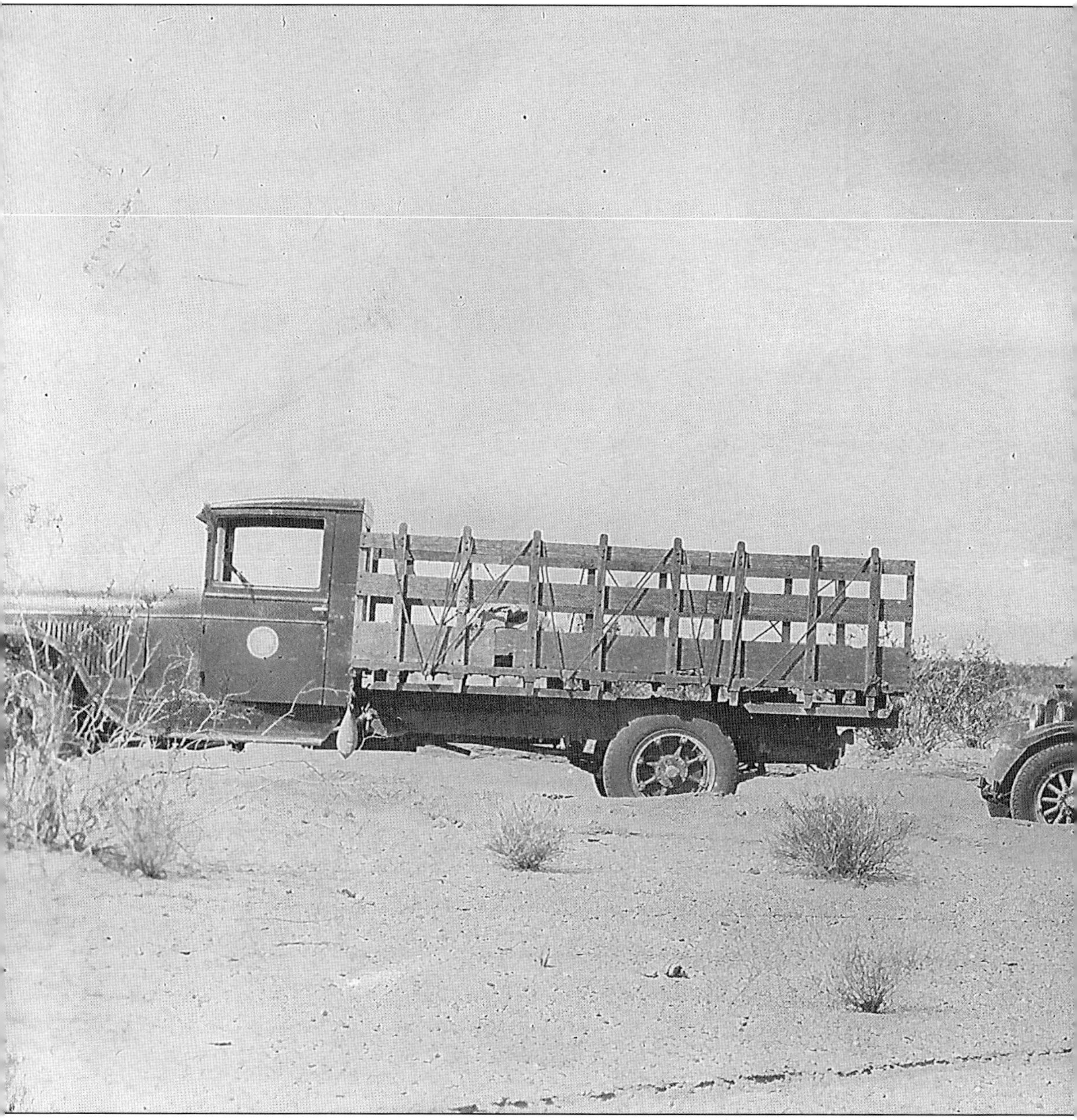

Here the survey crew takes a much-deserved break. The conditions in which the crew members worked were less than desirable. The vehicles they used continually needed maintenance because of the miles of travel across desert sand. If the vehicles were not buried up to their axles in sand,

the sand getting into the motor could be quite damaging. The survey crew also had to deal with the desert's blistering heat without much shade or protection from the elements.

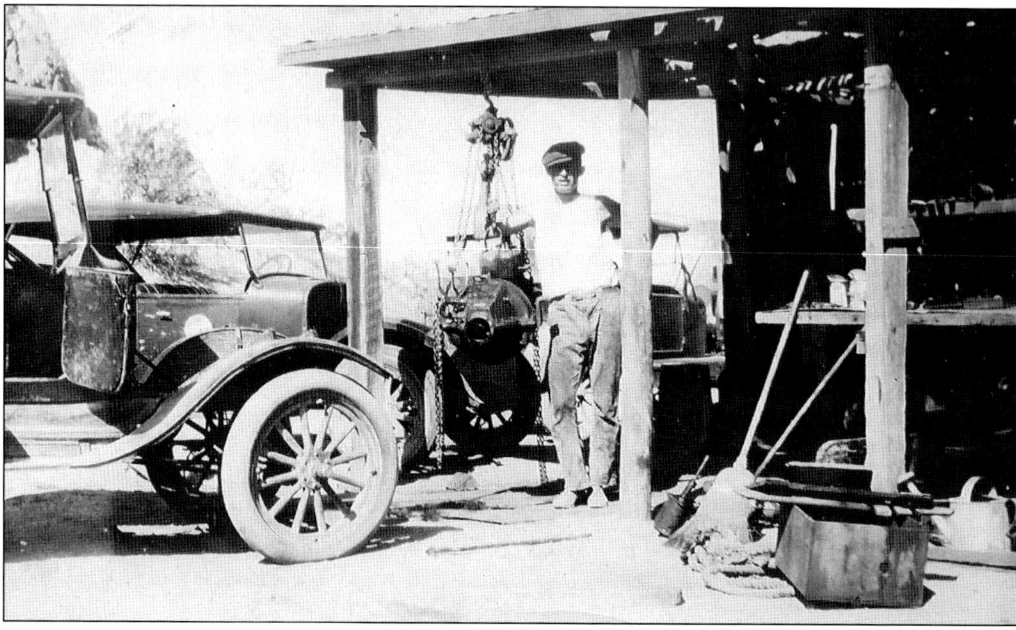

Back at camp, survey crew members spend much of the time with their vehicles in the repair shop.

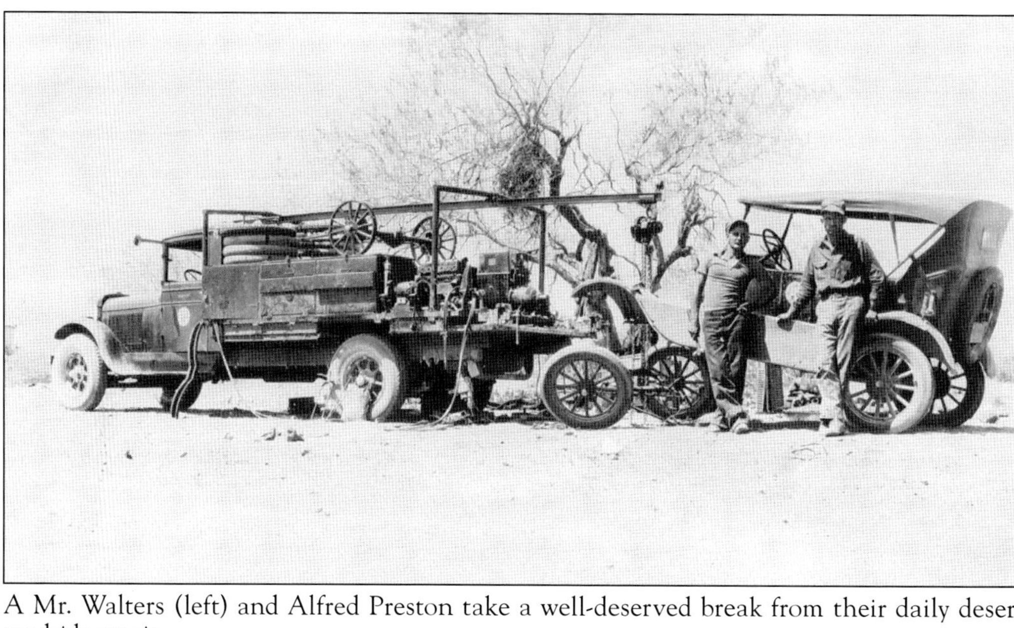

A Mr. Walters (left) and Alfred Preston take a well-deserved break from their daily desert roadside repair.

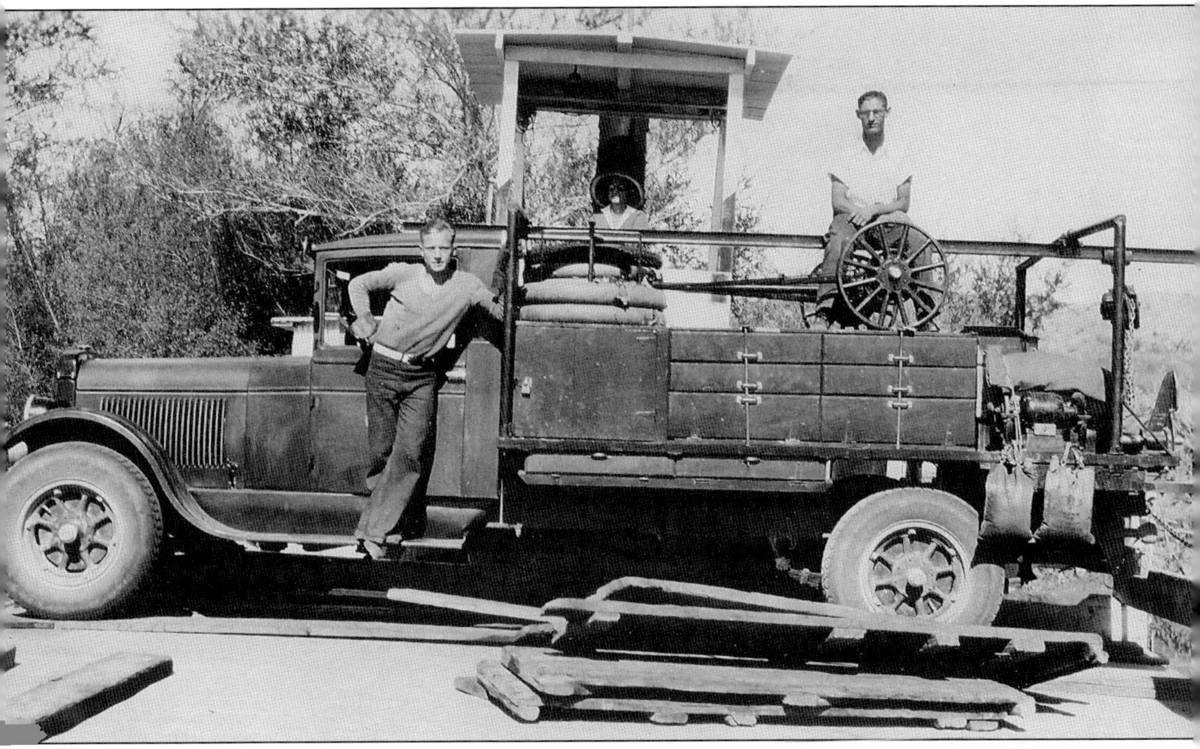

Nellie Bush is seen at the helm of the ferryboat after transporting the repair truck used by the Metropolitan Water District survey crew.

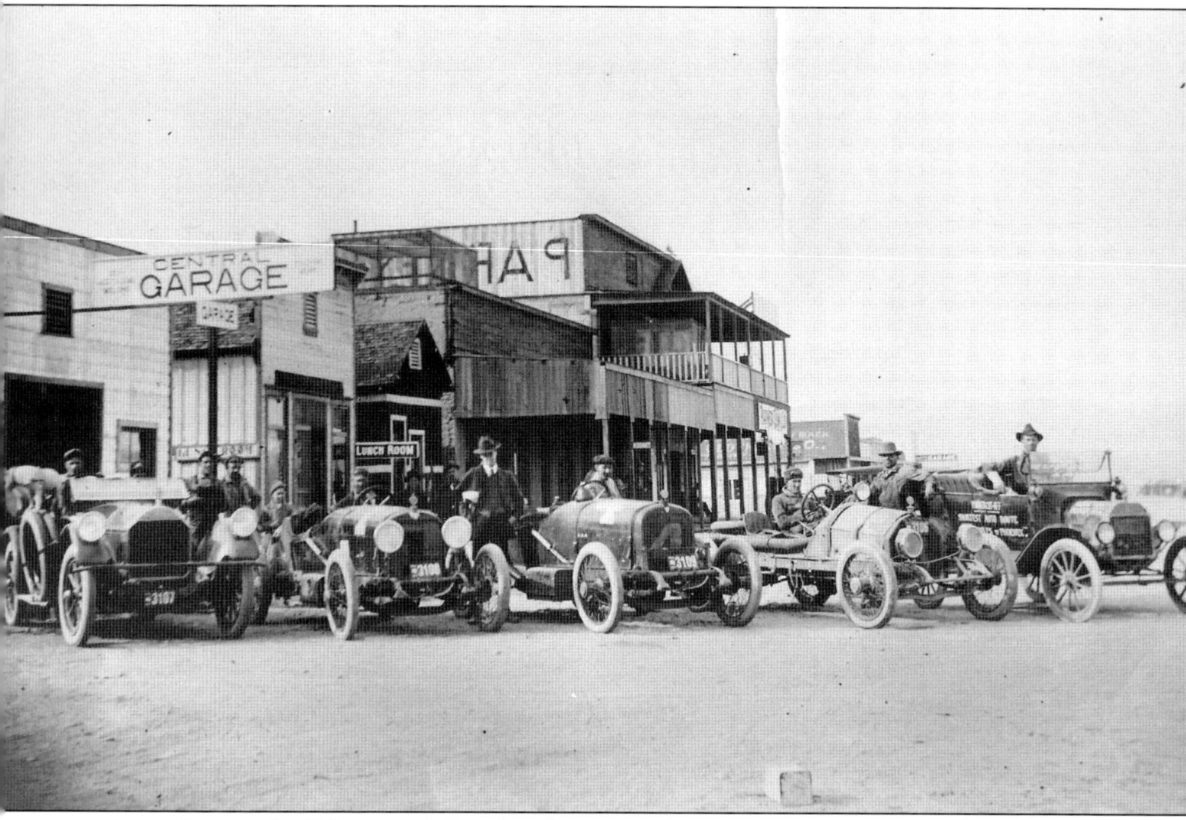

According to the February 1968 *Lakeside Desert Sun*, "Barney Oldfield and Louis Chevrolet were among the early automobile pioneers with whom Joe Bush was acquainted, having ferried them across the river when they were driving across country to obtain publicity. Racers line up across Parker's main street, which was only used once as an alternate route in 1916. Standing between the cars at center is Harold Bell Wright. The drivers, pictured from left to right, are Bill Hutt, Louis Chevrolet, Barney Oldfield, Ralph Hamlin, and Joe Bush. Bush accompanied the group of racers as far as Wenden and was ahead of the field after approximately 80 miles." This desert road rally was organized as an annual event by the California Automobile Association to promote automobile travel. The race started in downtown Los Angeles and finished at the state fair in Phoenix.

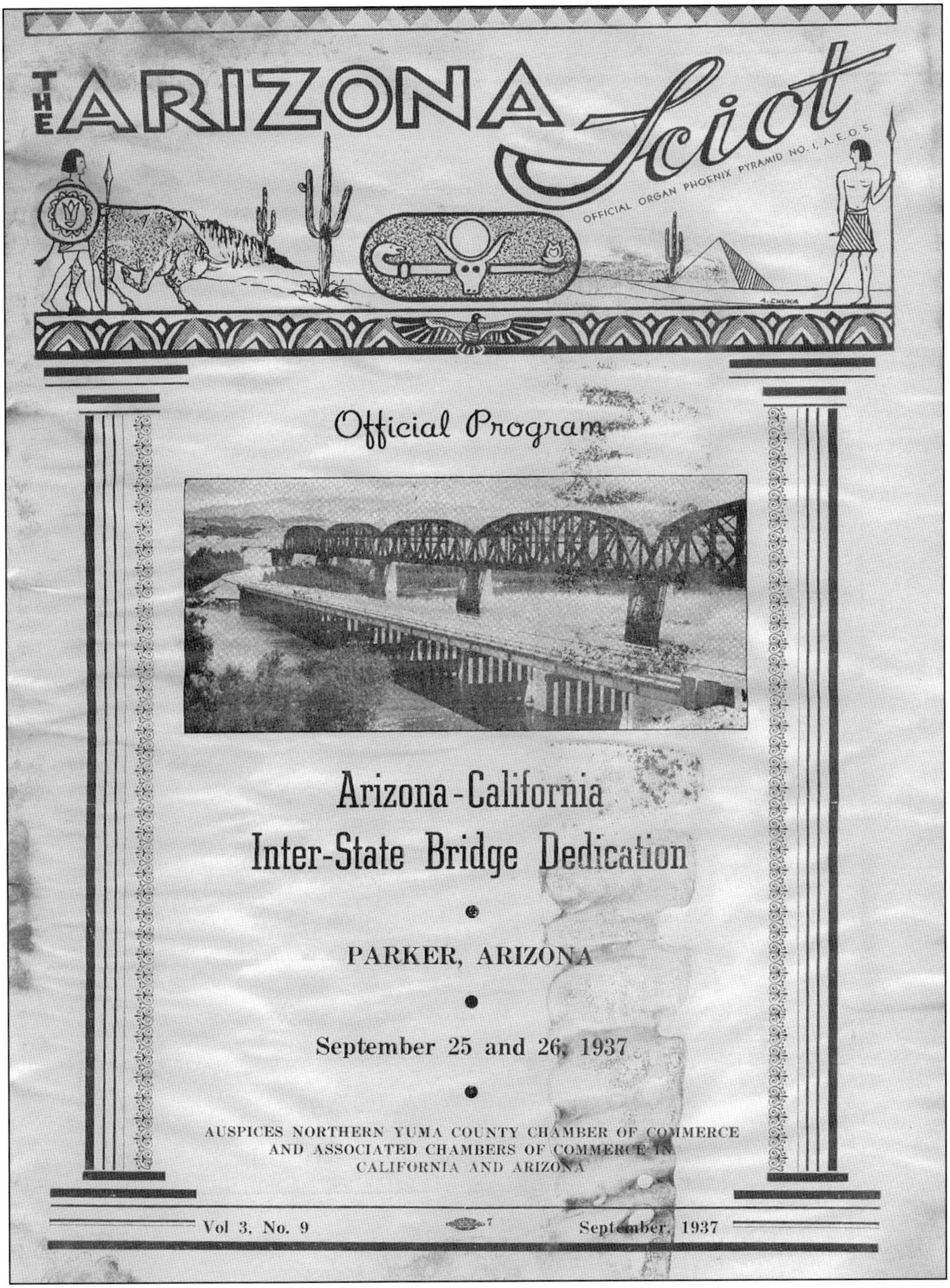

The official program cover for the 1937 Arizona-California Interstate Bridge Dedication identifies the fraternal organization of the Arizona Sciot as responsible for producing the program. The Northern Yuma County Chamber of Commerce recognizes the contributions of all federal, state, and county officials as well as civic, commercial, and industrial organizations.

Program of Events

ARIZONA-CALIFORNIA INTER-STATE BRIDGE DEDICATION AND CELEBRATION

PARKER, ARIZONA

Sept. 25-26, 1937

	Arizona Time	California Time	
Arrival Sciots and other fraternal organizations and visitors.	11:00 A.M.	10:00 A.M.	Arrival Official Guests at U.S.B.R. Guest House at the Parker Dam.
Buffet Barbecue at Parker continuous during entire celebration. Eat when hungry.	12:00 Noon	1:30	Luncheon for official guests at the Parker Dam.
		2:30	Official Motorcade to review Aqueduct Project.
See the $220,000,000 Aqueduct, including the $13,000,000 Parker Dam.	1:00		
		3:00	Trip through district and return to Parker.
Sciot Ritualistic Secret Work —High School Bldg.	3:00		
Parade of all Sciots and all civic bodies from Parker to Bridge.	5:30	4:30	Parade of all Sciot Officials and all civic bodies from Parker to Bridge.
Parker Bridge Dedeication Ceremonies.	6:00	5:00	Parker Bridge Dedication Ceremonies.
Sciot Public Ceremonial and presentations other organizations at Parker.	7:30	6:30	Sciot Public Ceremonial and presentations other organizations at Parker.
Dance and Frolic on Parker Bridge to the tantalizing strains of festive music.	9:00	8:00	Dance and Frolic on Parker Bridge to the tantalizing strains of festive music.
Sciots Funmakers and Hi-Jinks at Stephan Dude Ranch. Open to public.	9:30	8:30	Sciots Funmakers and Hi-Jinks at Stephan Dude Ranch. Open to public.
Departure Santa Fe Specials to Phoenix starts at—	2:00	1:00	Departure Santa Fe Specials for Los Angeles starts.

Other Interesting Features—Hi-Jinks Party at Stephan's Dude Ranch and Hacienda will be an outstanding event, as every Sciot Pyramid will stage a seven-minute fun-makers stunt. Wild West and diversified entertainment will be continuous in Parker, and all places of amusement in the district for your GOOD TIME.

Be assured that a most cordial greeting and joyous time awaits you at the Parker Bridge Dedication-Celebration

PARKER, ARIZONA, SEPTEMBER 25-26

ATTENTION—There is an hour's difference between Arizona and California time at Parker. All Sciots and other organizations participating in this function with drill teams, bands, fun units, dance orchestras and other featured entertainment representatives upon arrival report to Geo. Stetson, Chairman Entertainment Committee, located at the PARKER THEATRE BLDG., where information will be available regarding the program.

The 1937 Arizona-California Interstate Bridge Dedication activities planner includes a reminder regarding the time differential between Arizona and California.

Official Souvenir Program

●

ARIZONA-CALIFORNIA INTER-STATE BRIDGE DEDICATION
PARKER, ARIZONA
September 25 and 26, 1937

CALIFORNIA, HERE I COME
(Sing)

California, here I come,
Right back where I started from;
Where bowers of flowers bloom in the sun,
Each morning at dawning,
Birdies sing an' eve'ything.
A sunkist miss said, "Don't be late,"
That's why I can hardly wait;
Open up that Golden Gate—
California, here I come.

MASTER OF CEREMONIES—Wm. M. Balsz

AMERICA ---------- Official Band

Salute to Flag

Invocation ---------- Rev. Geo. McClure

Presentation of Governors---------- Clara Osborne Botzum
Hon. R. C. Stanford, Governor of Arizona------Address of Welcome
Hon. F. E. Merriam, Governor of California----------Response

A Vision---------- Hon. Carl Hayden
U. S. Senator of Arizona

The United Span—Poem---------- Hon. John S. McGroarty
U. S. Representative of California

California, Its Natural Resources---------- Hon. John R. Murdock
U. S. Representative of California

A Great Barrier Broken Down---------- Geo. D. Whittle
Bridge Engineer, U. S. Bureau of Public Roads

Official Band

The Parker Bridge ---------- Ames Crawford
Representing Northern Yuma County Chamber of Commerce

DEDICATION ADDRESSES

Pointing the Way---------- Howard S. Reed
Director, Federal Public Works Administration, Arizona

United Front---------- Hon. Frank S. Shaw
Mayor of Los Angeles, Representing All Mayors

Unity of Purpose---------- W. P. Whitsett
Chairman Metropolitan Water District of Southern California

Fraternalism ---------- Charles Foye
National Pharaoh, Ancient Egyptian Order of Sciots

Transportation---------- F. G. Mackie
Asst. General Manager, Santa Fe. R. R. Co., Coast Lines

Address---------- Wm. C. Hogoboom
National President, American Association of Engineers

The Significance of Co-operation---------- Byron T. Hanna
President, Los Angeles Chamber of Commerce

A New Highway---------- E. E. East
Engineer, Automobile Club of Southern California

Civic Good Will---------- Grace M. Sparks
President, Arizona Chambers of Commerce Secretaries

Address---------- V. H. Householder
Representing American Association of Engineers, Arizona

A Bridge Is More Than a Thoroughfare---------- Chas. A. Horrworth
Director, All-Year Club of Southern California

ARIZONA, HERE I COME
(Sing)

Arizona, here I come,
Right back where I started from;
Where sagebrush and cactus bloom in the sun,
Each morning at dawning,
Birdies sing an' eve'thing.
A native miss said, "Don't be late."
That's why I can hardly wait;
Open up that Parker Bridge—
Arizona, here I come.

The Northern Yuma County Chamber of Commerce wishes to express a sincere appreciation to all federal, state and county officials as well as civic, commercial and industrial organizations that have contributed to this program and have so generously aided in the development and completion of the Parker Dam project.

Committee of Welcome

E. A. BROWNE, chairman of committee.

E. A. MORITZ, supervising engineer, U. S. Bureau of Roads.

M. N. FOREMAN, chairman Yuma County Board of Supervisors.

S. DeCORSE, member Yuma County Board of Supervisors.

GEO. HAGELY, member Yuma County Board of Supervisors.

ARTHUR DORAN, member San Bernardino County Board of Supervisors.

PAUL B. MURPHY, Phoenix Chamber of Commerce.

HAROLD W. WRIGHT, Los Angeles Chamber of Commerce.

C. OSBORNE BOTZUM, Northern Yuma County Chamber of Commerce.

GRACE SPARKS, Yavapai County Chamber of Commerce.

W. A. SULLIVAN, Gila County Chamber of Commerce.

VERNON FOSTER, Phoenix Junior Chamber of Commerce.

C. F. THOMALLO, Graham County Chamber of Commerce.

EVELYN SMITH, Yuma County Chamber of Commerce.

S. J. ARNOLD, San Bernardino Chamber of Commerce.

A. H. CONDRON, Tucson Chamber of Commerce.

WILLIAM DUNKERLY, Pasadena Chamber of Commerce.

CORNELIUS BACKSEY, San Bernardino County Chamber of Commerce.

L. H. MYERS, Glendale Chamber of Commerce.

ARCHIE M. HALL, Needles Chamber of Commerce.

J. D. WALKUP, Flagstaff Chamber of Commerce.

C. R. MICHAELS, Bisbee Chamber of Commerce.

M. O. REESE, Mohave County Chamber of Commerce.

CHARLES H. FOYE, National Pharaoh, Ancient Egyptian Order of Sciots.

ARTHUR JUDISCH, Chairman Arizona-California Sciot Ceremonial Parker Bridge Dedication.

The Arizona-California Interstate Bridge Dedication ceremony was held on September 25 and 26, 1937. The list of dignitaries who attended was quite impressive. Gov. R. C. Stanford of Arizona and Gov. F. E. Merriam of California spoke. Among the others addressing those in attendance was the U.S. senator from Arizona, Hon. Carl Hayden.

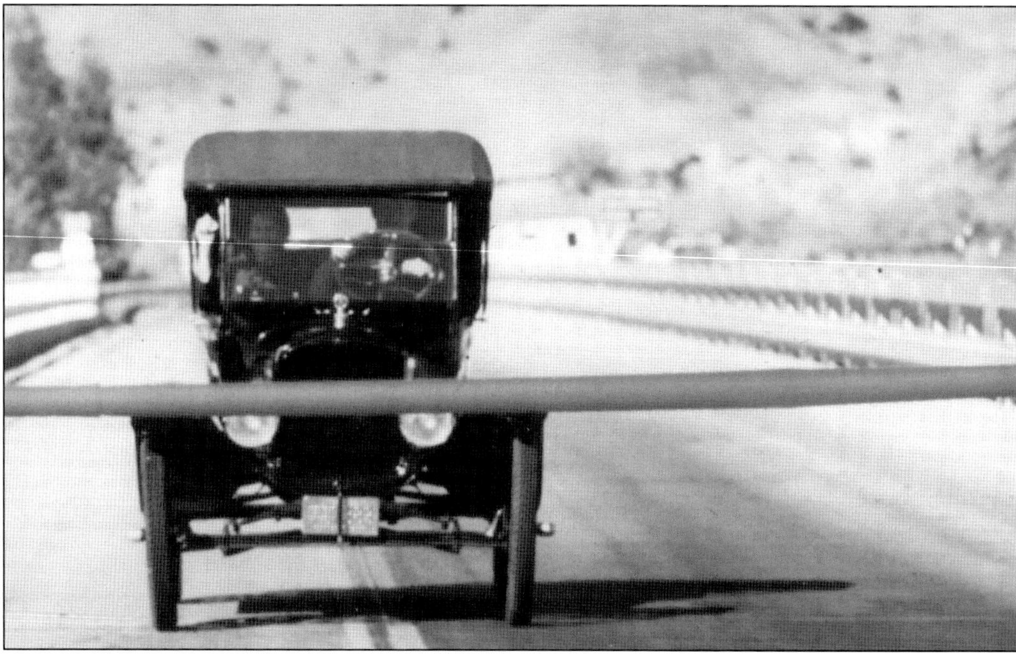

On January 4, 1979, a 1925 Ford transports Clara Osborne Botzum across the Colorado River highway bridge, which was renamed the Clara Osborne Botzum Bridge in her honor. Marion Beaver, a member of the Yuma County Board of Supervisors, drives the car.

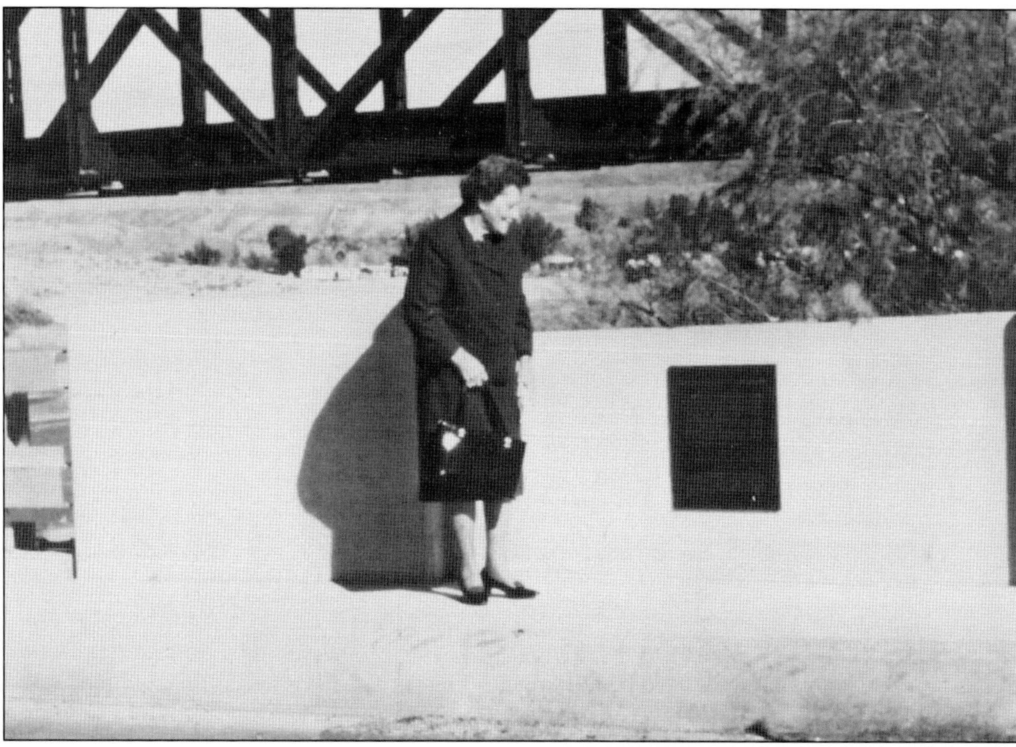

Clara Osborne Botzum, whose tireless efforts resulted in the construction of the Colorado River highway bridge, views the dedication plaque in 1979.

Five

THAT DAM WAR
BRING OUT THE NATIONAL GUARD!

A little-known but significant conflict between the State of California and the State of Arizona began over the construction of Parker Dam. Had the disagreement not occurred, the Arizona water rights that exist today may have looked very different.

Having first been elected to the Arizona legislature in 1920, Nellie Bush was already familiar with the politics of government. The Colorado River Compact was negotiated in 1922 to address the Colorado Basin states' anxiety over their share of the water resource. California contributed the least amount of runoff to the river but had the greatest demand. By 1934, California had the audacity to start construction of a dam near Parker, Arizona.

Nellie Bush was quite familiar with the area, as one of her business enterprises was ferrying people and supplies up and down the stretch of river that would be adversely affected by the building of the dam. Nellie's interest in blocking California's dam project was undoubtedly motivated by several different factors.

On November 10, 1934, at the behest of Nellie Bush, Arizona governor B. B. Moeur declared martial law and mobilized 100 troops of the Arizona National Guard to resist the invasion on Arizona soil. Upon arrival in Parker, the National Guard began a plan of action that included the use of two Bush ferryboats flying the Arizona flag. Soon thereafter, they were dubbed "the Arizona Navy."

The dispute may have been short-lived, but it resulted in the U.S. Supreme Court decision (295 U.S. 174) in favor of Arizona on March 4, 1935.

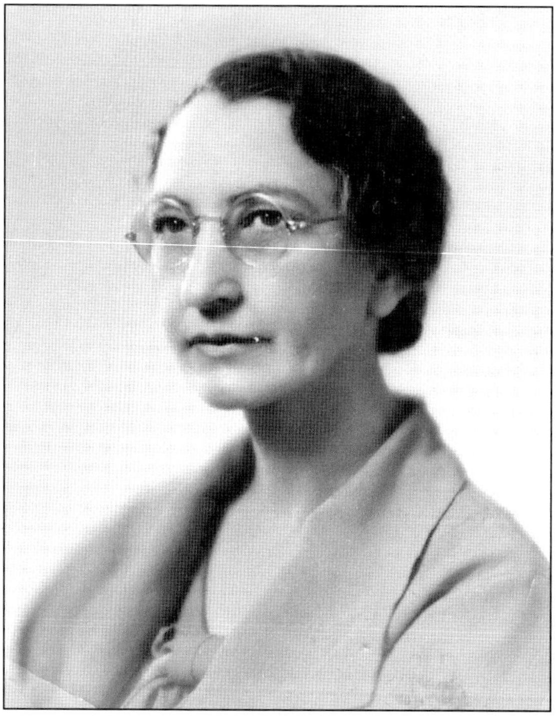

First elected as a representative in 1920, Nellie T. Bush served in the Arizona legislature for 16 years, working for her district and Northern Yuma County. The second woman to serve in the Arizona House of Representatives, she later became the first female state senator.

Nellie T. Bush, never one to consider women incapable of succeeding in a male-dominated society, received her steamboat license in 1931. It allowed her to pilot the family ferryboats on the Colorado River.

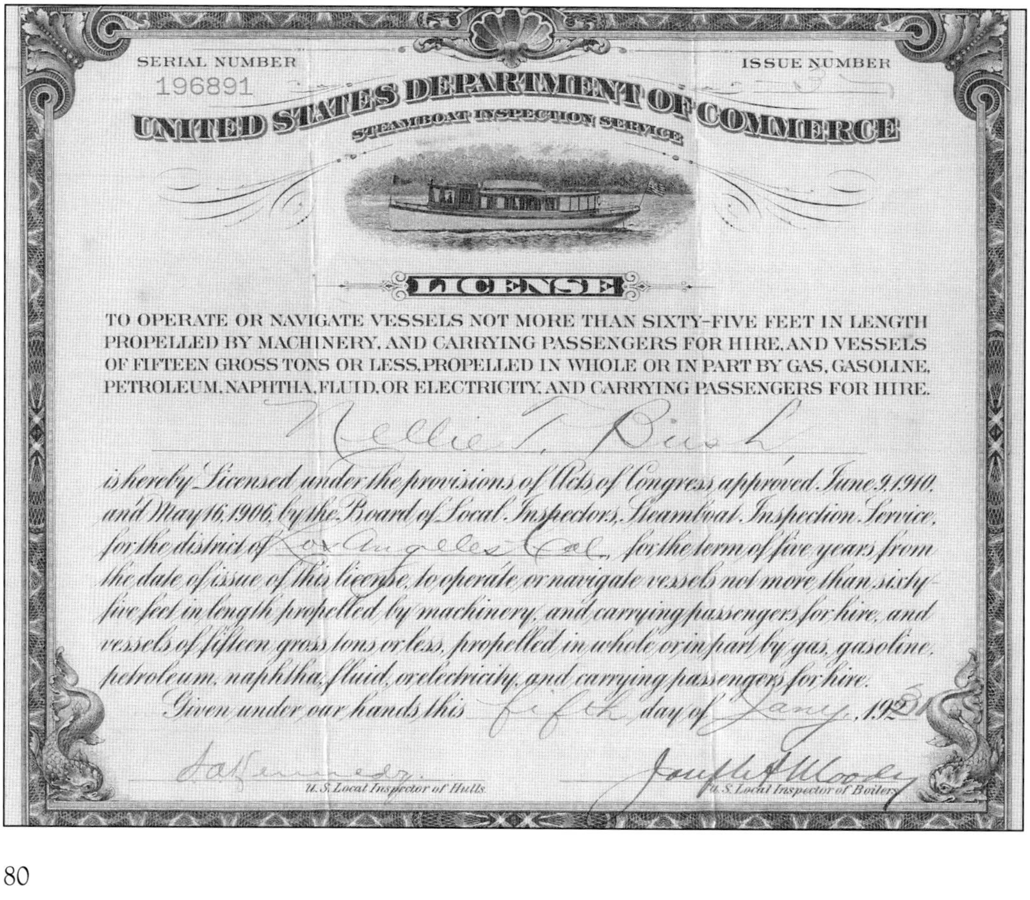

SERIAL NUMBER 196891

ISSUE NUMBER

UNITED STATES DEPARTMENT OF COMMERCE

STEAMBOAT INSPECTION SERVICE

LICENSE

TO OPERATE OR NAVIGATE VESSELS NOT MORE THAN SIXTY-FIVE FEET IN LENGTH PROPELLED BY MACHINERY, AND CARRYING PASSENGERS FOR HIRE, AND VESSELS OF FIFTEEN GROSS TONS OR LESS, PROPELLED IN WHOLE OR IN PART BY GAS, GASOLINE, PETROLEUM, NAPHTHA, FLUID, OR ELECTRICITY, AND CARRYING PASSENGERS FOR HIRE.

Nellie T. Bush

is hereby Licensed under the provisions of Acts of Congress approved June 9, 1910, and May 16, 1906, by the Board of Local Inspectors, Steamboat Inspection Service, for the district of Los Angeles Cal, for the term of five years from the date of issue of this license, to operate or navigate vessels not more than sixty-five feet in length propelled by machinery, and carrying passengers for hire, and vessels of fifteen gross tons or less, propelled in whole or in part by gas, gasoline, petroleum, naphtha, fluid, or electricity, and carrying passengers for hire.

Given under our hands this fifth day of Jany. 1931

U. S. Local Inspector of Hulls.

U. S. Local Inspector of Boilers.

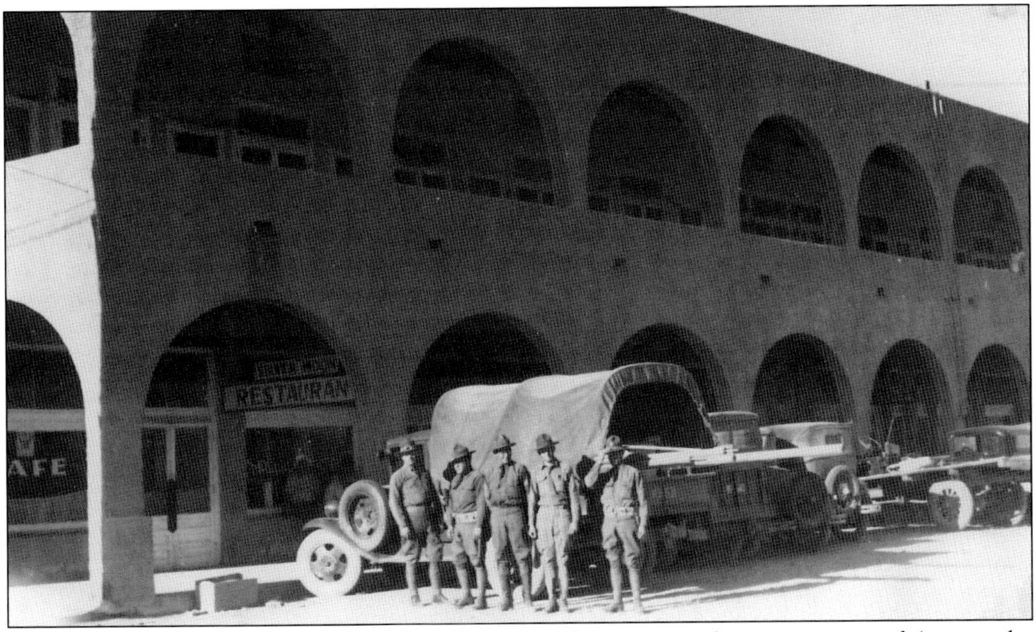

Gov. B. B. Moeur called upon the National Guard to protect the sovereignty of Arizona by declaring martial law to prevent the construction of Parker Dam. The National Guardsmen are seen here upon their arrival in 1934.

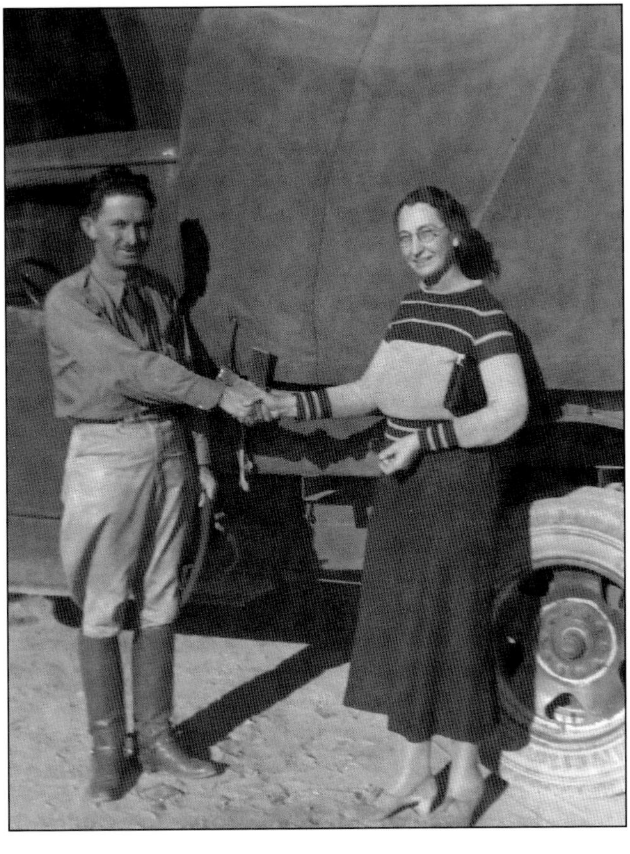

Nellie Bush greets commanding officer Maj. Franklin I. Pomeroy as he arrives at the Grandview Hotel.

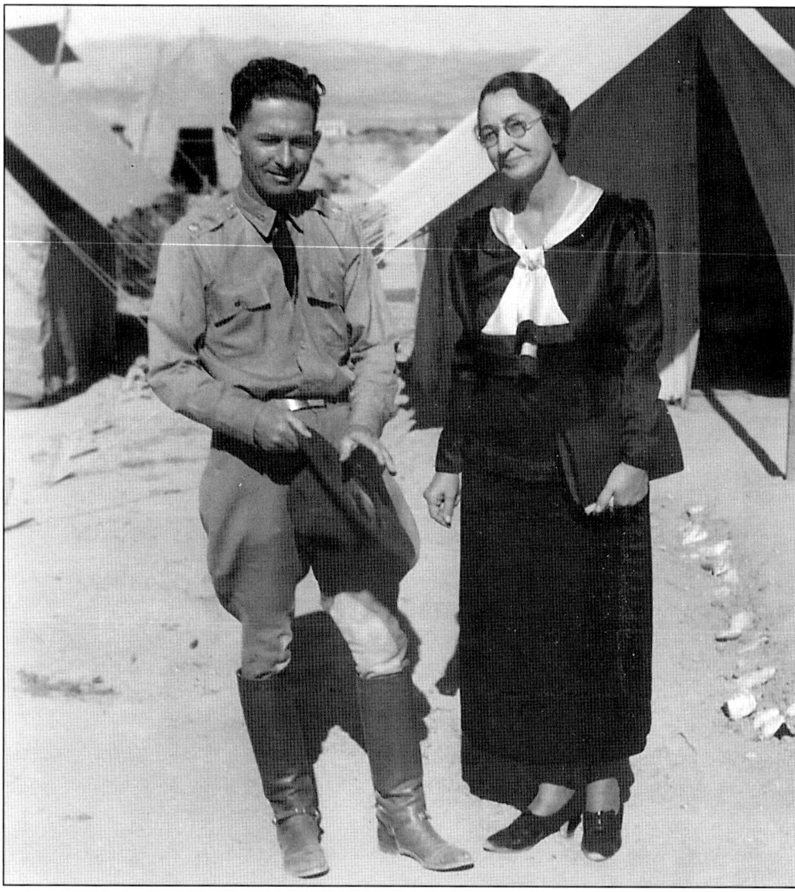

Nellie Bush meets with Maj. Franklin I. Pomeroy while visiting the National Guard campsite in Parker. The barracks, actually tent cabins, were very similar to the type used by area miners. The guardsmen were able to use the campsite as a command center for planning their activities.

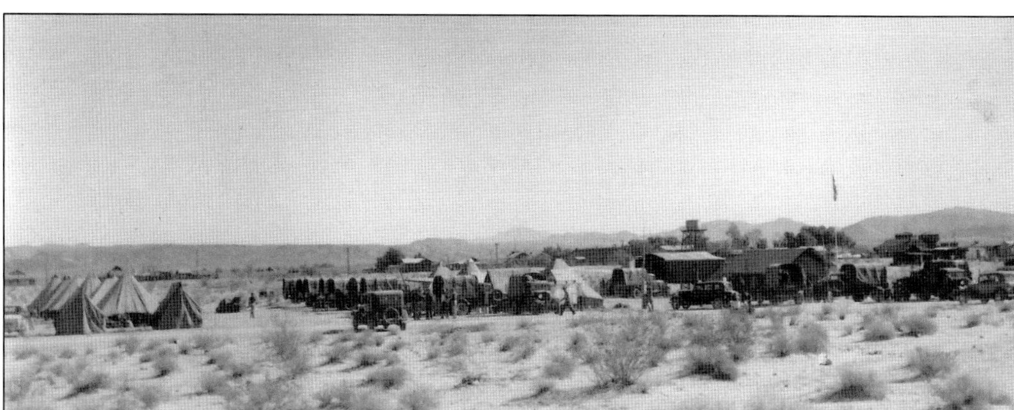

This panoramic view shows the Arizona National Guard campsite and command center during the monitoring of the Parker Dam construction site.

Arizona took a stand to protect its sovereignty in spite of California's attempts to forge ahead with the construction of Parker Dam. Nellie Bush spoke with the media to get the story out. Her efforts proved successful both in the press and all the way to the U.S. Supreme Court.

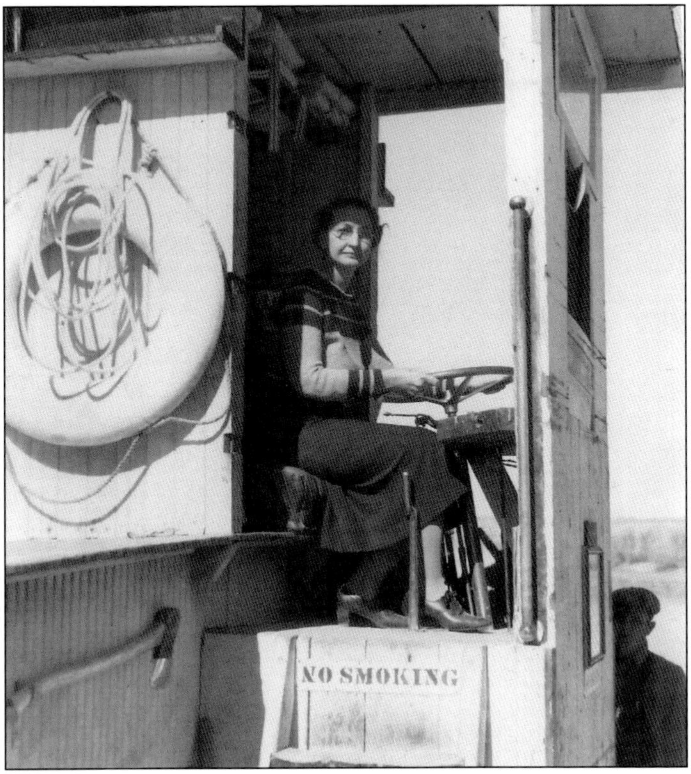

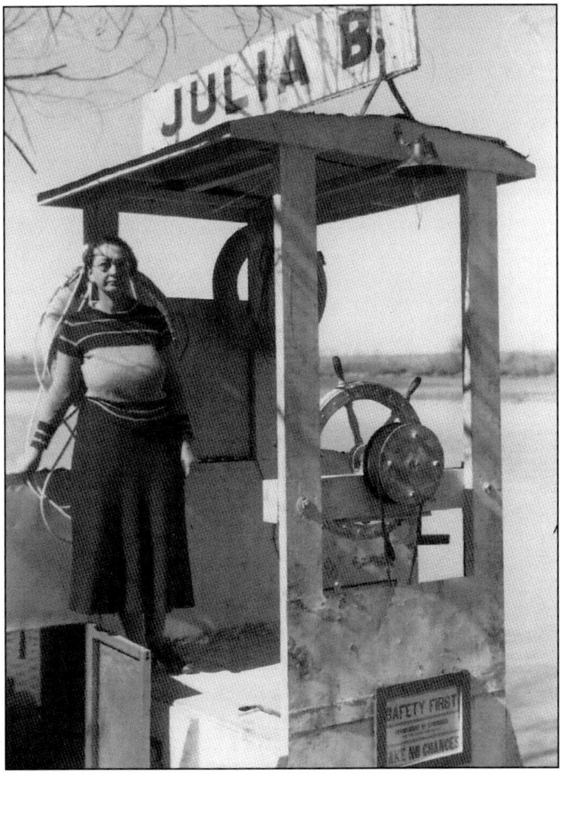

Nellie Bush stands on the ferryboat *Julia B*, commissioned to fly the Arizona flag and carry the National Guardsmen up the Colorado near the mouth of the Bill Williams River. The vessel became part of "the Arizona Navy," with Nellie made an honorary admiral.

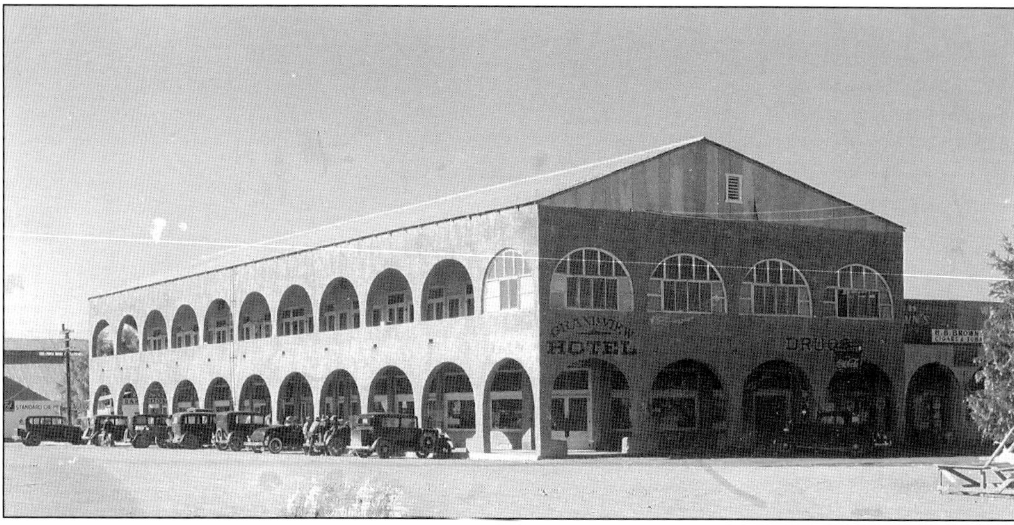

This scene of the Grandview Hotel was captured during the holiday season, as the community Christmas tree so aptly reflects.

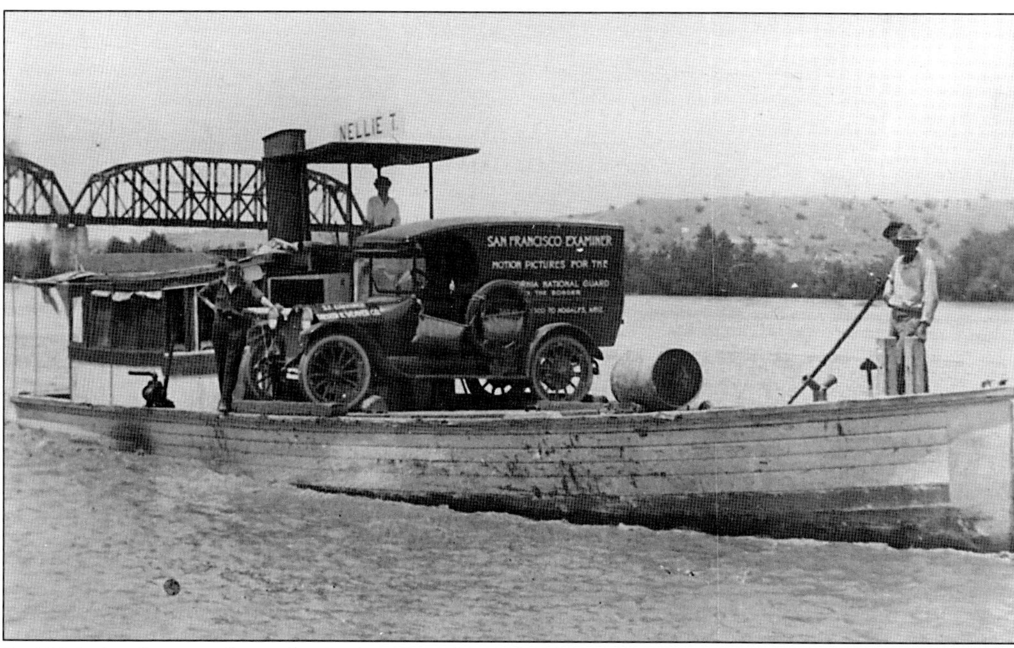

In 1934, the dispute about the Parker Dam brought the *San Francisco Examiner*, which needed its vehicle ferried in order to report firsthand on the status of "the Dam War."

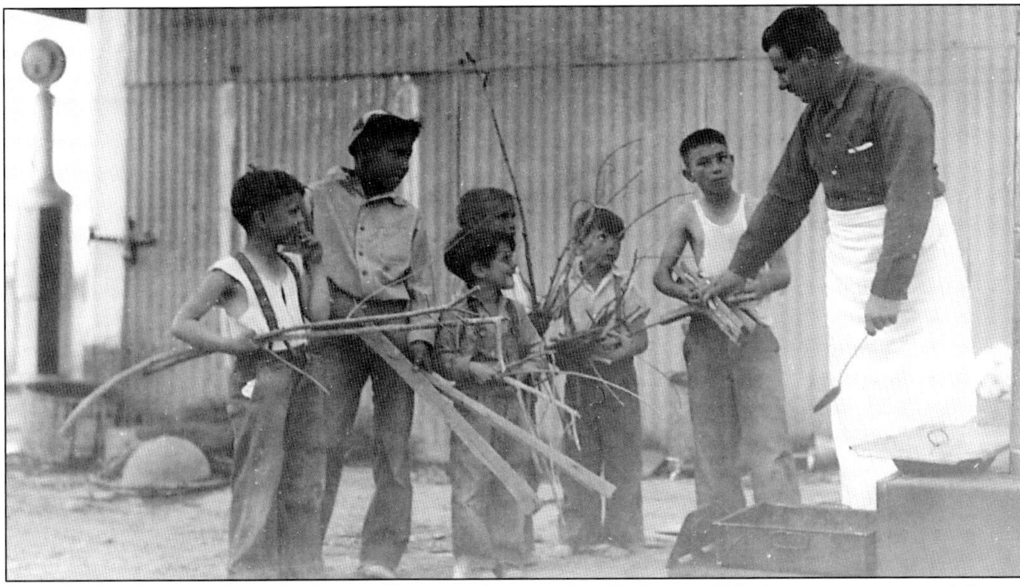

The Arizona National Guardsmen who were dispensed to Parker in 1934 became instant celebrities to the local boys, who were eager to collect the firewood used for cooking the men's meals.

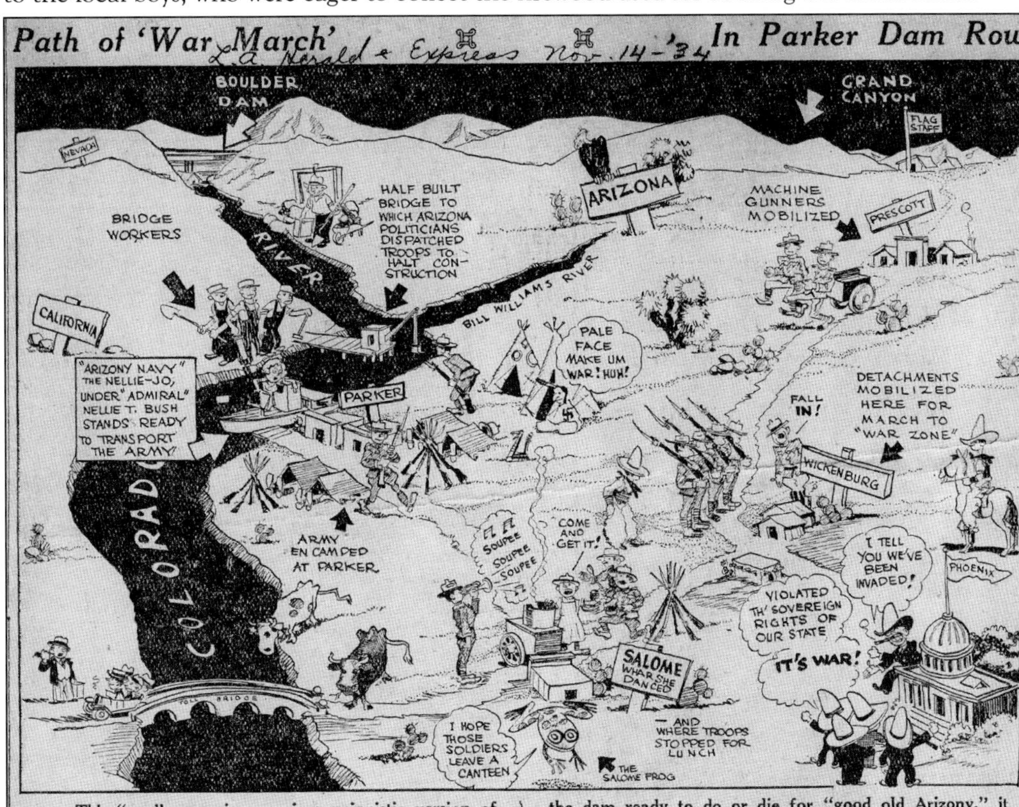

The disagreement over the construction of a dam created quite a stir with the Associated Press. In this 1934 *Los Angeles Herald* cartoon entitled "Path of Dam War," the California newspaper has attempted to put a humorous twist on the event.

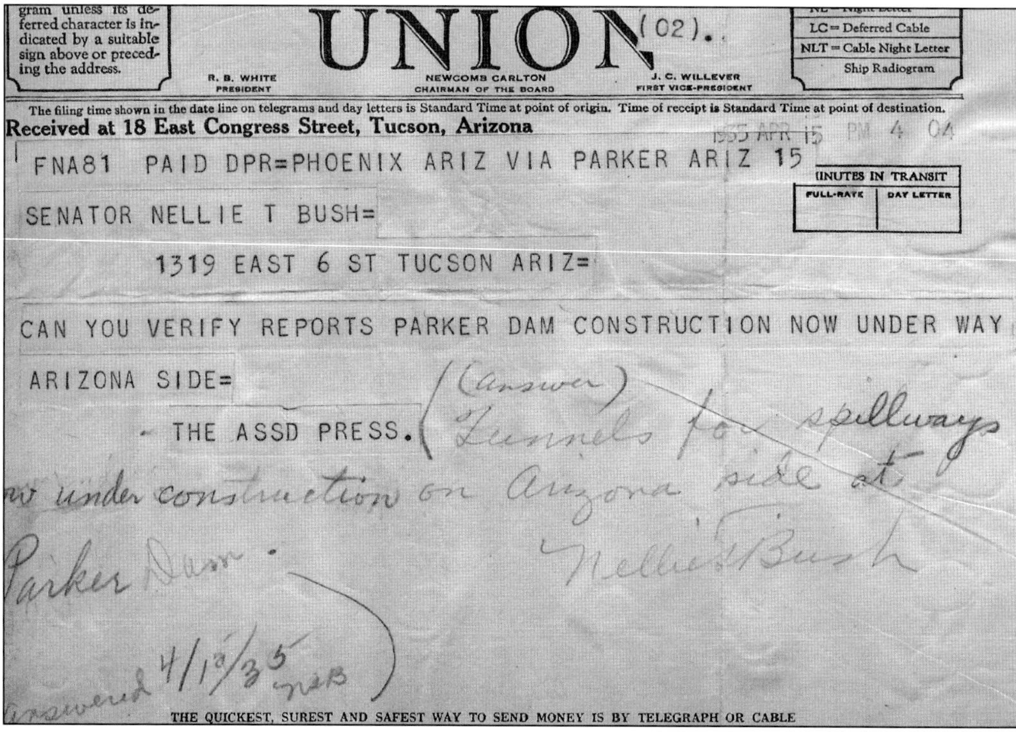
gram unless its deferred character is indicated by a suitable sign above or preceding the address.

UNION (02).

R. B. WHITE PRESIDENT — NEWCOMB CARLTON CHAIRMAN OF THE BOARD — J. C. WILLEVER FIRST VICE-PRESIDENT

LC = Deferred Cable
NLT = Cable Night Letter
Ship Radiogram

The filing time shown in the date line on telegrams and day letters is Standard Time at point of origin. Time of receipt is Standard Time at point of destination.

Received at 18 East Congress Street, Tucson, Arizona 1935 APR 15 PM 4 04

FNA81 PAID DPR=PHOENIX ARIZ VIA PARKER ARIZ 15

MINUTES IN TRANSIT — FULL-RATE — DAY LETTER

SENATOR NELLIE T BUSH=

1319 EAST 6 ST TUCSON ARIZ=

CAN YOU VERIFY REPORTS PARKER DAM CONSTRUCTION NOW UNDER WAY ARIZONA SIDE=

- THE ASSD PRESS.

(Answer) Tunnels for spillways now under construction on Arizona side at Parker Dam. Nellie T Bush

Answered 4/15/35 NTB

THE QUICKEST, SUREST AND SAFEST WAY TO SEND MONEY IS BY TELEGRAPH OR CABLE

On April 15, 1935, Nellie Bush received a telegram from the Associated Press for verification about the status of Parker Dam on the Arizona side. Nellie's response the same day was that tunnels for spillways were under construction.

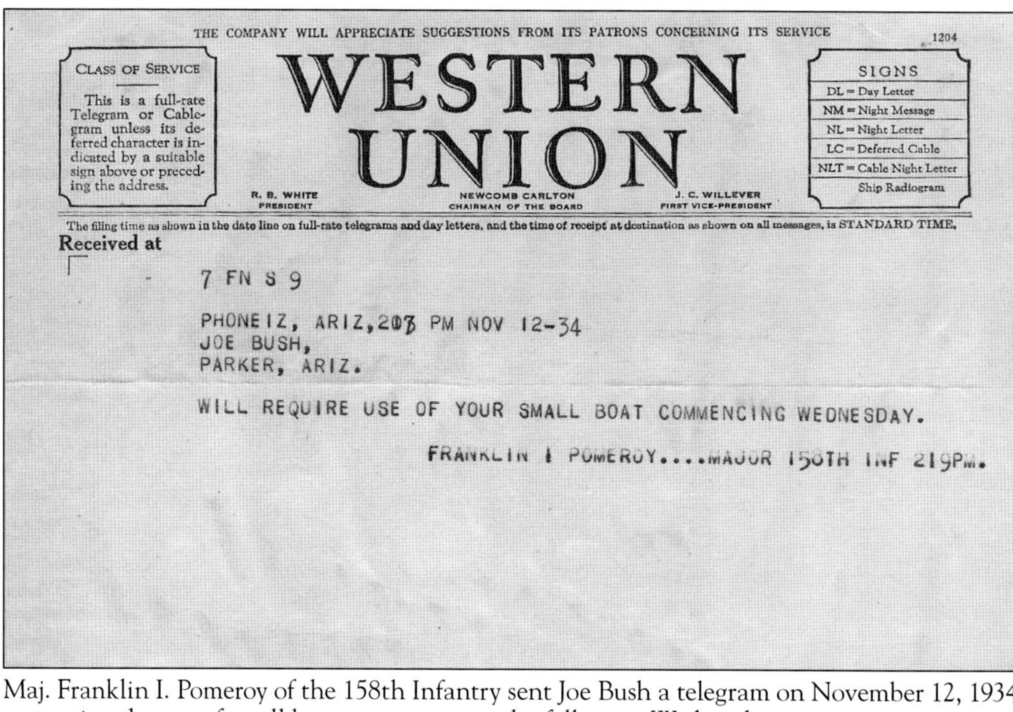
THE COMPANY WILL APPRECIATE SUGGESTIONS FROM ITS PATRONS CONCERNING ITS SERVICE 1204

CLASS OF SERVICE
This is a full-rate Telegram or Cablegram unless its deferred character is indicated by a suitable sign above or preceding the address.

WESTERN UNION

R. B. WHITE PRESIDENT — NEWCOMB CARLTON CHAIRMAN OF THE BOARD — J. C. WILLEVER FIRST VICE-PRESIDENT

SIGNS
DL = Day Letter
NM = Night Message
NL = Night Letter
LC = Deferred Cable
NLT = Cable Night Letter
Ship Radiogram

The filing time as shown in the date line on full-rate telegrams and day letters, and the time of receipt at destination as shown on all messages, is STANDARD TIME.

Received at

7 FN S 9

PHONEIZ, ARIZ,203 PM NOV 12-34
JOE BUSH,
PARKER, ARIZ.

WILL REQUIRE USE OF YOUR SMALL BOAT COMMENCING WEDNESDAY.

FRANKLIN I POMEROY....MAJOR 158TH INF 219PM.

Maj. Franklin I. Pomeroy of the 158th Infantry sent Joe Bush a telegram on November 12, 1934, requesting the use of small boats commencing the following Wednesday.

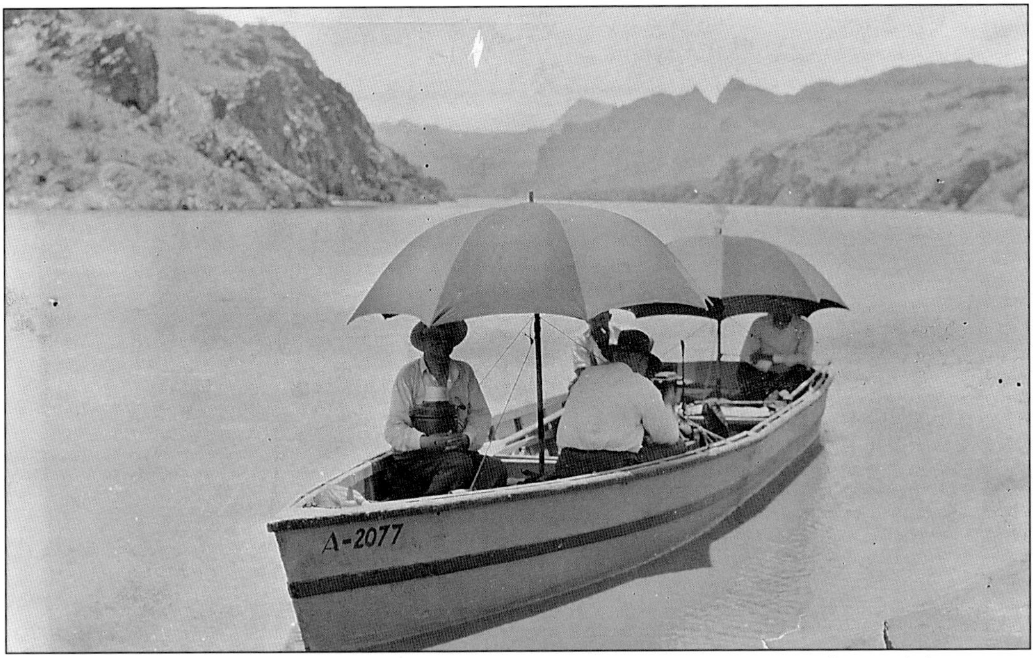

By 1923, thirteen California cities were seeking an additional water source, collectively becoming the Metropolitan Water District of Southern California, which began engineering studies in conjunction with surveying to discover the best and most economical route for an aqueduct from the Colorado River. Construction of the aqueduct would also necessitate the creation of a dam.

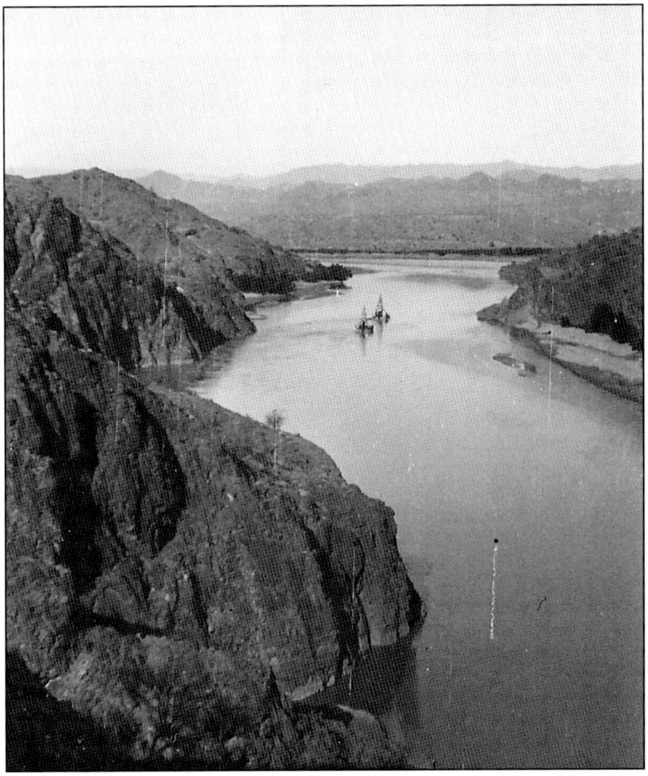

Core drilling from a barge can be seen in the distance in this view of the future Parker Dam site. This image also provides a glimpse of how the water flowed at the Bill Williams Fork prior to the dam.

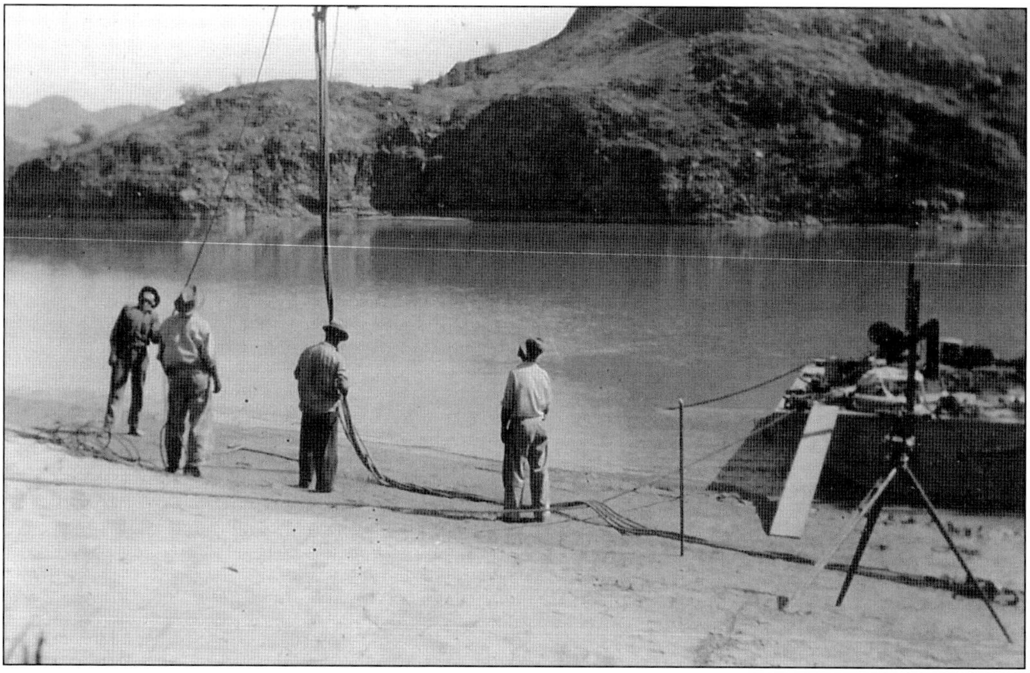

Workers prepare equipment for core drilling at the Parker Dam site in 1933. Diamonds are used for core drilling because they are the strongest stone, able to penetrate and not break.

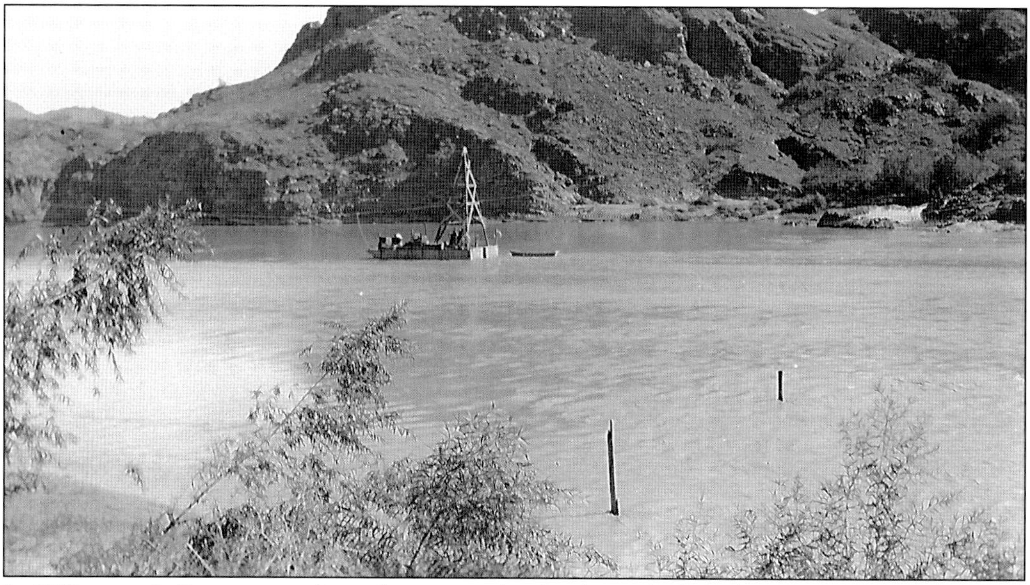

In 1933, core drilling was performed to assess the depth at which bedrock could be located.

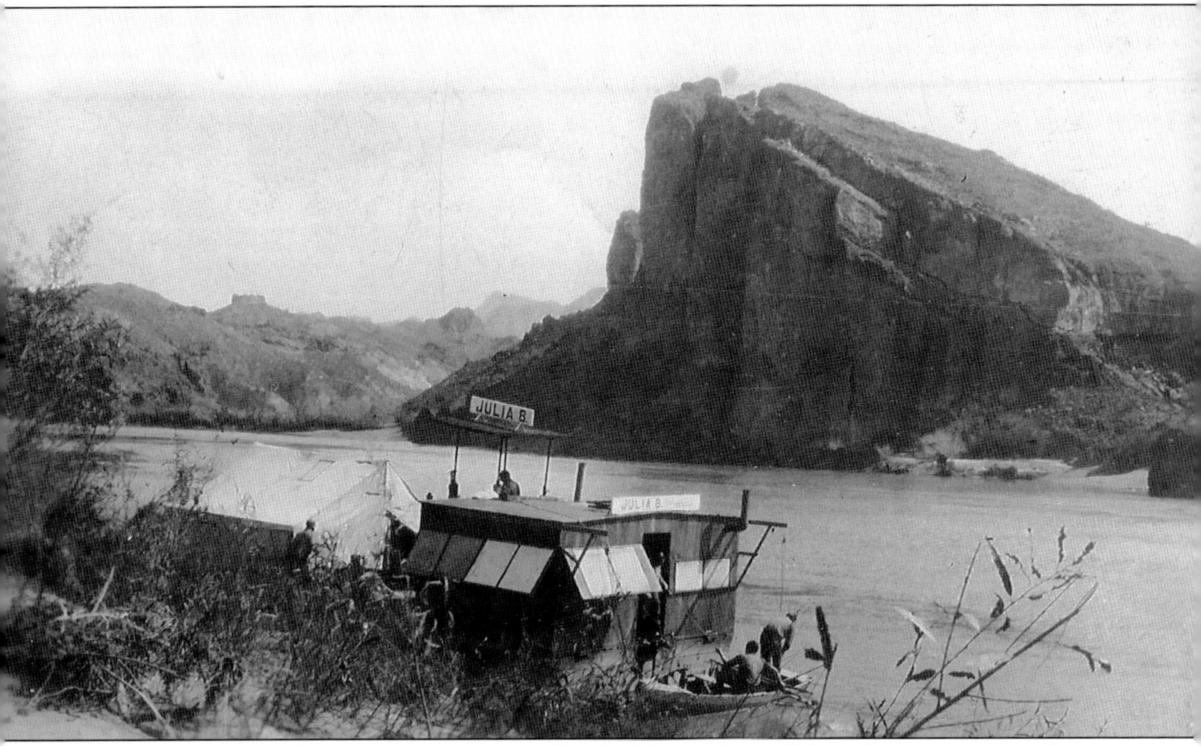

The *Julia B*, employed to ferry a survey crew for the Metropolitan Water District, is moored on the California side of Parker Strip in proximity to Echo Lodge. In the distance, a big rock outcrop towers over the river. This section of county road can no longer be traveled because of concern over possible rock slides.

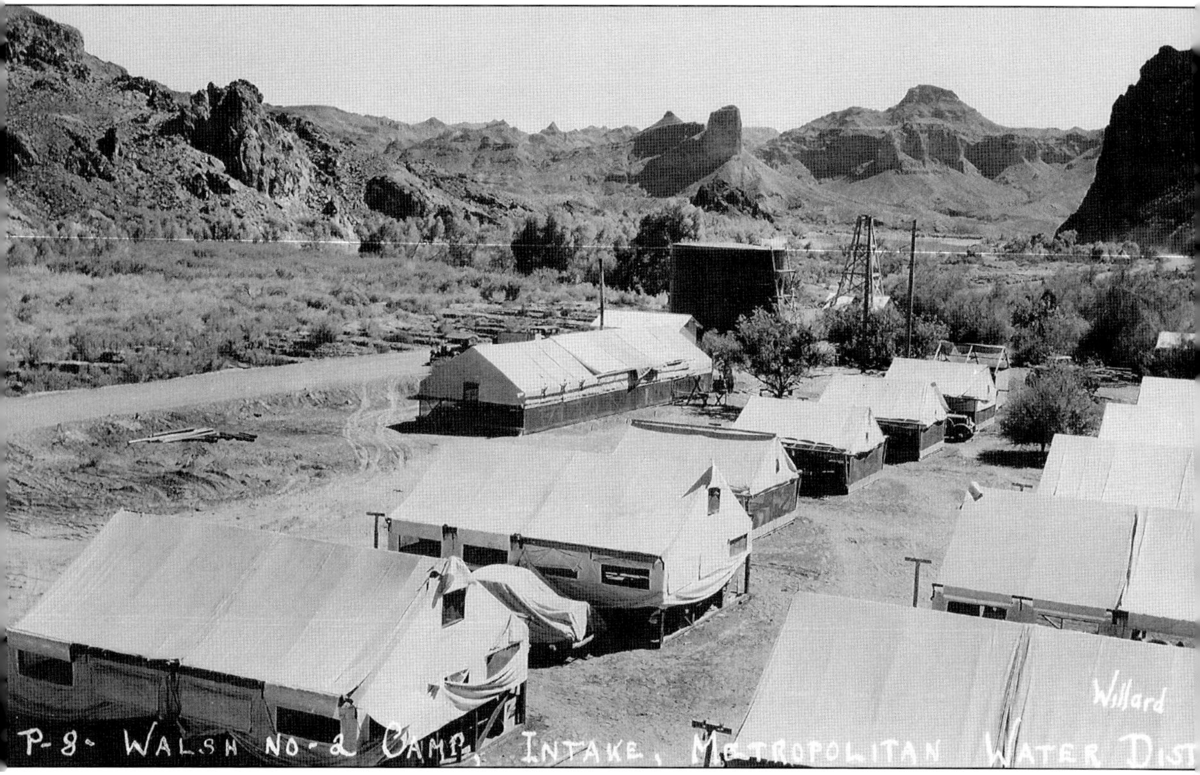

The use of tent cabins was quite common, as depicted at this campsite used by the construction crew of Parker Dam in the early 1930s.

Six

The Little Desert Town that Could
The Spirit of the Community

The town of Parker has maintained a strong sense of community, readily noticeable by the available services from the all-volunteer Parker Fire Department, established in 1944, and the many civic organizations, churches, and schools that contribute to the overall quality of life.

One of the highlights each year is the annual barbecue hosted by the Parker Fire Department. The barbecue would not be complete without country music from local musicians or the ride around town on the fire truck for both children and adults. From the 1940s through the 1960s, the volunteers at the fire department also served as ambulance drivers. They would be parked on the sidelines at football games if ever an emergency arose.

Civic organizations have played a significant role in the community. These groups include the Elks and Does, Soroptimist, Rotary, Lions, Women's, Masons, Eastern Star, Hustlers, Kiwanis, Junior Women's, and Eagles Clubs; the Veterans of Foreign Wars; the American Legion; and the neighborhood Boy and Girl Scouts. Parker's best are the tireless volunteers who continue to give to others. The community is forever grateful.

Early in the town's history, only one church existed. Soon one more was built, and then another and another, until most religious faiths are now represented with a place to gather in fellowship and shared spiritual belief. The Community Church, which later became Parker United Methodist, and the Sacred Heart Catholic Church provided the use of their receptions halls as nonsectarian USO Centers for American servicemen and women who found themselves in Arizona during Patton's desert training maneuvers and again in the 1960s for army–air force joint maneuvers.

Education is the foundation of the American way of life. Parker's original one-room schoolhouse has long since evolved into a unified kindergarten-through-12th-grade school district representative of three primary cultures: Anglo, Native American, and Hispanic. School is a common bond that brings local children together, whether participating in the classroom, sports, or extracurricular activities.

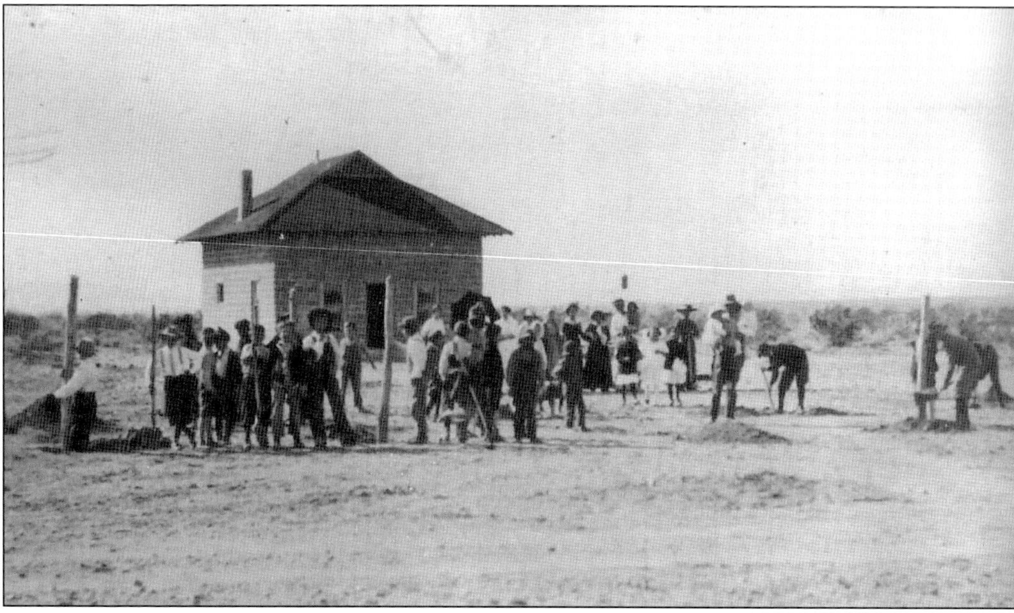

With the establishment of the Parker town site and settlers moving into the area, Yuma County determined a need for building a jail in its northern section in 1914. The Old Jail, listed on the National Register of Historic Places, is located in Pop Harvey Park—the same site where it was originally constructed in Block 140.

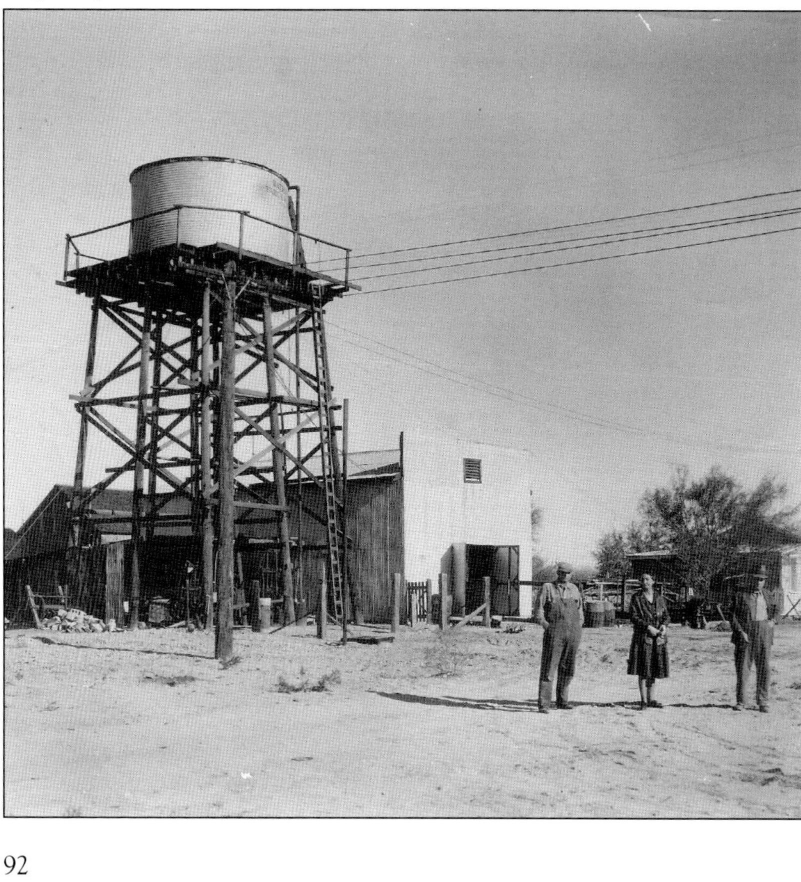

Joe and Nellie Bush purchased the Parker Water Company from owner James Gillen (standing at left) in 1931. With 11 water meters, the company was pumping 5,000 gallons every 24 hours by 1932.

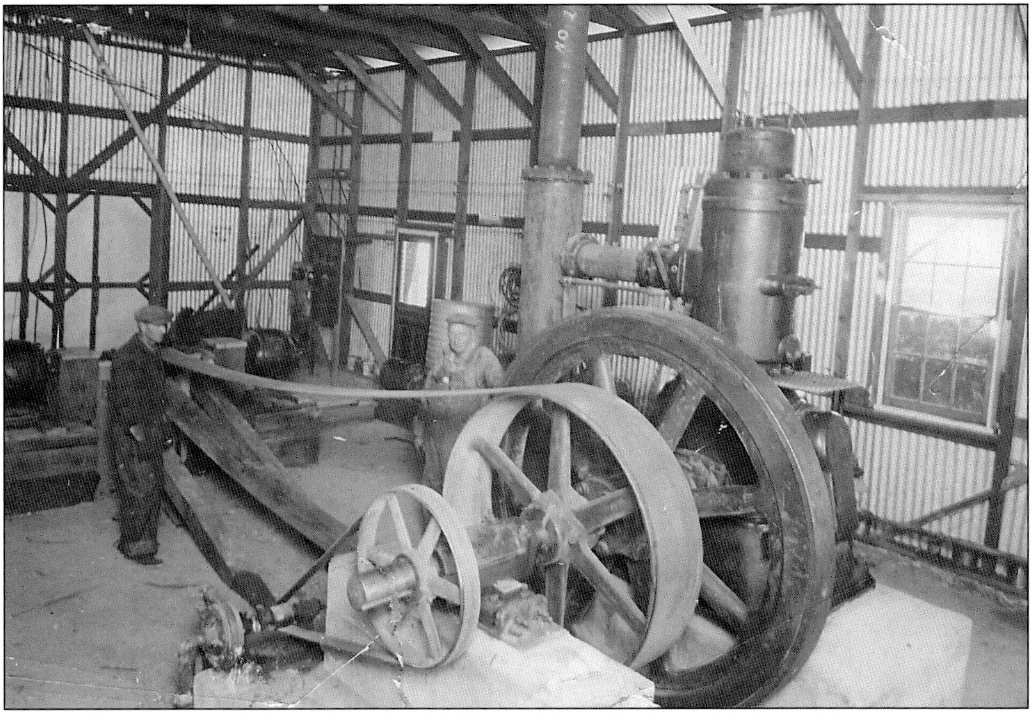

The Bushes established the Parker Electric and Light Plant, which operated from 1924 to 1946. Between 1924 and 1941, it ran with a direct current (DC) of 110 to 220 volts; from 1941 to 1946, the power was changed to an alternating current (AC) of 25 to 115 volts. This photograph depicts Plant No. 2 in 1932.

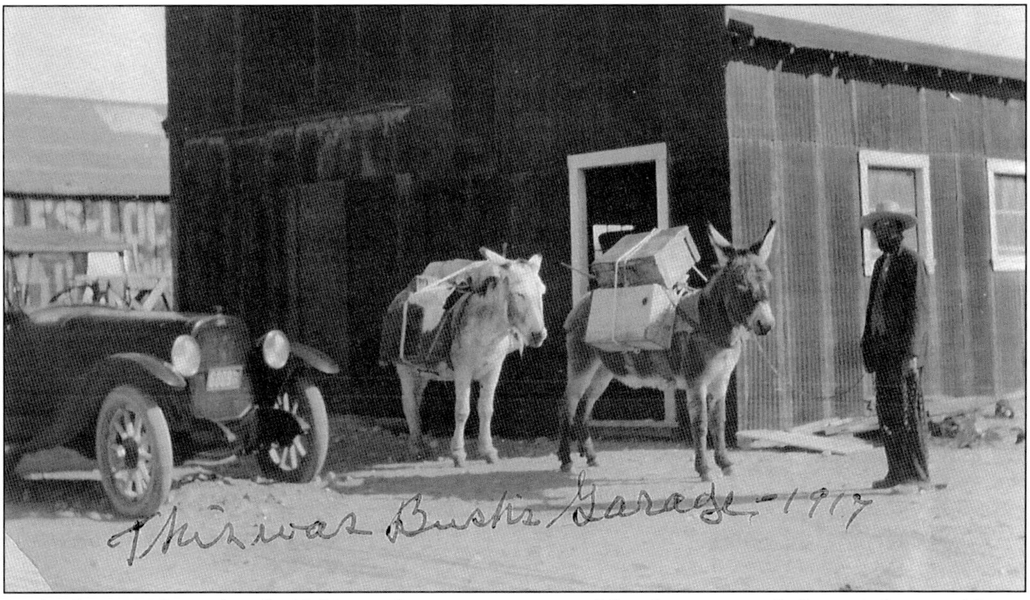

In the late 1800s and early 1900s, mules were recognized for their strength despite their stubborn temperament. Mules could haul supplies out to desert mining camps, carry the mail to outback destinations such as Swansea, and transport luggage from the train depot to accommodations at the Grandview Hotel. Here mules stand in front of the Bush garage in 1917.

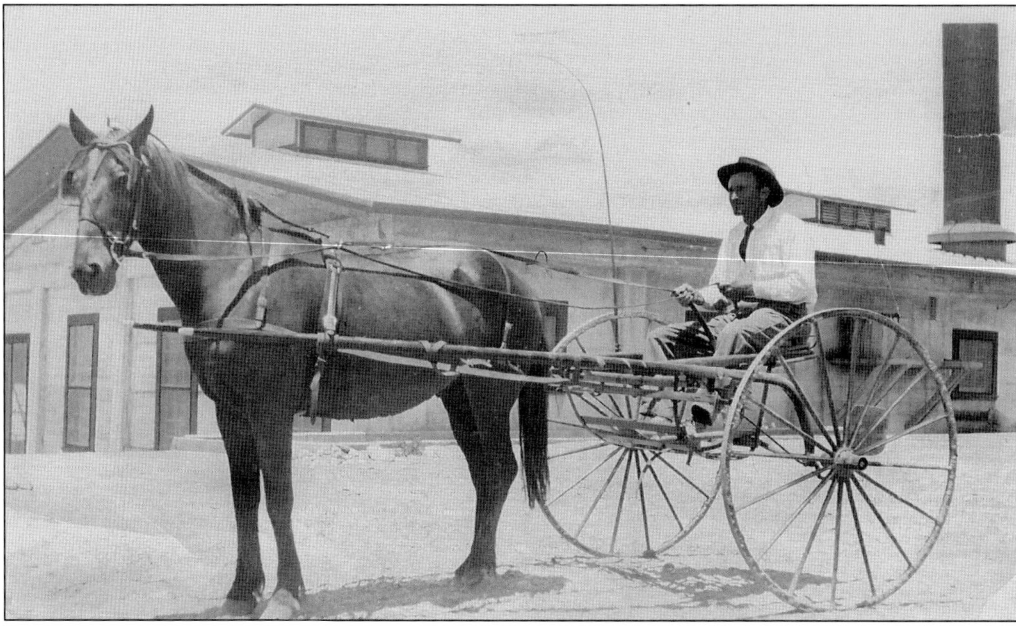

A man and his horse and buggy pause near the Parker Indian Agency pumping plant in the early 1920s.

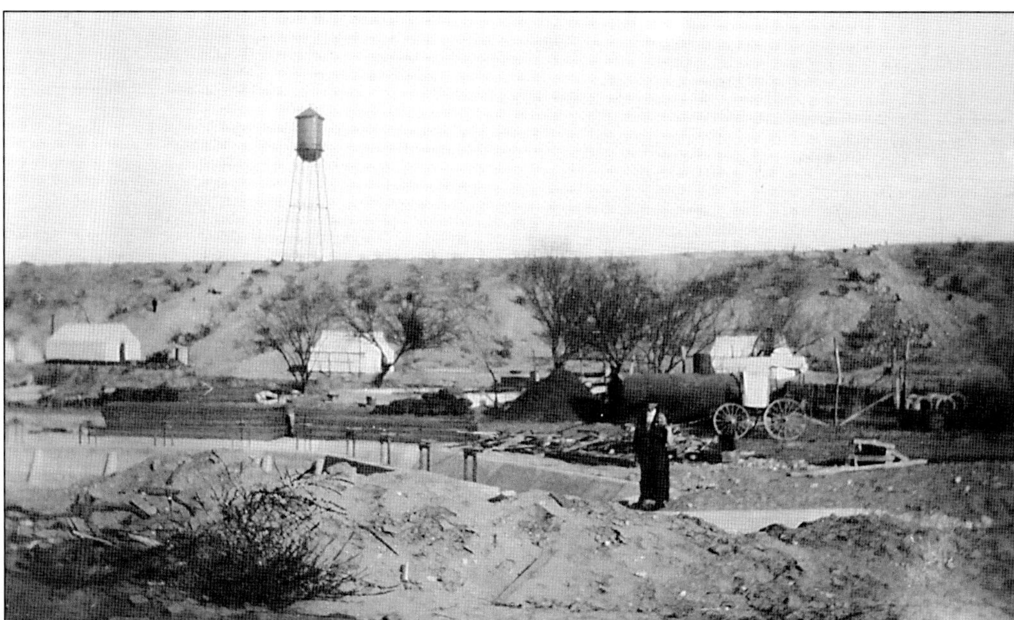

A couple stands on a dirt mound near the construction site of the main canal, below the mesa where the Parker Indian Agency is located. Visible in the background are the tent cabins commonly used for housing in the early 1900s.

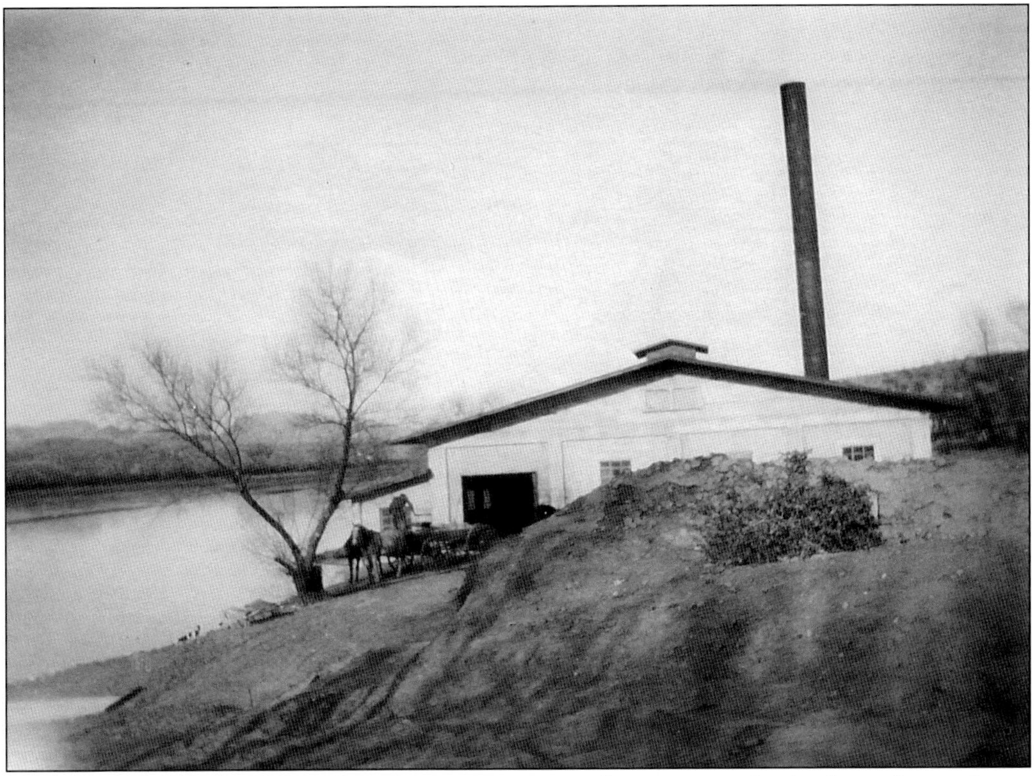

In this view of the Parker Indian Agency pumping plant, a man climbs down from a horse and wagon.

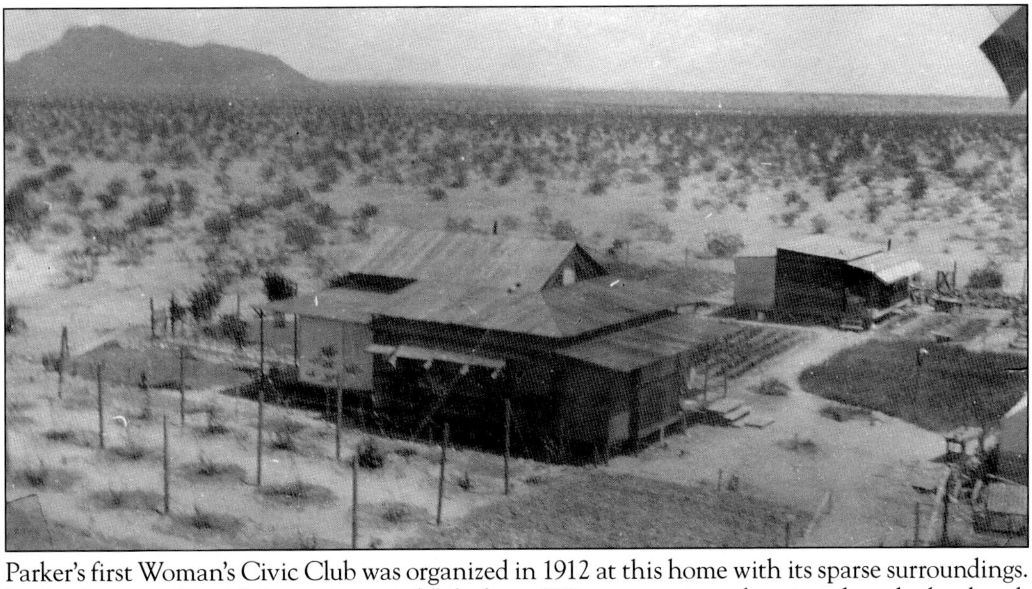

Parker's first Woman's Civic Club was organized in 1912 at this home with its sparse surroundings. In the distance, Black Mountain is visible before a "P" was prominently painted on the landmark by high school students as a spirit activity beginning in 1938.

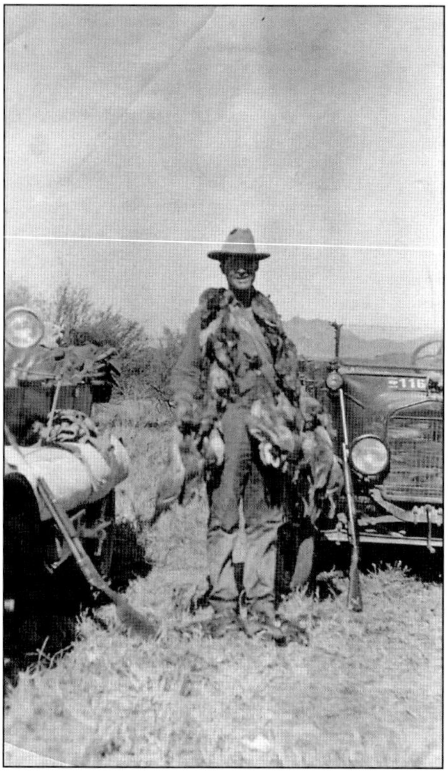

When not out prospecting, Claude Fugatt was hunting. This 1915 photograph is supportive of the chance for a good rabbit hunt.

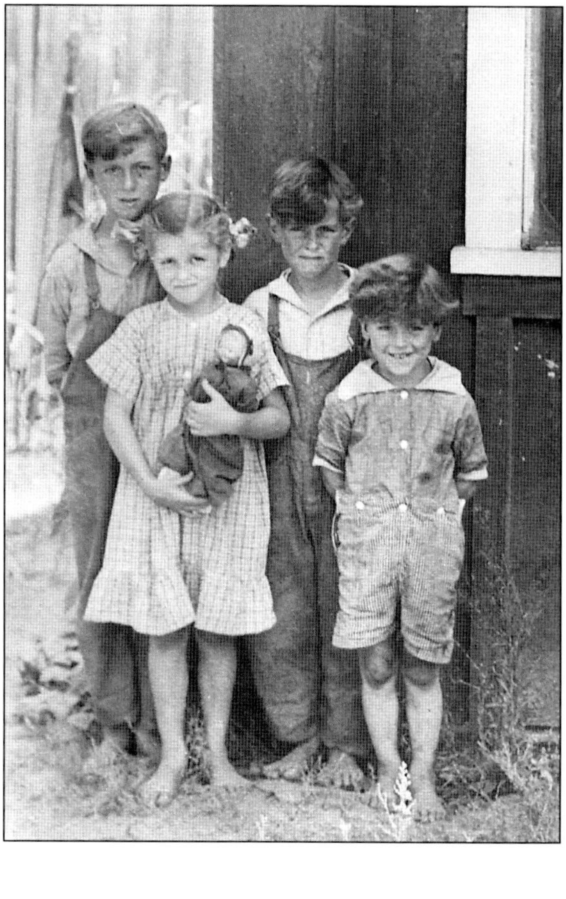

Seen here from left to right are John, Pearl, Vernon, and Barney Fugatt. The Fugatt children looked forward to coming into town from the Cienega Springs area because they were able to go to Fuqua's Store to buy a soda or candy.

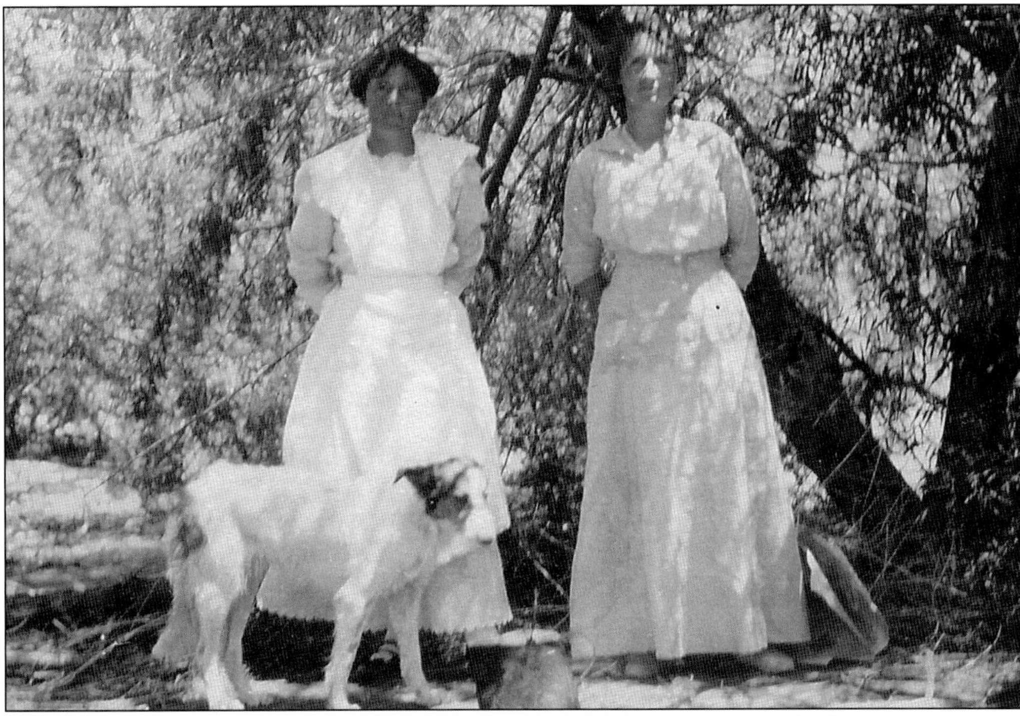

Jenny Fugatt (right) stands with a friend. Both women served as camp cooks for the miners, who included Jenny's husband, Claude.

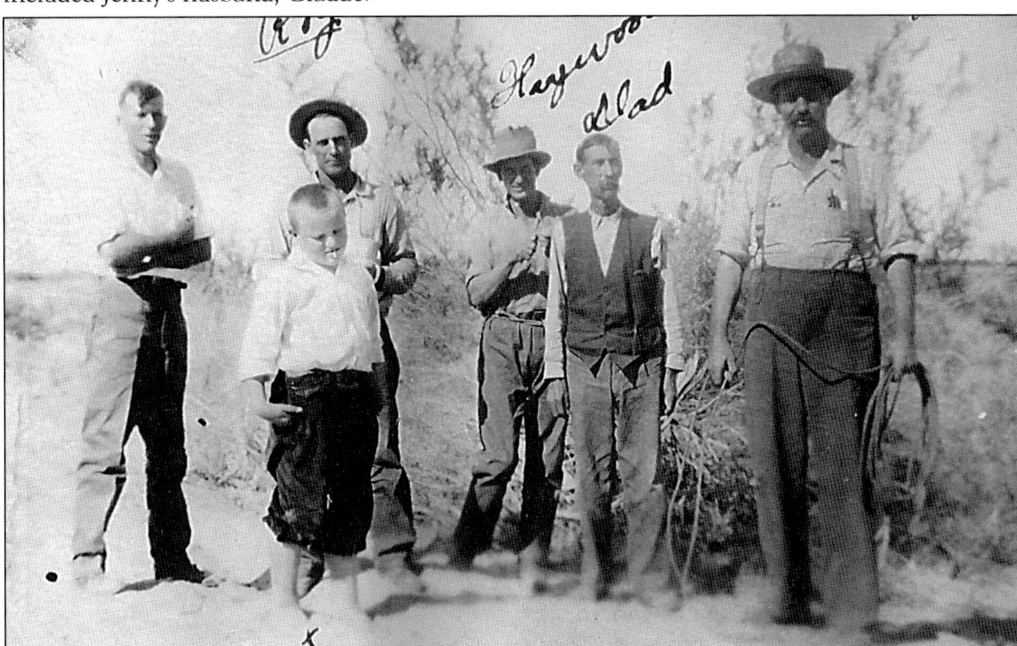

Mr. Short (second from right) and his sons pose with Mr. Raney (far right) around 1910. Short lived and worked in Swansea, which is now a ghost town not far from Parker. Short's son Haywood (center) moved to Parker and married, though he never had children. His home was originally one of the many barracks used in Poston to house Japanese Americans during World War II.

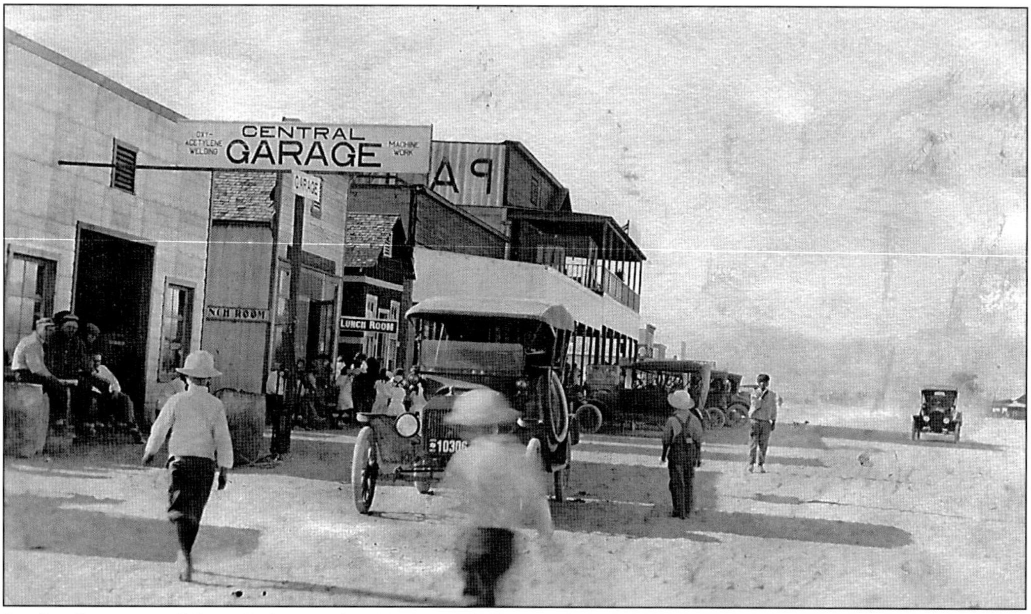

In the foreground from left to right, Vernon, John, and Barney Fugatt, all wearing white hardhats, take advantage of the opportunity to purchase a sweet treat as they head toward the Parker Commercial Company about 1918.

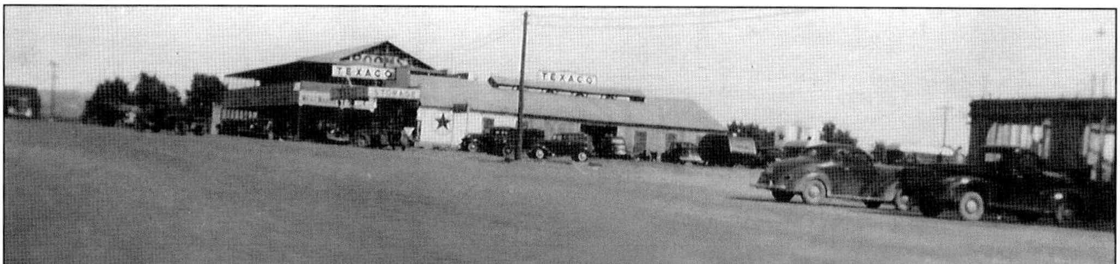

In this northeast view of Arizona Avenue, the back of the Parker Commercial Company building can be seen. The Shrubbery Flower Shop is now located on the site of the Texaco station.

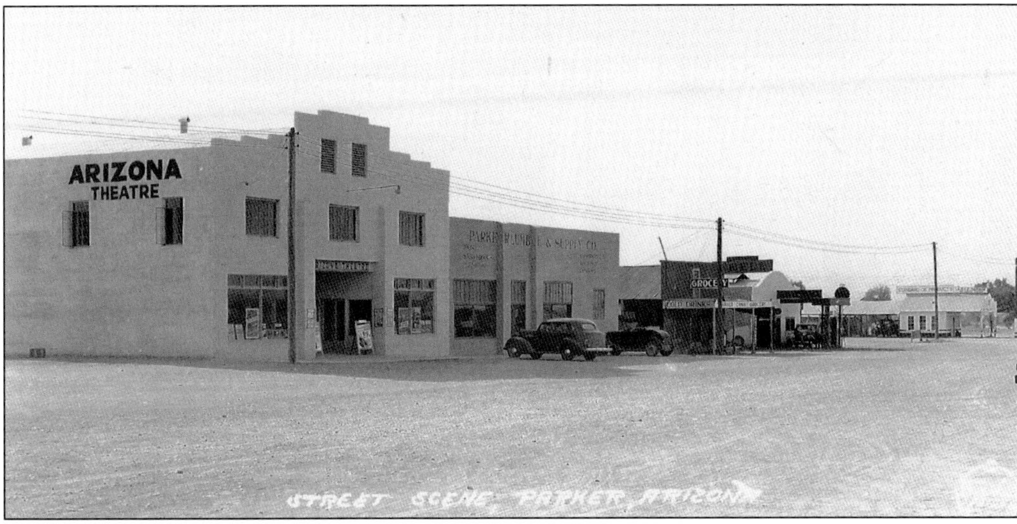

The downtown Parker Arizona Theatre has provided decades of entertainment, surviving through multiple ownerships and even fire. Transformed into a bar and restaurant in more recent years, it is now undergoing renovations to become the Colorado River Indian Tribes Museum.

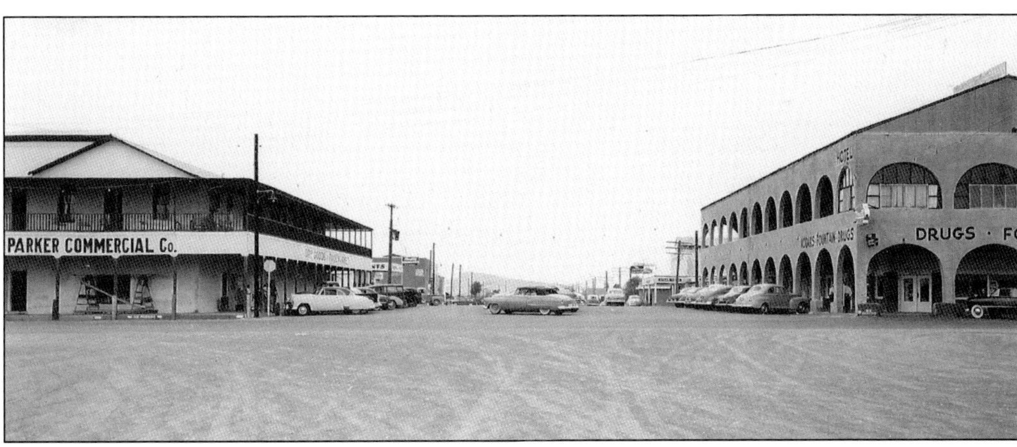

This 1950s street scene, looking west, shows the heart of Parker's business district. On the left is the Parker Commercial Company, originally built in 1905. On the right is the Grandview Hotel, built in 1916 and remaining a community landmark until it was destroyed by fire in 1974.

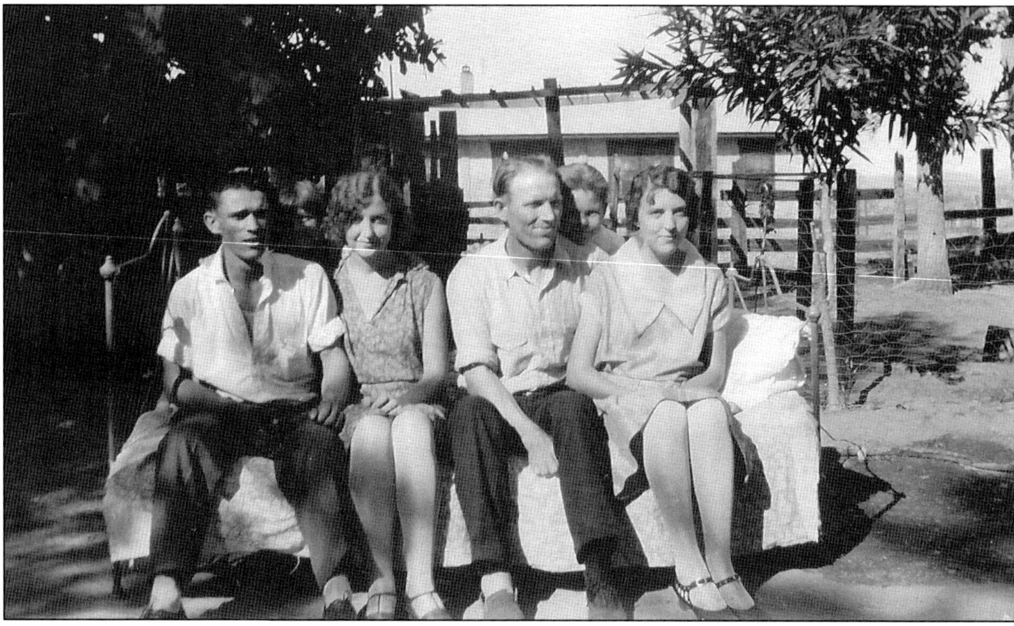

These young people posing for the camera in the late 1920s are, from left to right, Ronald Brown, Marvell Richter, Bill Langendorf, and Merle Richter. The younger Glen Strohm sneakily looks over their shoulders.

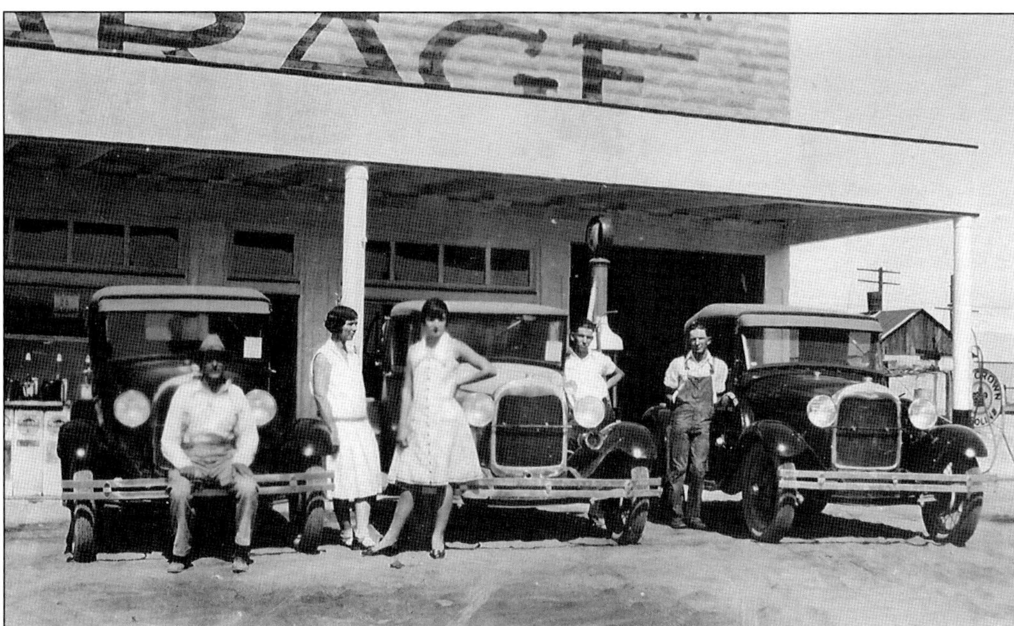

Lined up in front of Parker Motor Company are three newly delivered Ford Model As, which were manufactured from 1928 to 1931. Fashion was not lost on this desert town, as evidenced by the women dressed in "flapper" fashion in this 1929 photograph.

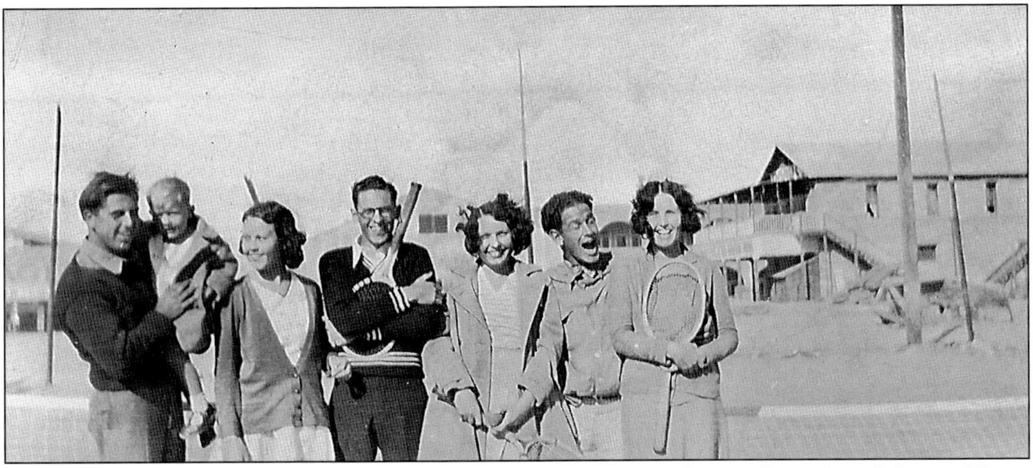

Many youth activities were held on the cement courts located near the railroad depot. These young adults enjoy a game of tennis in the 1940s.

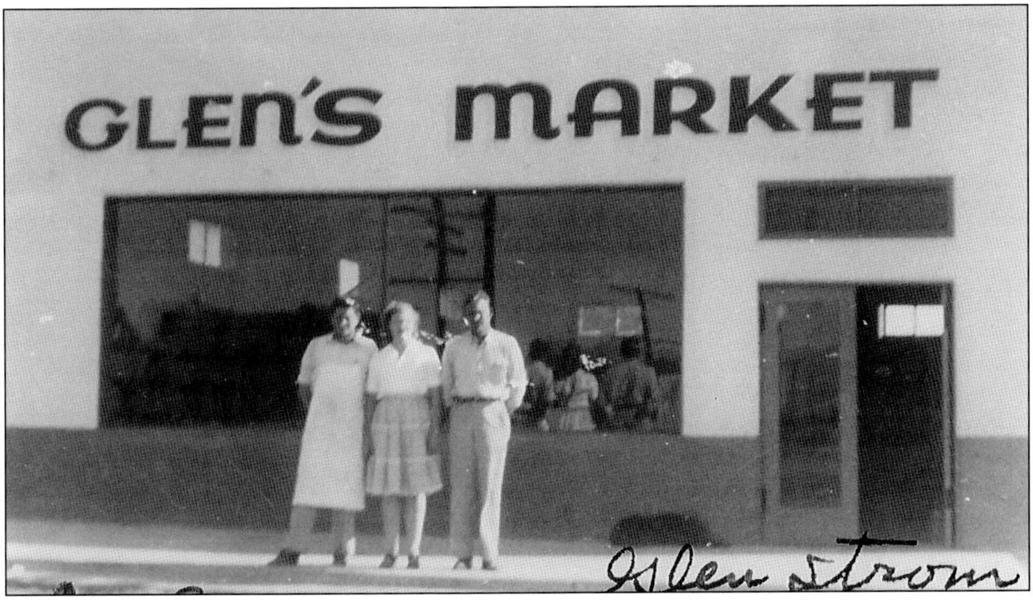

Glen Strohm (right), who would become Parker's first mayor, is pictured with employees Charlie Bennem and Imogene Cole at his market. Glen's Market stood on Parker's main street, generally identified today as California Avenue or State Route 95. It was a full-service grocery store with a meat butcher.

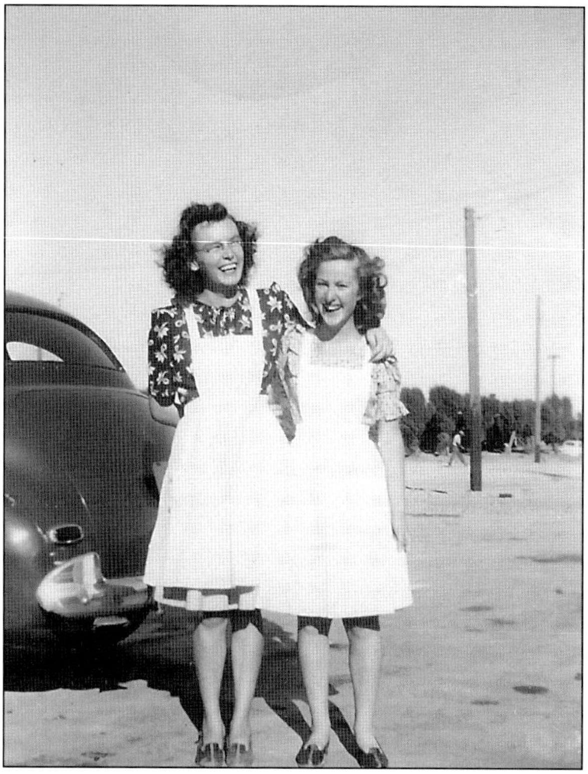

In this July 1946 photograph, two unidentified teenage girls have fun while sharing a humorous moment.

Marion Beaver piloted the plane at the time of this 1946 aerial view of Parker facing northwest.

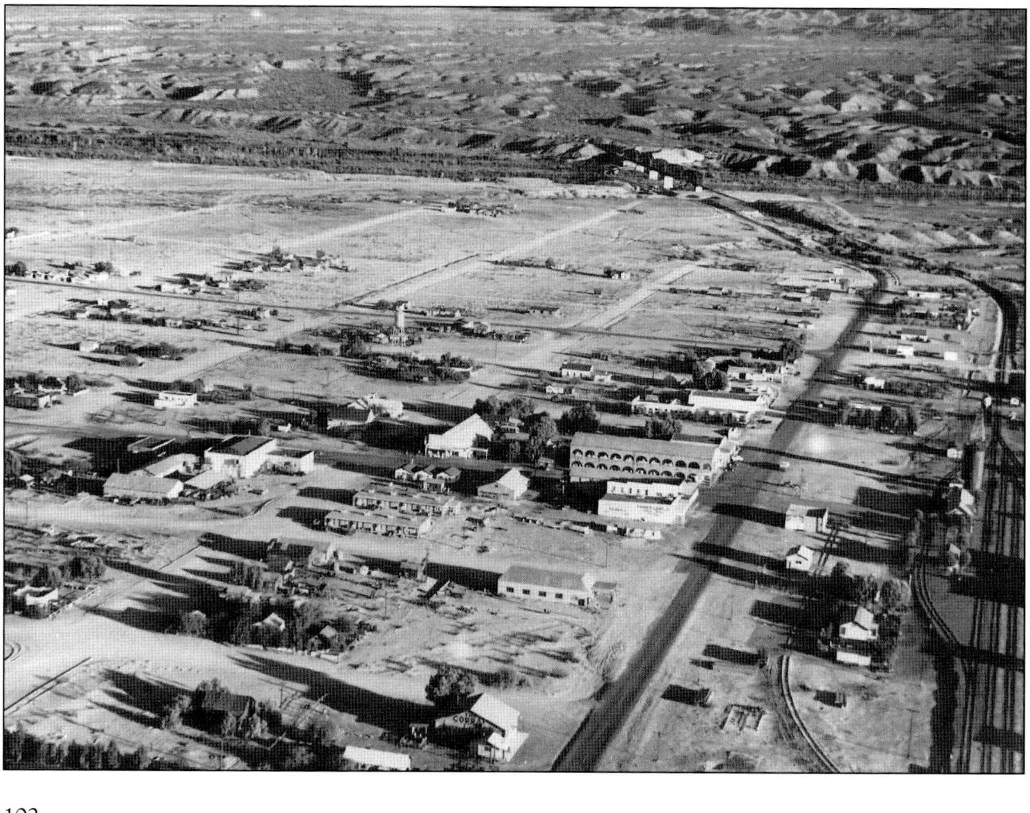

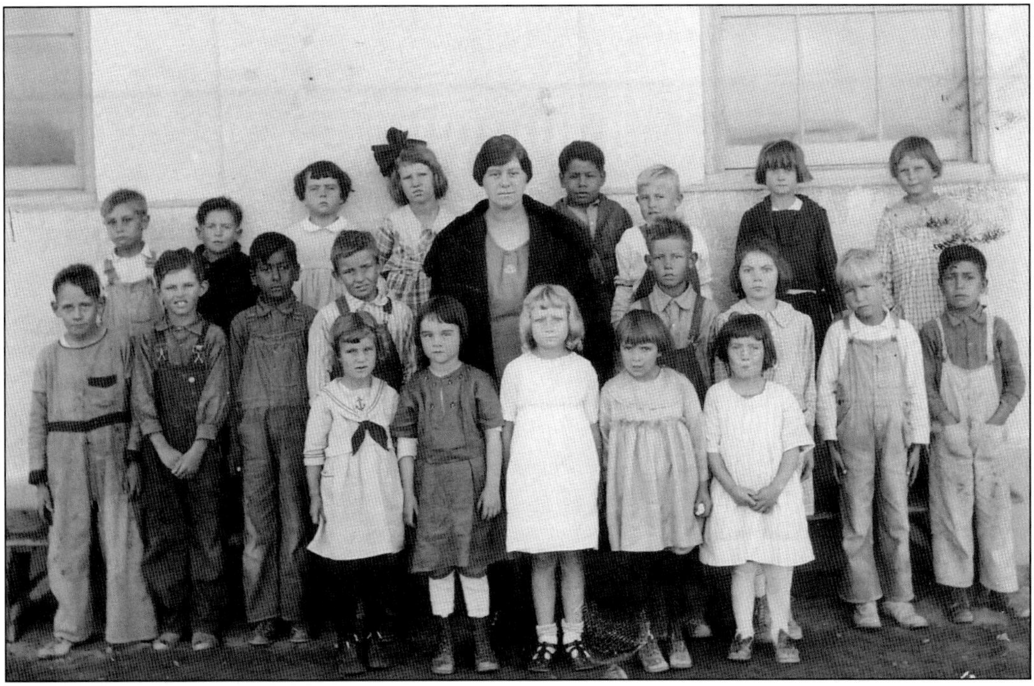

The first public school in Parker began in a one-room schoolhouse. Soon thereafter, an elementary school district was created, followed by the eventual construction of Wallace Elementary School, seen in the background of this 1923 class photograph. The original structure, though modified, continues to be used in the education of Parker's youth.

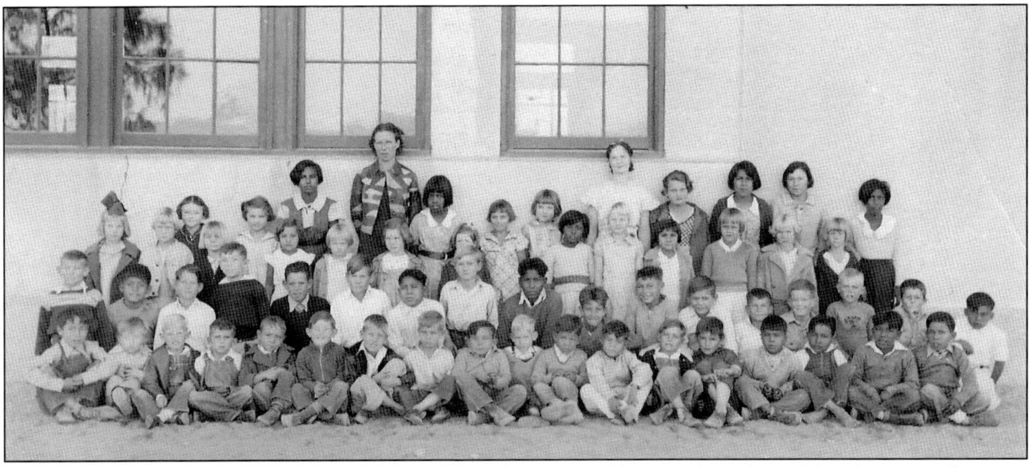

Wallace Elementary School grades one through four are featured in this 1934 photograph.

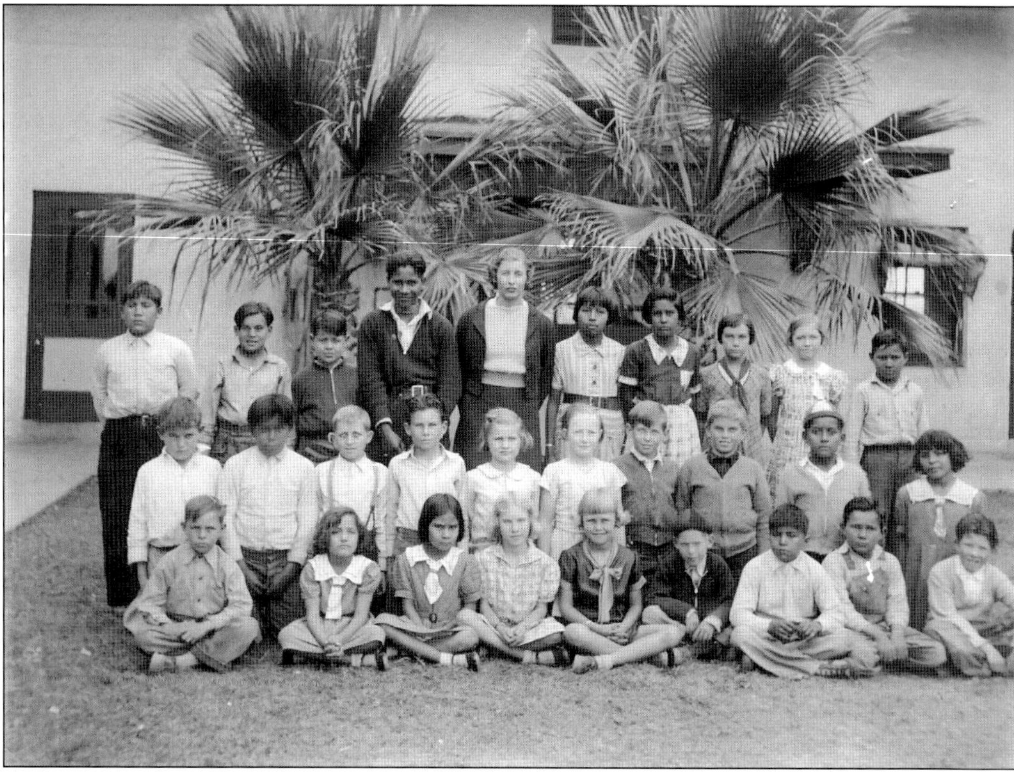

Seen here in 1936 are Wallace Elementary grades three and four.

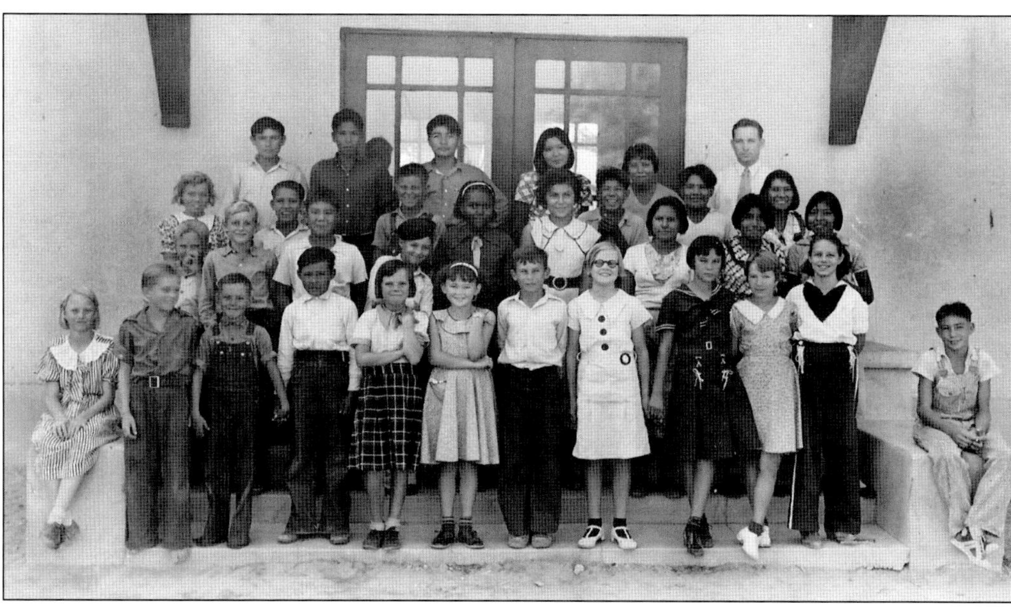

Fifth- and sixth-grade students from Wallace Elementary School pose in 1936.

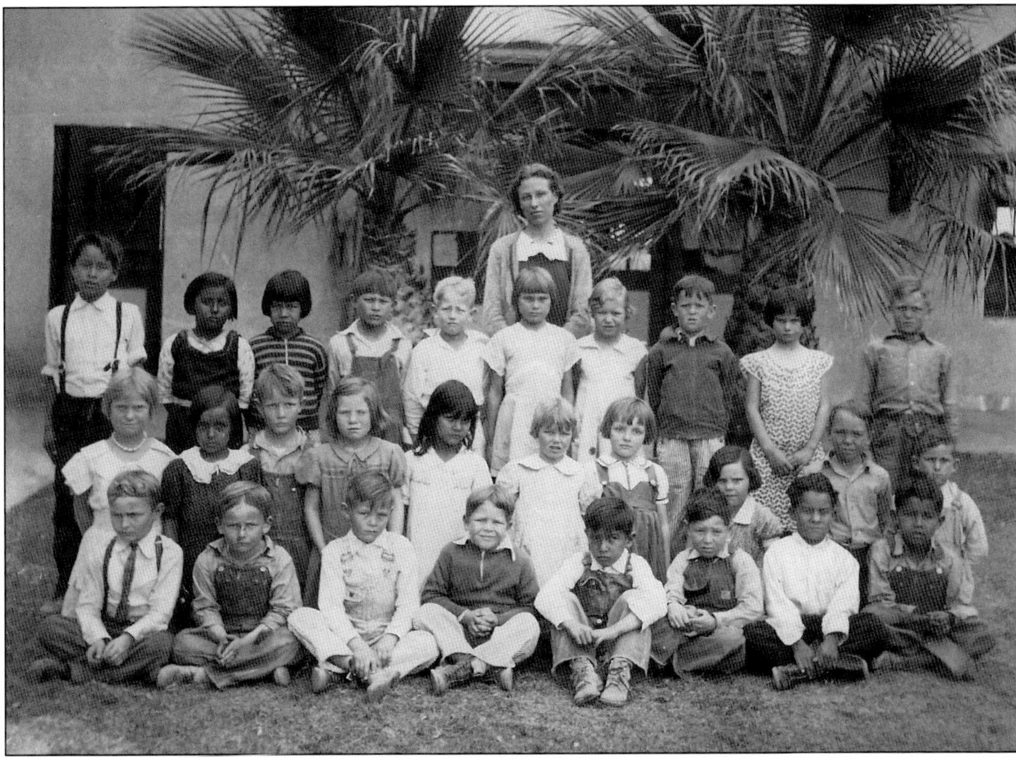

Wallace Elementary School students are pictured here in 1936.

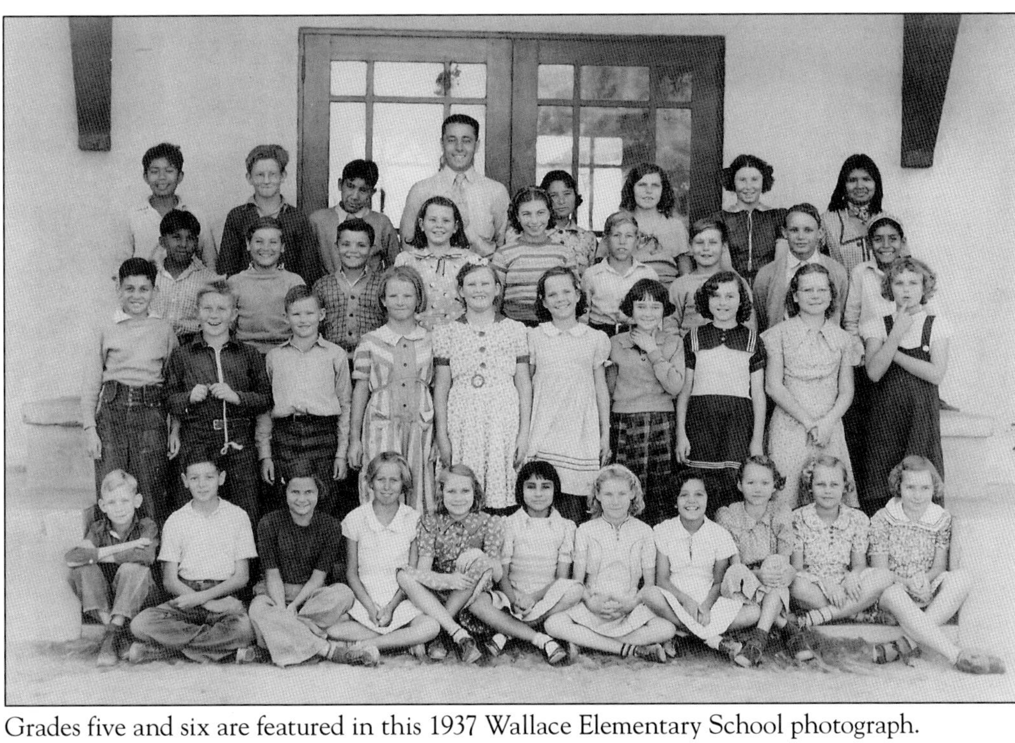

Grades five and six are featured in this 1937 Wallace Elementary School photograph.

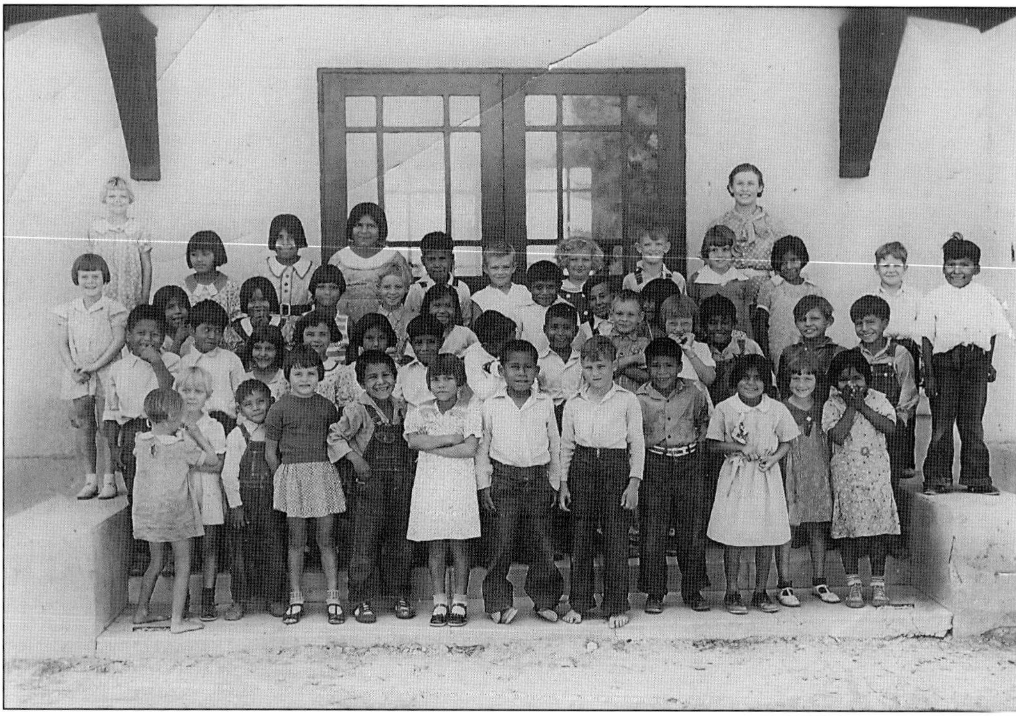

Wallace Elementary students are pictured with teacher Blanche Turnbow-Thompson in 1937.

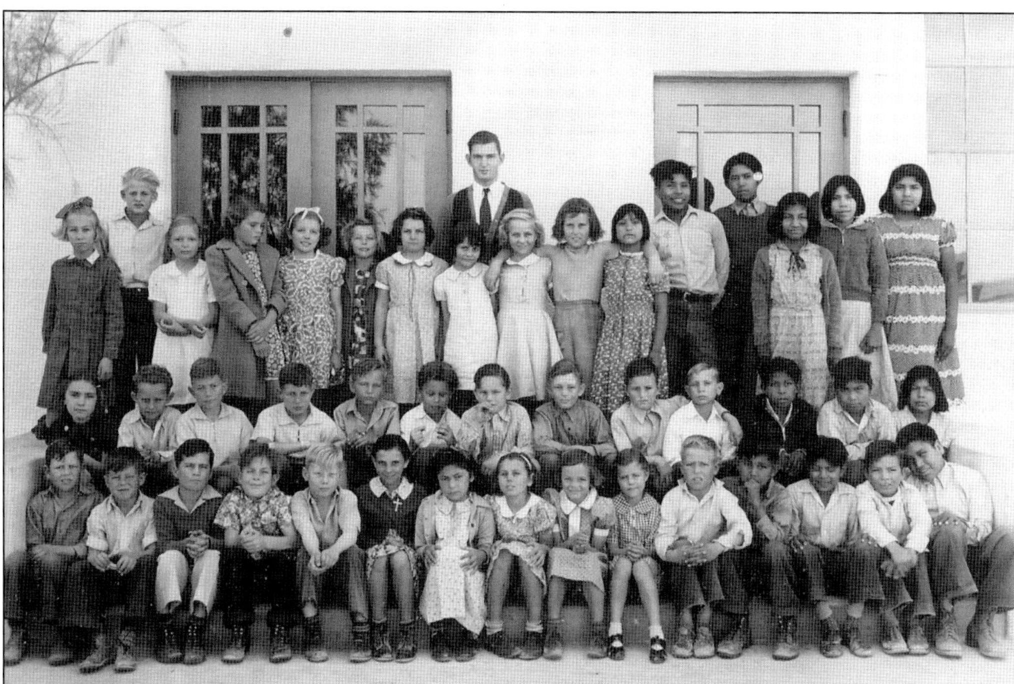

In 1939, Wallace Elementary School students pose with teacher Francis Blake, who went on to become a school principal. Later the new primary school was named in his honor.

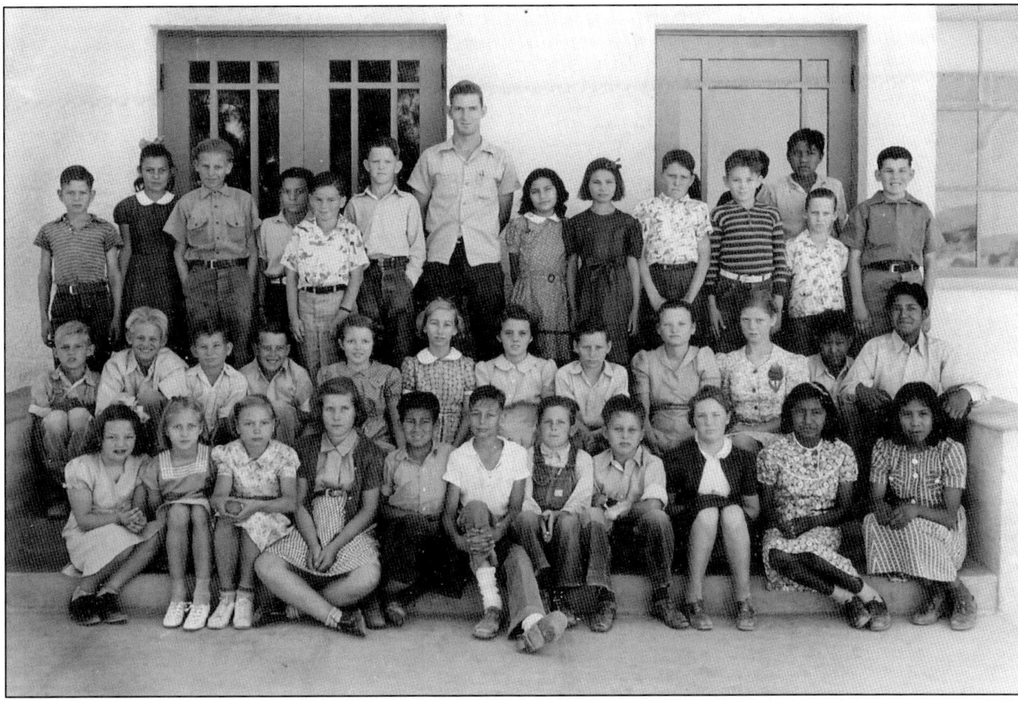

Students from Wallace Elementary School gather for a portrait with teacher Francis Blake in 1940.

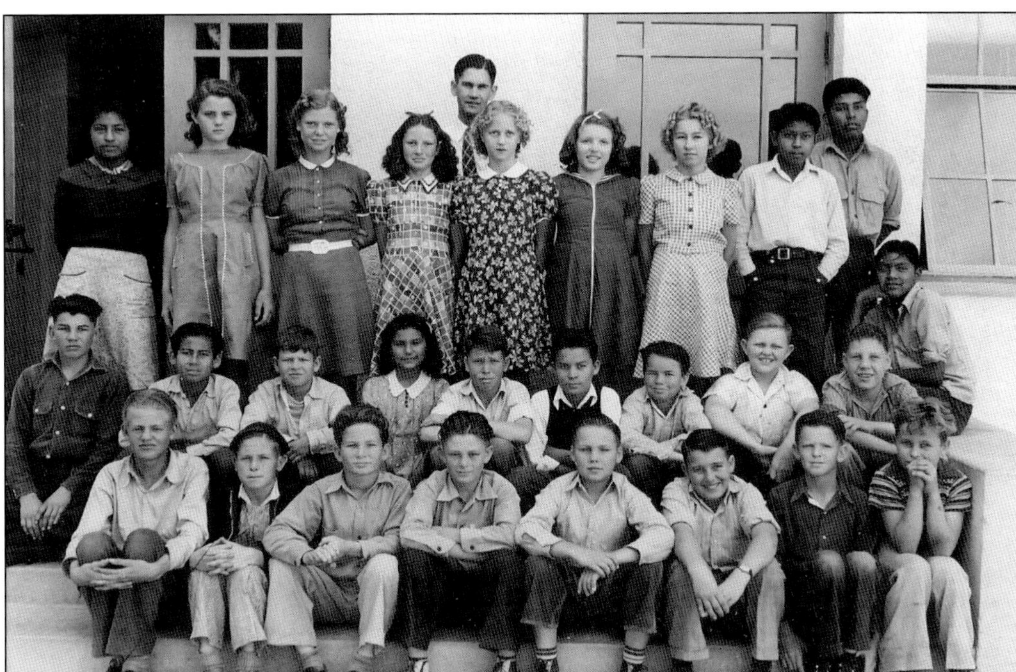

Teacher Glenn Nicholson stands with his Wallace Elementary School students in 1941.

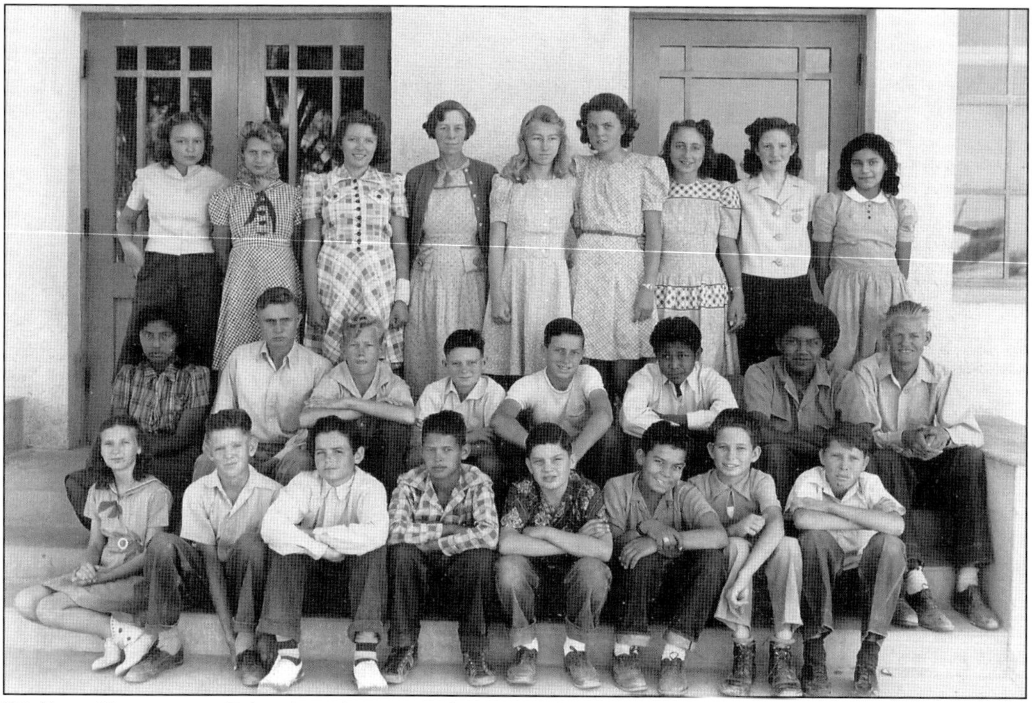

Wallace Elementary School students are shown in this 1942 photograph.

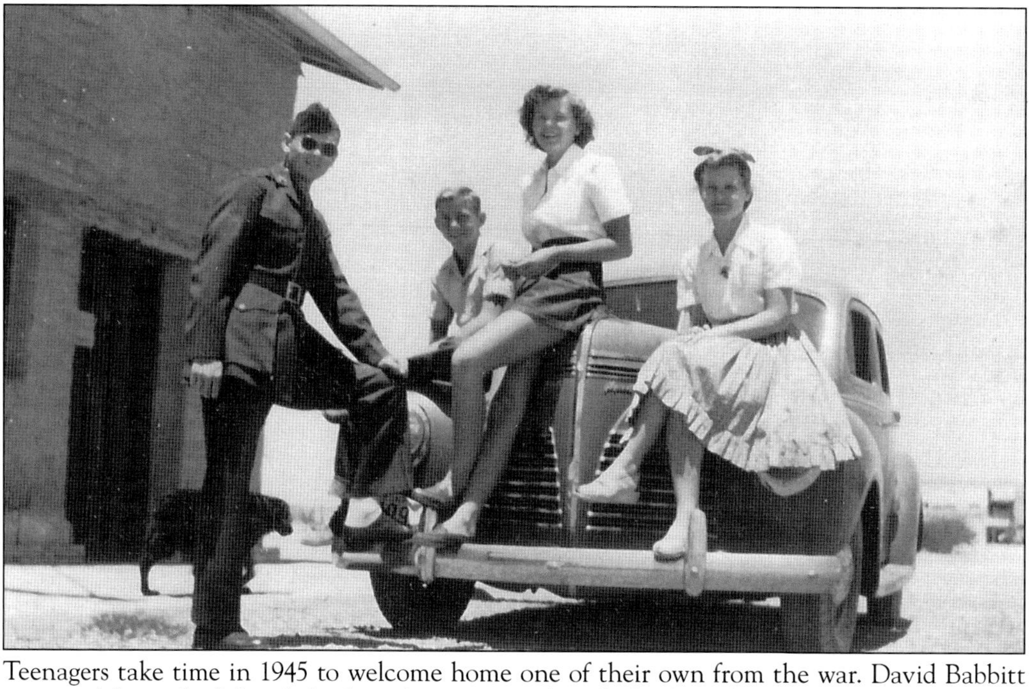

Teenagers take time in 1945 to welcome home one of their own from the war. David Babbitt is second from the left, while the others are unidentified. The Old County Jail is visible in the background.

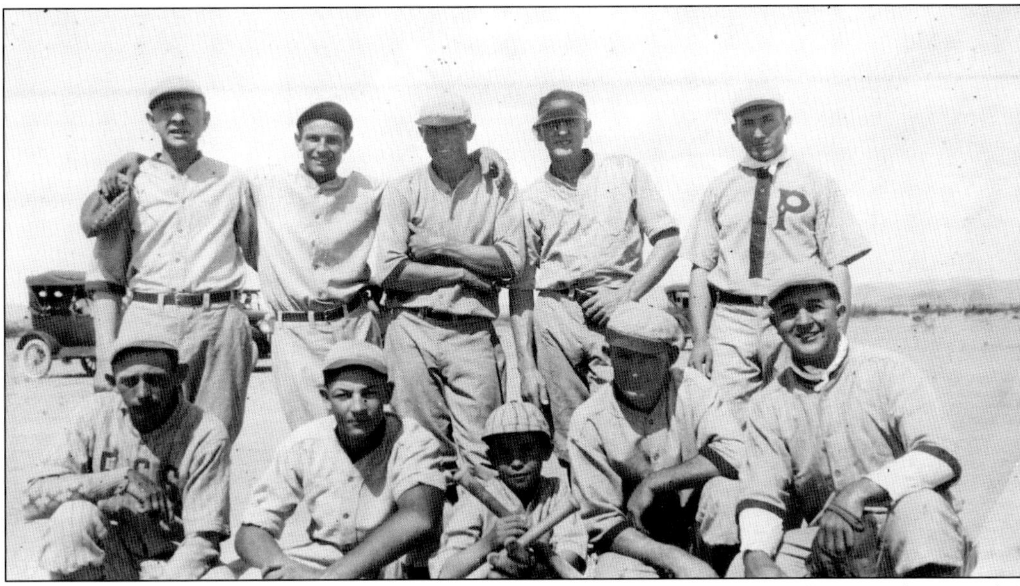

Parkerites had an early fondness for baseball, as seen in this 1924 team photograph. From left to right are (first row) B. Norman, G. Edmonds, M. Beaver (batboy), ? Thurston, and J. Dudley; (second row) A. Robinson, J. Harger, B. Langendorf, D. Robinson, and L. Hoover.

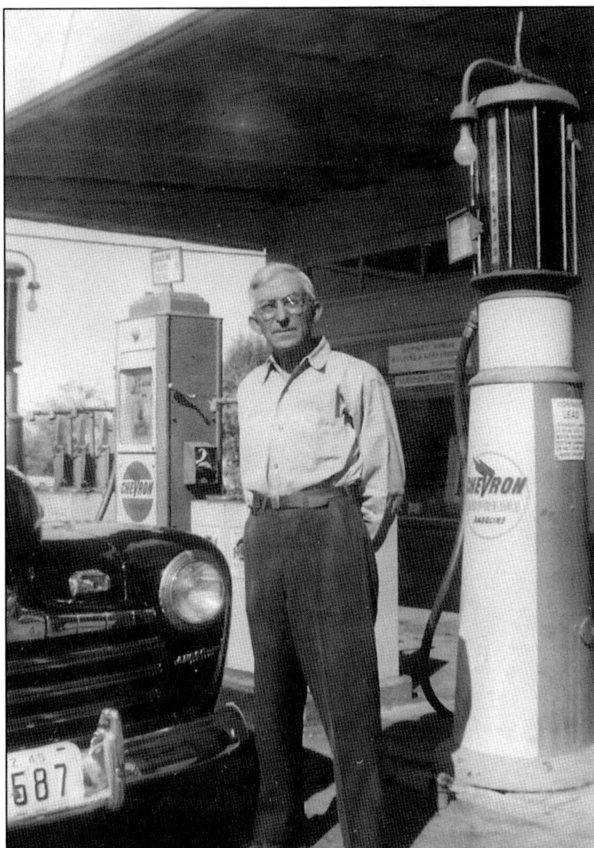

Dan Beaver II relocated to Prescott, Arizona, from Missouri in 1920 while working for the Atchison, Topeka, and Santa Fe Railroad. Stranded in Parker because of a railroad strike, Dan sent for his wife, Floy, because there was a good life to be had in this small desert town. Shortly thereafter, Dan and Floy bought into a partnership with J. D. Mathews, the original owner of the Parker Motor Company, the local Ford dealership. Floy also owned and operated a café on Parker's main street, where her homemade rhubarb pies were even requested by Wyatt Earp when he was in town picking up supplies to take back to his Happy Day Mines.

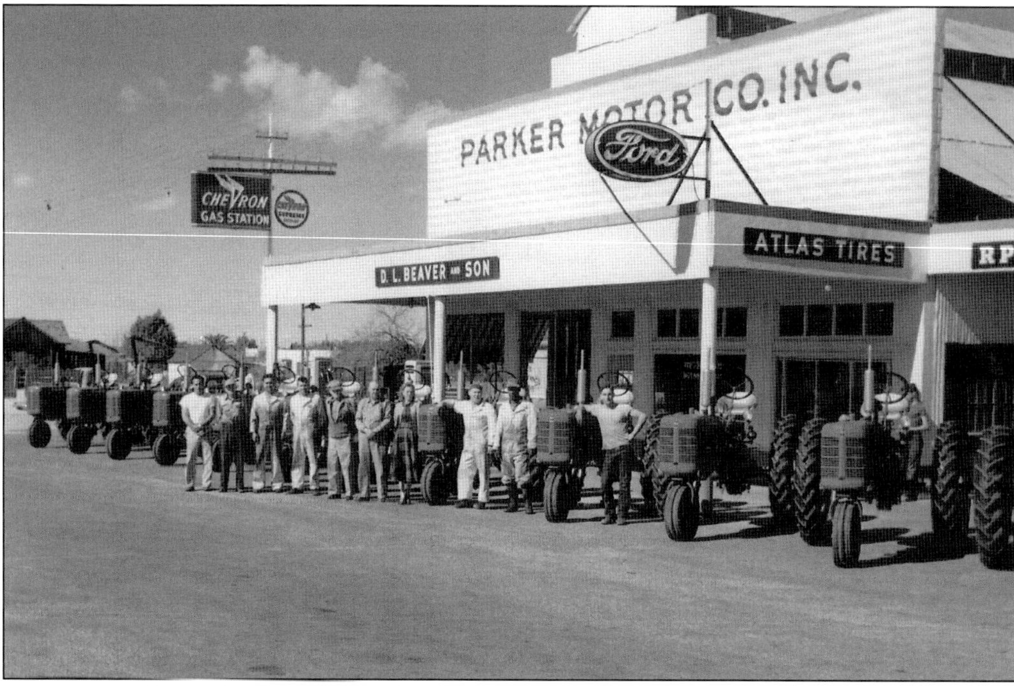

During agricultural development in the Parker Valley, the Parker Motor Company expanded to become a franchise dealer for both Ford and International tractors. The initial delivery of tractors can be seen lined up on Arizona Avenue.

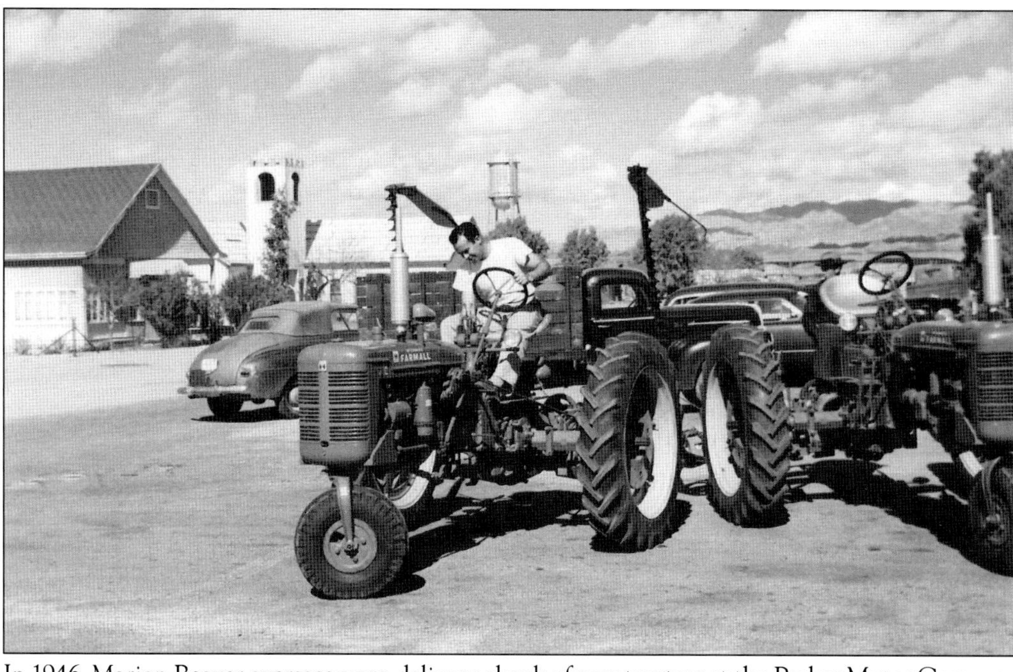

In 1946, Marion Beaver oversees a pre-delivery check of new tractors at the Parker Motor Company, located at the corner of Arizona Avenue and Joshua Street. The Parker Community Church's bell steeple is visible in the background. The church eventually became Parker United Methodist and moved to its current site at the corner of Ocotillo and Arizona Avenues.

Marion Beaver (right) familiarizes Henry Shorty with the details of his new tractor in 1950.

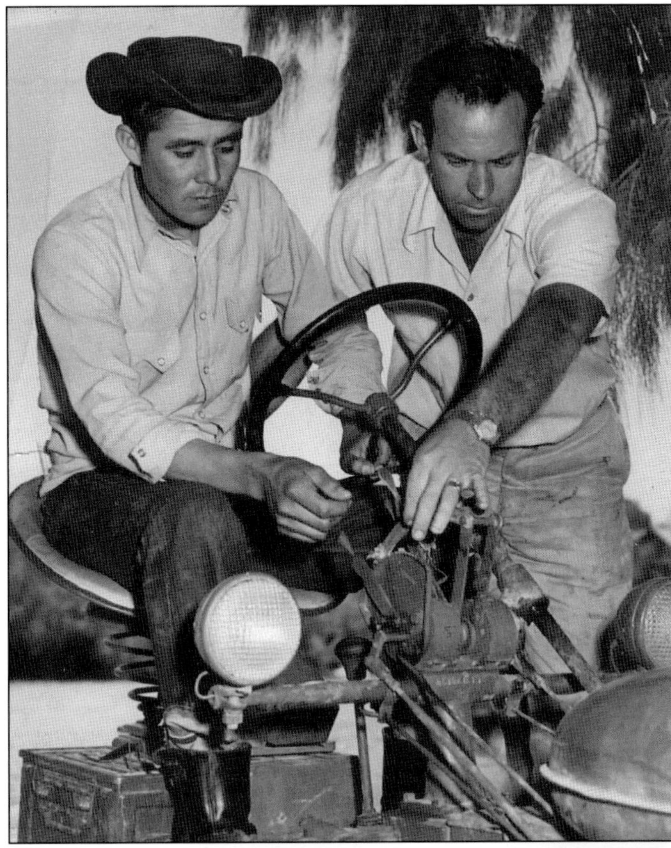

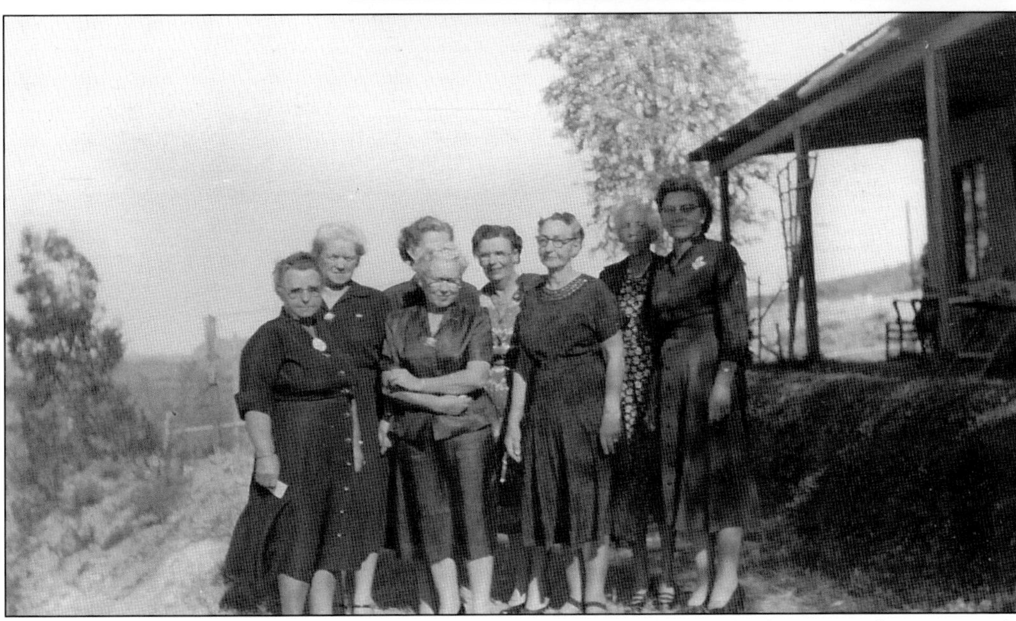

Parker Woman's Civic Club members pose in the yard of Nellie Bush's home on the river in the late 1950s. Seen from left to right are Floy Beaver, Sara Short, Mrs. Ewing, Mrs. McVey, Mildred McVey, Nellie Bush, Winnie Barrett, and Eileen Gnau.

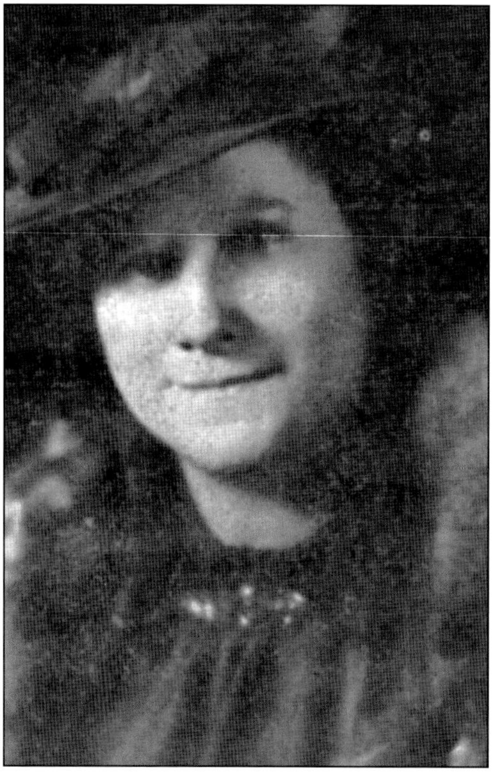

In 1936, Clara Osborne Botzum, as secretary of the Northern Yuma County Chamber of Commerce, began advocating for the development of roads in the Parker area. In 1937, Clara was instrumental in seeing the completion of the Parker–Colorado River highway bridge. By 1940, notes recorded by Clara described, "The CCC [Civilian Conservation Corps] camp was built about a mile down stream from the Parker Dam on Arizona side of the Colorado River with several hundred men and equipment. After a short work period the entire camp, crew and equipment were moved to the Parker Valley as an emergency to prepare for the evacuation of the Japanese from the Coastal area in 1942."

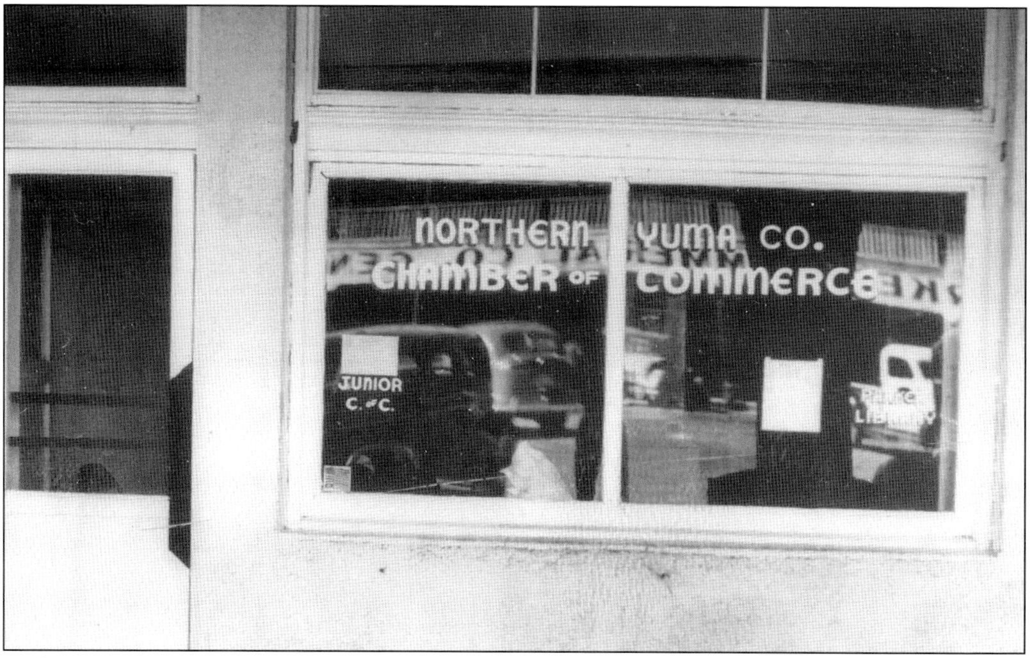

Parker was home to two significantly powerful political women. One was Nellie T. Bush, owner of the Grandview Hotel building, which by 1952 was providing office space for the Northern Yuma County Chamber of Commerce. The other was Clara Osborne Botzum. Both women advocated for roads and highways.

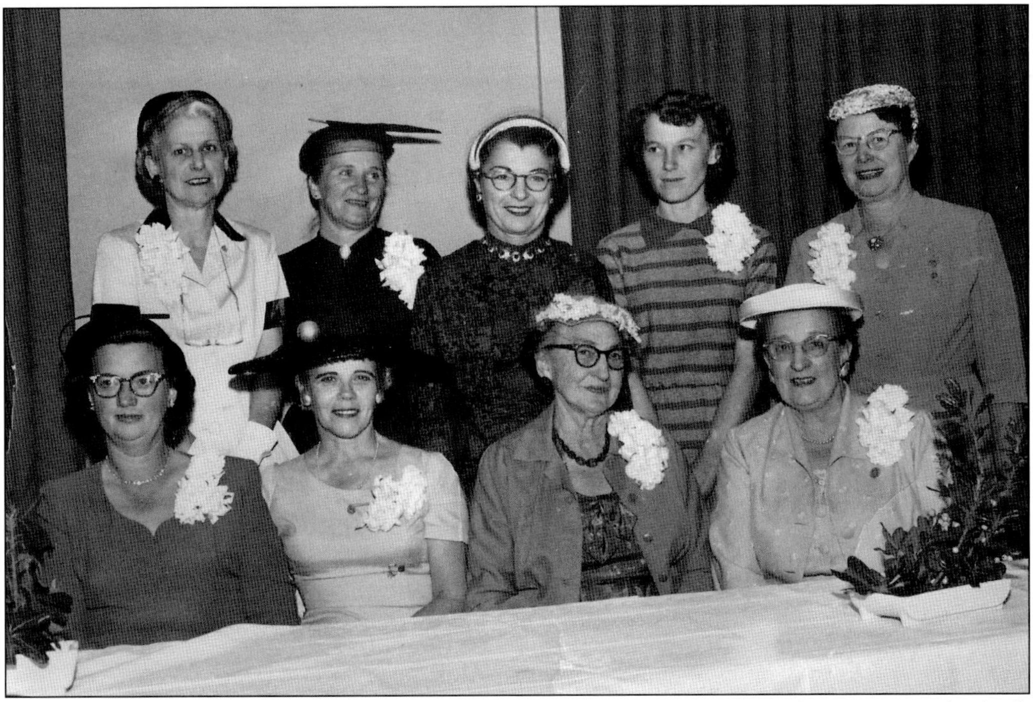

This 1956 Woman's Civic Club leadership photograph includes two Parker women: Elizabeth Solper (standing second from the left), Parker Woman's Civic Club president; and Nellie Bush (seated third from the left), Arizona State Woman's Civic Club president.

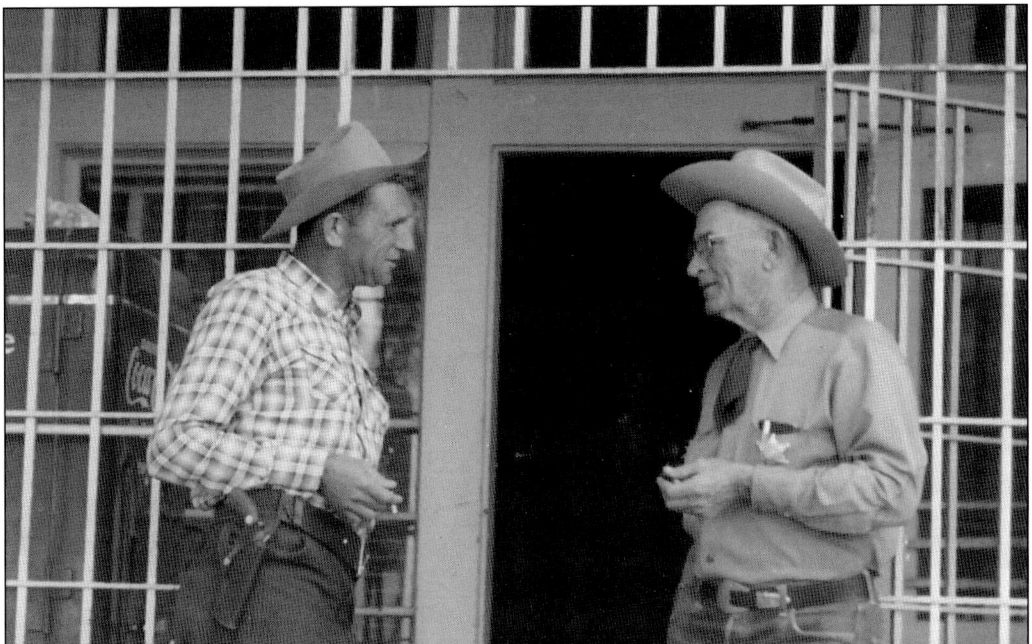

Around 1953, deputy sheriff Jack Pool (left) and an unidentified officer confer outside the entrance to the old Northern Yuma County Jail, located on Arizona Avenue between Kofa and Laguna Avenues.

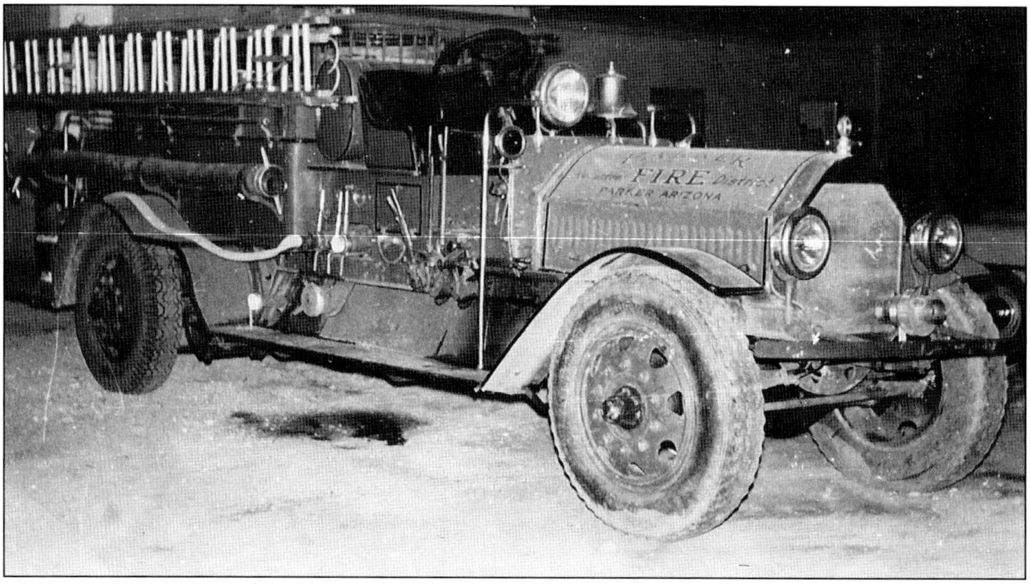

The original truck used by the Parker Fire Department is identified by the logo painted on its hood. The fire truck was affectionately referred to as "Ole Leaky."

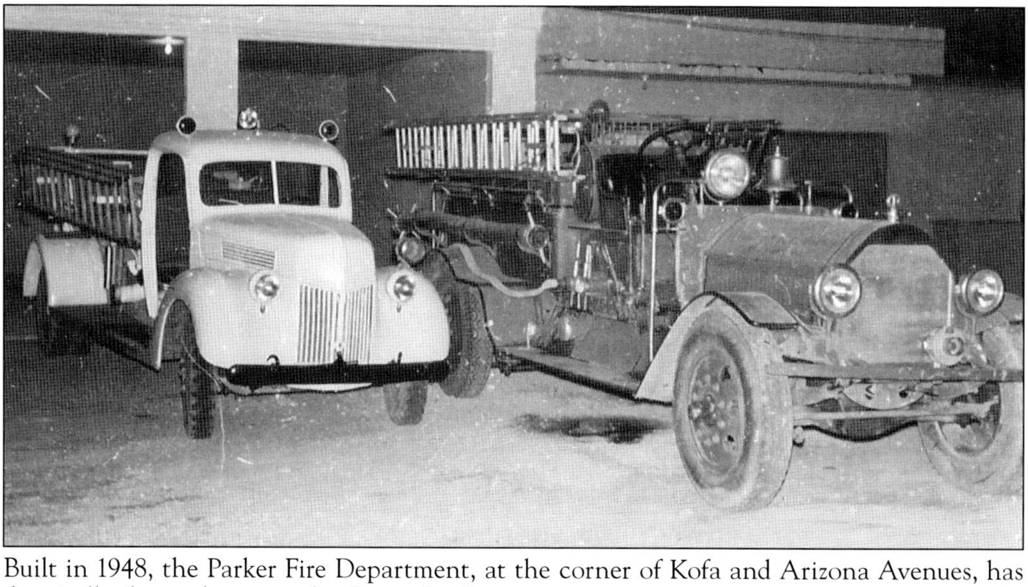

Built in 1948, the Parker Fire Department, at the corner of Kofa and Arizona Avenues, has drastically changed to meet the demands of a new era.

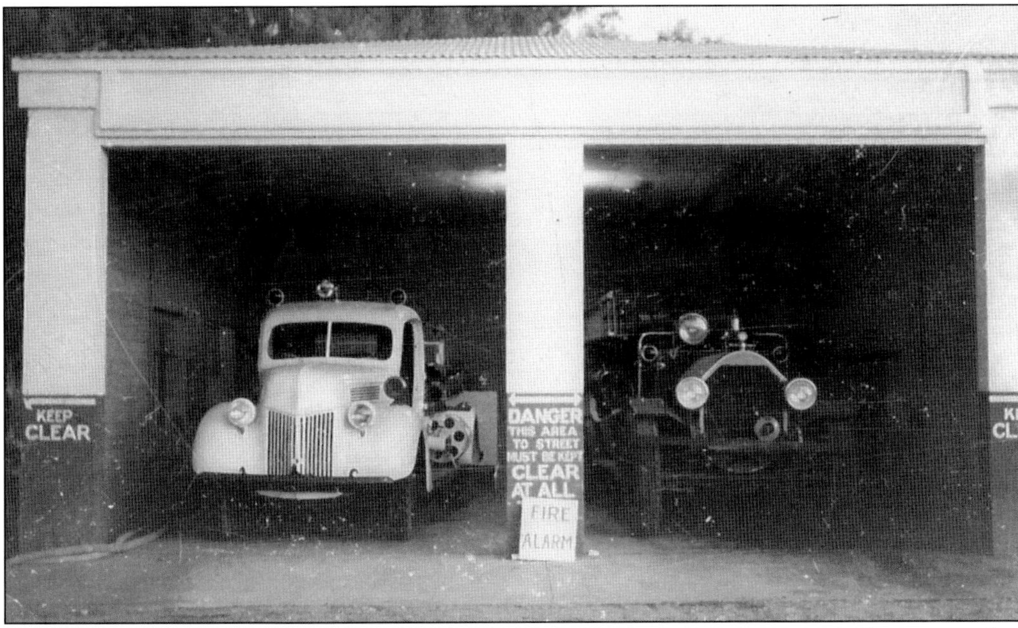

Community members started Parker's all-volunteer fire department in 1944. Those providing their services were chief E. C. "Johnnie" Johnson; assistant chief M. Beaver; secretary J. G. Fuqua; marshal G. Heinz; drivers R. Vanegas and C. Rushing; firefighters R. Vasarhely, H. Schnack, S. Davis, R. Critchlow, A. Hoover, W. O'Dell, J. King, H. Johnson, V. D. Baker, S. Hall Jr., F. Stephan, G. Strohm, C. Slane, R. Patrick, D. Patrick, T. C. Hollis, and F. Esquerra; peace officers J. Poole, C. Dick, J. Cawley, and J. Harold; and physicians Dr. D. Gallaher and Dr. T. Horton.

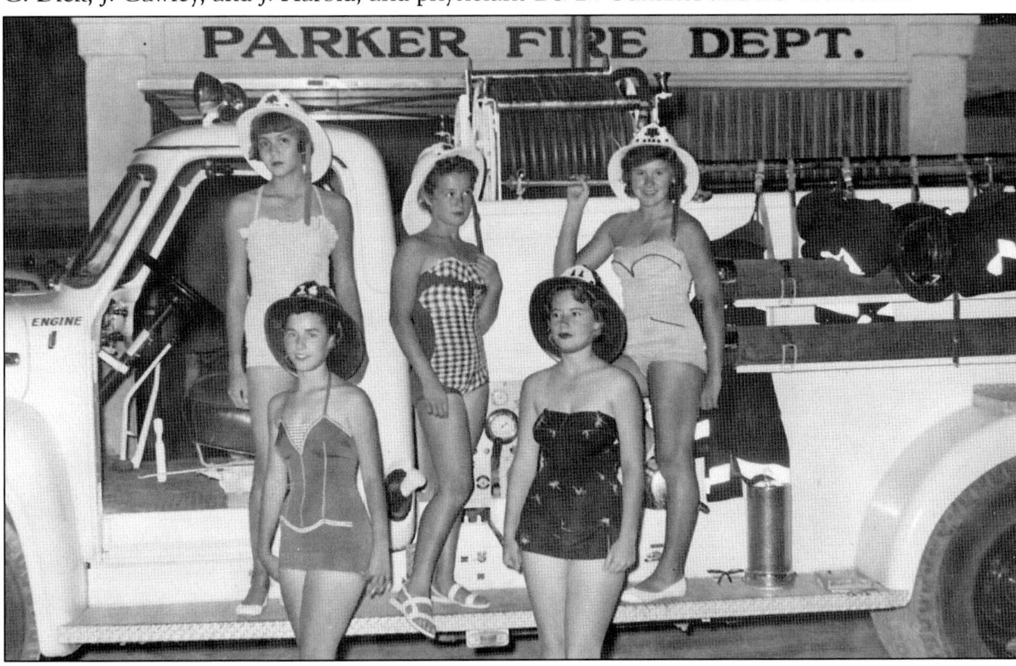

The Parker Fire Department always supported community activities, one being the annual Miss Firecracker Contest held during Fourth of July activities. Participants welcomed the opportunity to pose on the fire truck in the late 1950s.

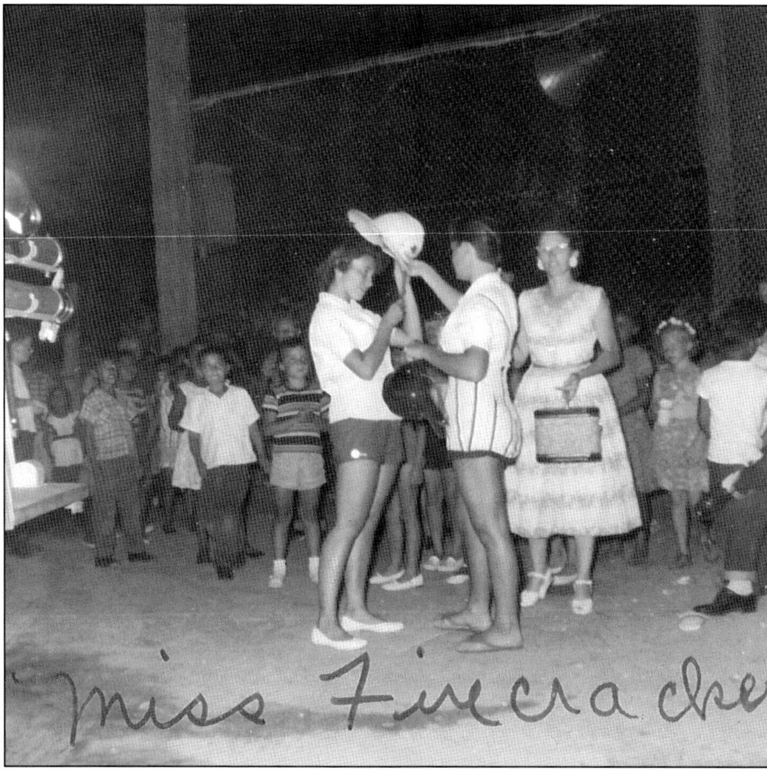

Each year, the Parker Fire Department sponsored fireworks at the local baseball field, which was located in the vicinity of the current police department and the town water tanks on the corner of Eleventh Street and Mohave Avenue. Miss Firecracker 1957, Roberta Beaver, is crowned with a fireman's helmet as children look on.

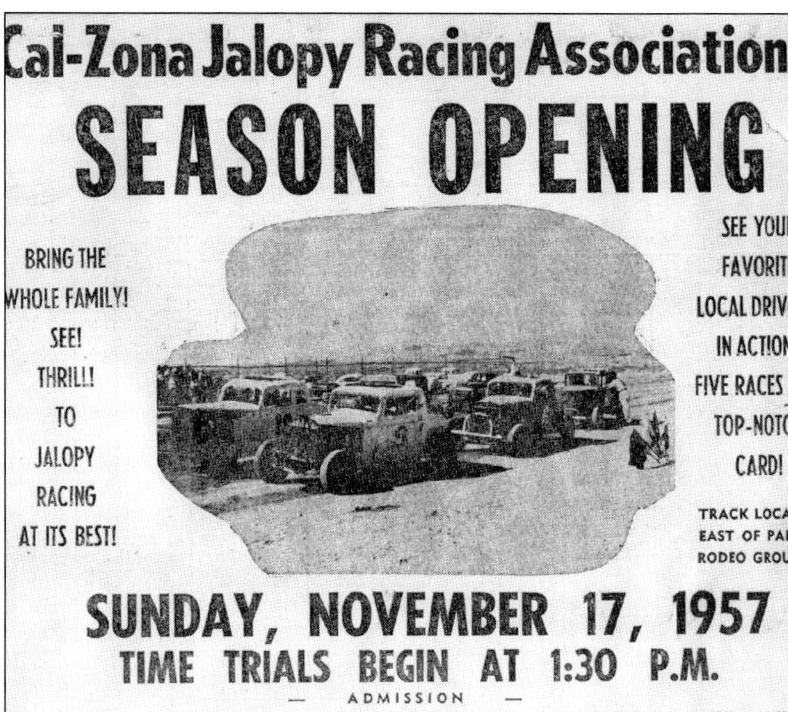

The Calzona Jalopy Racing Association's season opening in 1957 occurred on November 17. The advertisement reads, "Bring the whole family, see, thrill to jalopy racing at its best." Remnants of the Parker track berm are still visible at the edge of town to those traveling on Riverside Drive. The other track was located at Jack Ass Flats (now known as Burro Flats), on the California side of the river.

Interested locals began jalopy racing, calling themselves the Calzona Auto Race Association. The audience enjoyed hearing the revving of race engines and the roaring of cars circling the track. Shown here are sisters Kelly (left) and Coni Patrick, who attended a jalopy race at the Parker track in 1956.

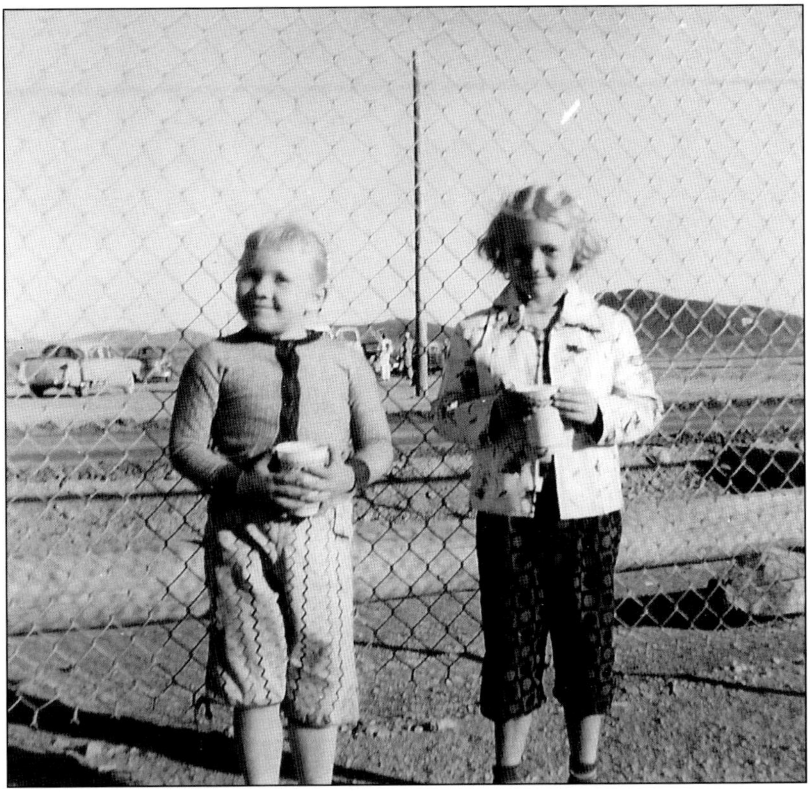

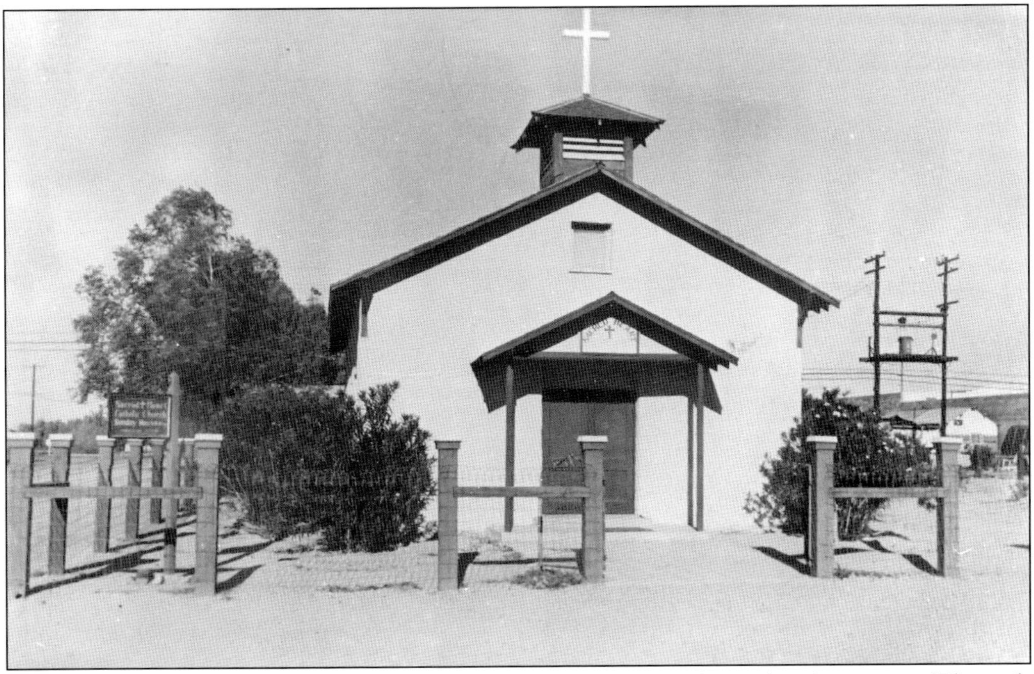

Parker's Sacred Heart Catholic Church, pictured around 1940, was located at the corner of Eleventh Avenue and Joshua Street. The building materials were locally made adobe bricks. The structure has since been razed and replaced with a modern church reception and fellowship hall.

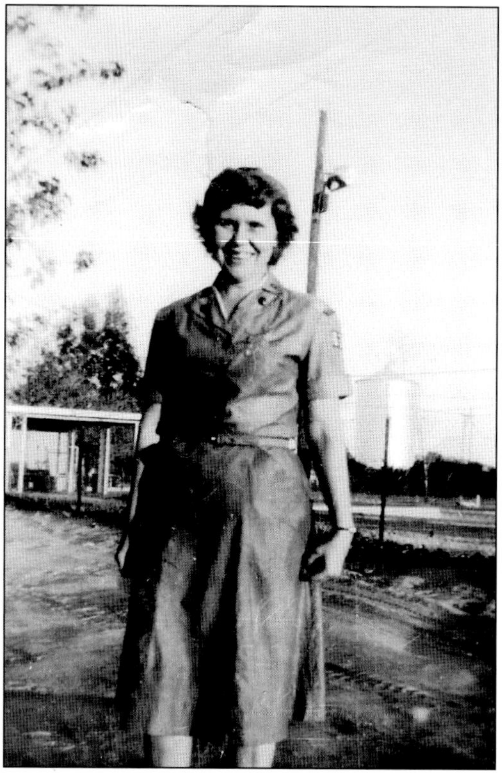

In 1961, Barbara Holdread organized the first neighborhood Girl Scout program in Parker, and it is still going strong. Norma Ray currently leads the program.

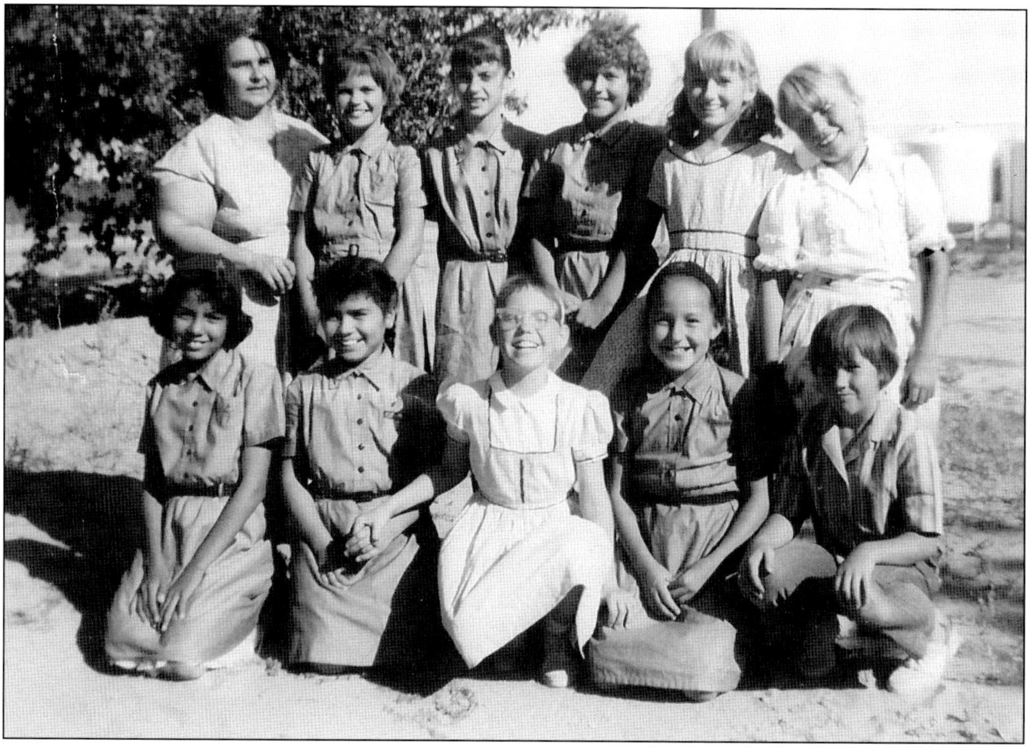

Delores Garcia, assistant Girl Scout troop leader, poses with her group of girls in 1962.

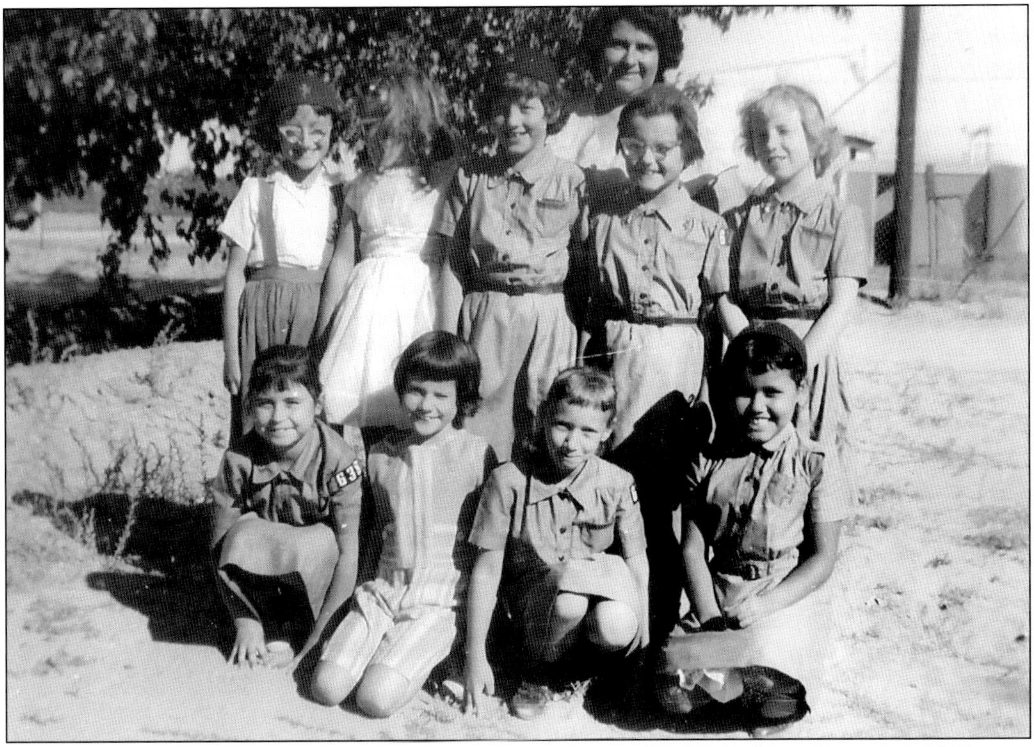

Younger Girl Scouts are pictured with their assistant troop leader, Delores Garcia, in 1962.

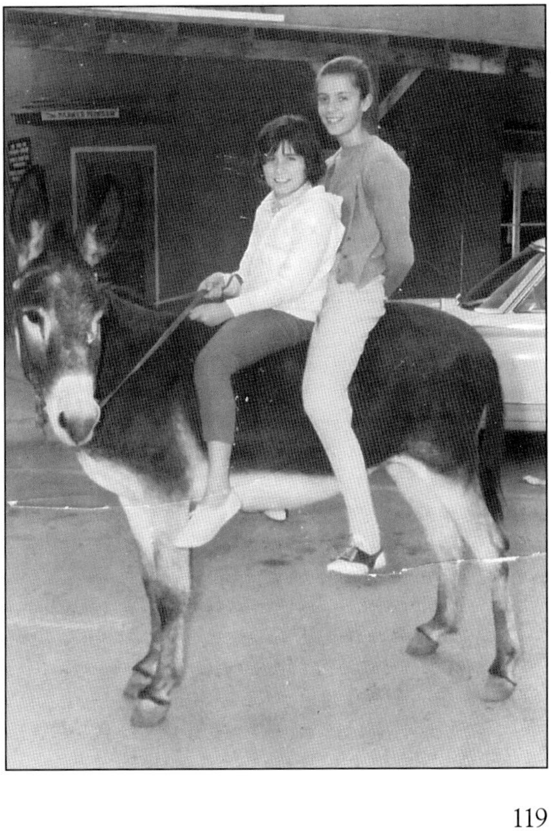

Bonnie (left) and Molly Magee pose while out riding their burro, Dreamboat, in 1964. The girls' parents, Bill and Jeanne McGee, had moved to Parker in 1949, when Bill went to work for the Parker Lumber and Supply Company. By 1951, Bill was employed by the U.S. Post Office, retiring after 22 years of service. In 1960, Jeanne began work at the First National Bank of Arizona branch office in Parker and retired after 25 years.

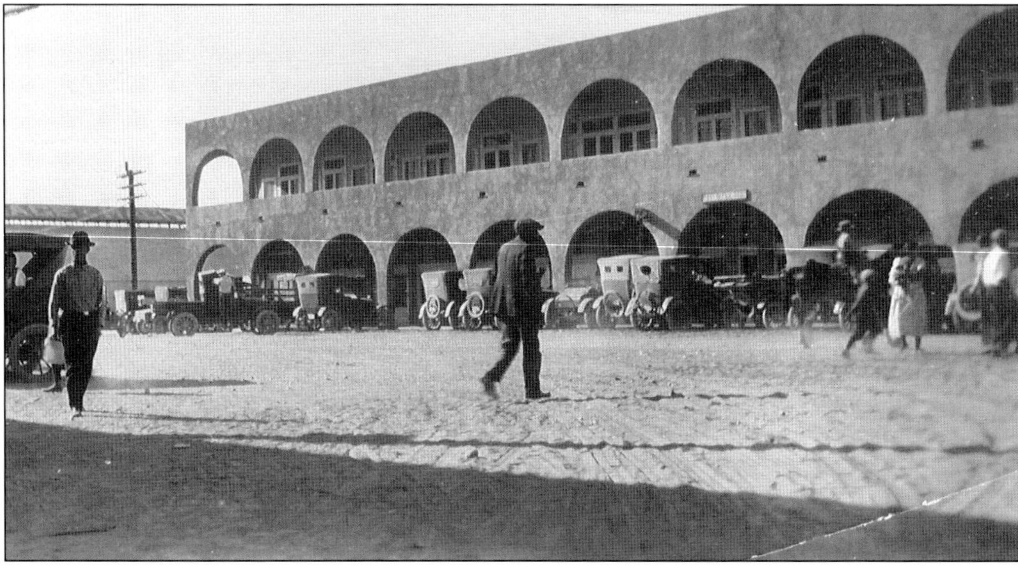

This early street scene shows a view of the Grandview Hotel from the corner of California and Arizona Avenues—busy with activity, as evidenced by the numerous vehicles parked along the street.

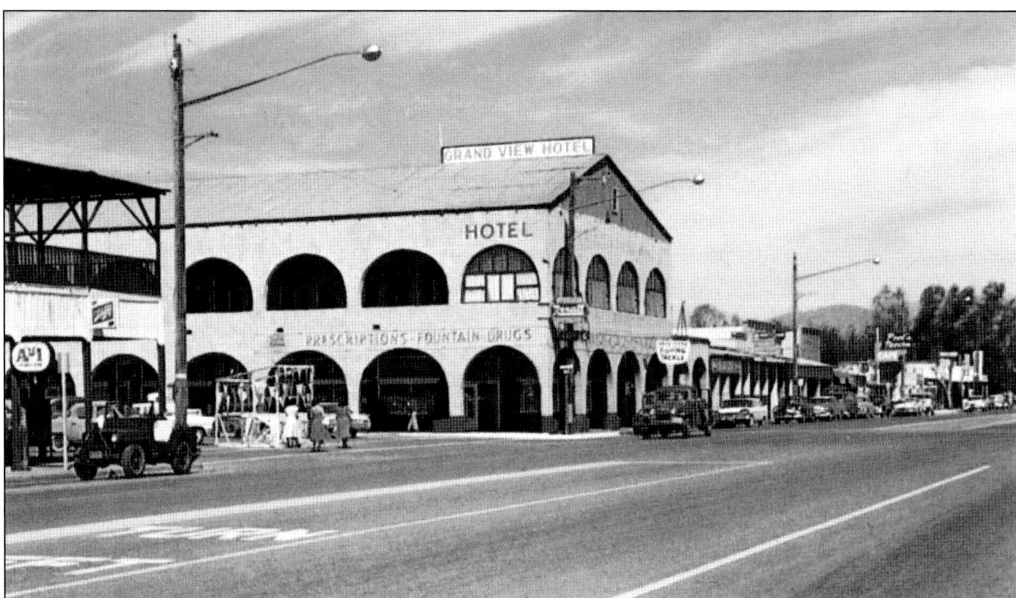

The Grandview Hotel must have been photographed during the rodeo in 1962 because of the booth set up in the intersection. The Does recently revived the fund-raiser Rodeo Jail, where friends turn in friends, who in turn have to get someone else to bail them out. It is all done in fun, with the Does also selling hot dogs and sodas and providing a smile or a friendly wave to passing motorists.

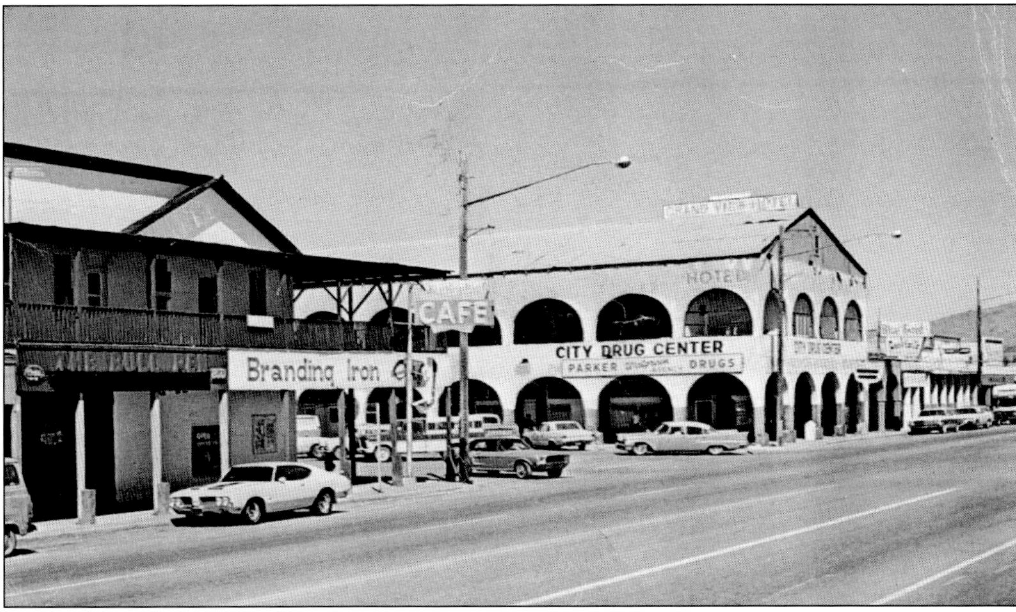

This late-1960s street scene depicts the Grandview Hotel, which served as the town landmark until burning in 1974.

The Oasis Bar, at the corner of Twelfth Street and California Avenue, was an early establishment in the Parker landscape. The Stephan family, who owned the Oasis, also owned the Parker area's oldest resort, Cienega Springs, which is still recognizable by the remaining palm trees that give the appearance of a dense jungle.

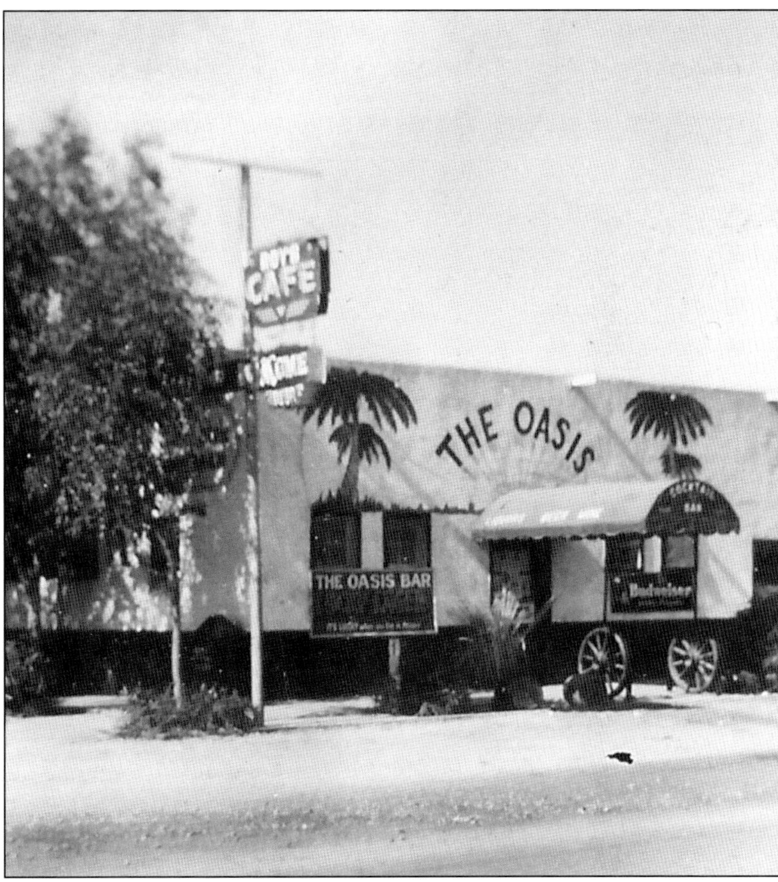

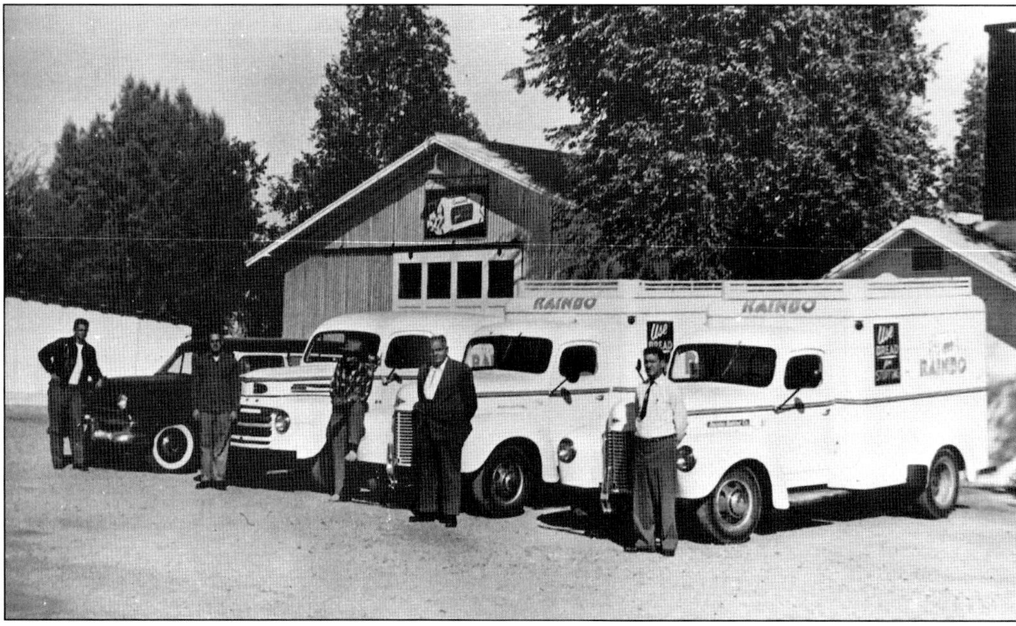

From the late 1930s through the early 1960s, Cecil Florence Jr. and Sr. owned and operated the Rainbo bread and milk distributorship, located on the current site of the NAPA store. Posing next to Rainbo delivery vehicles, Cecil Jr. is at far left. Cecil Jr. also boat raced in both circle and drag racing, where he would go on to specialize in drag racing, to which he lost his life in an accident.

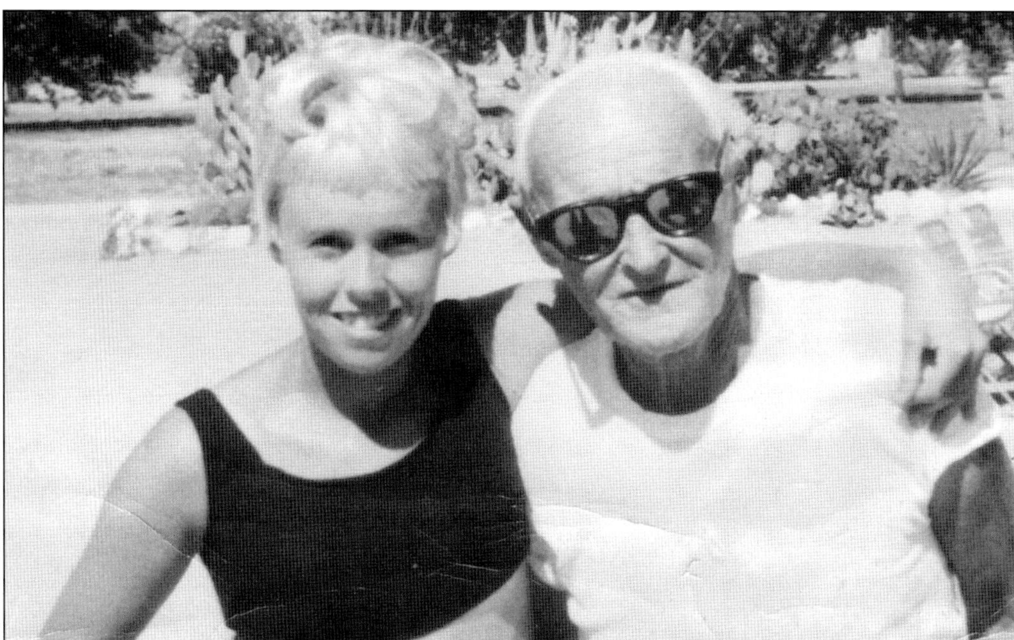

Pop Harvey and his daughter Buni moved to Parker in 1950. Pop had previously worked as a lifeguard at Coney Island, New York. He became manager of the Parker Public Pool and began teaching American Red Cross water safety classes in 1955. Buni started working at the pool in 1958, assuming the manager position in 1968 upon the passing of her father.

John T. Dockery Jr., formerly of Phoenix, became the branch manager in Parker when the First National Bank of Arizona opened its doors for business in 1952.

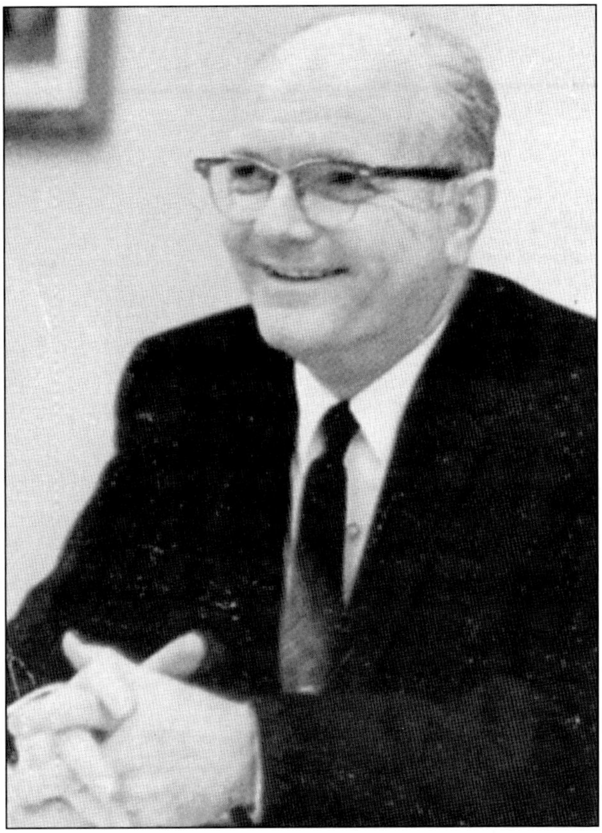

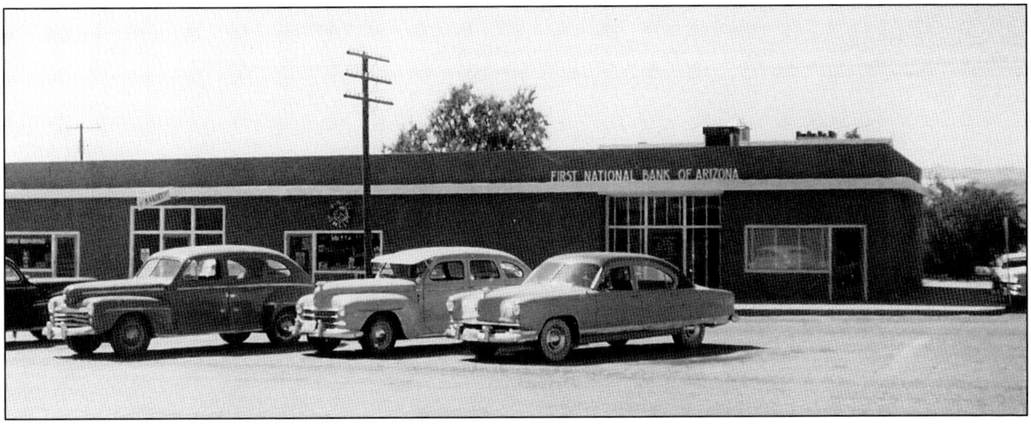

The First National Bank of Arizona was located at the corner of Joshua Street and Arizona Avenue in the early 1950s. With a local branch office, customers no longer had to travel the distance to Phoenix to take care of their banking needs.

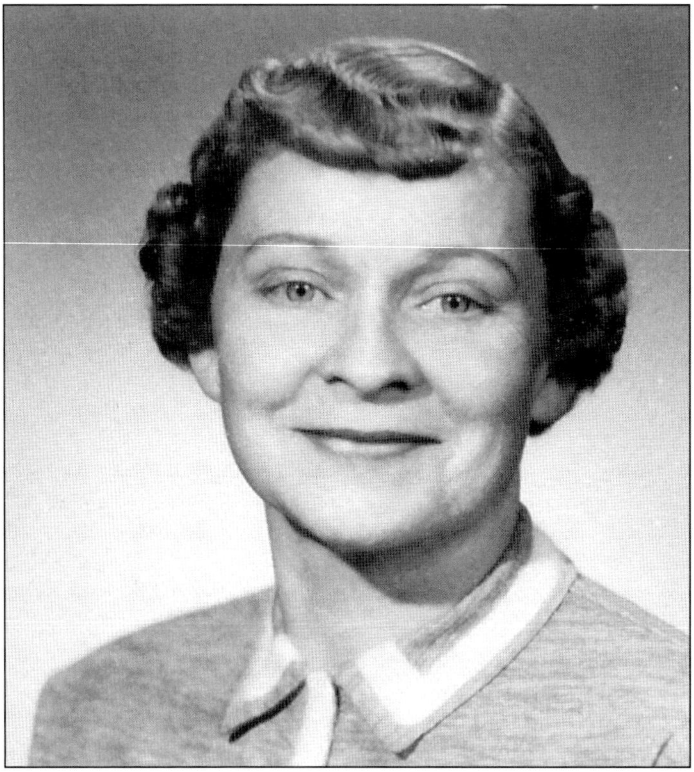

Berniece "Bea" Maddox and James Granville "Gran" Fuqua spent many years as justices of the peace at the Northern Yuma County Court in Parker. Bea and Gran were both well-respected judges, each serving until their respective retirements, Gran in 1969 and Bea in 1975.

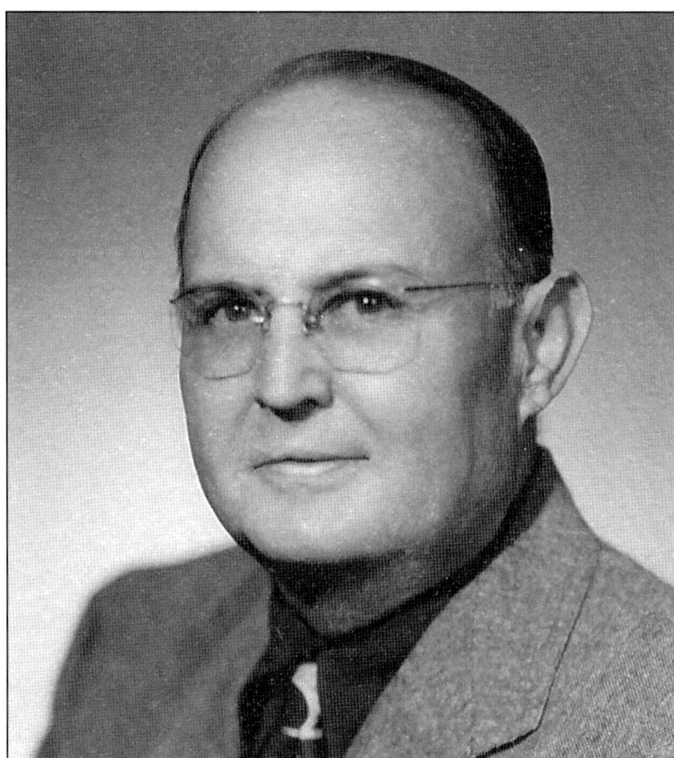

Gran Fuqua, justice of the peace in Northern Yuma County, was the only son of Berkeley M. Fuqua, one of Parker's earliest inhabitants. Gran had five sisters: Carrie King, Ellen Dick, Mabel Smith, Ruth Fuqua, and Senee Creighton.

Dottie Randall served as the Parker Area Chamber of Commerce director for over 30 years beginning in 1968. She promoted the area's tourism and economic development. Dottie's devotion to Arizona can be seen on her vehicle license plate, "ILUVAZ." Dottie and her late husband, Duke Randall, leased land on the California side of the river for their Bermuda Palms Mobile Home Park.

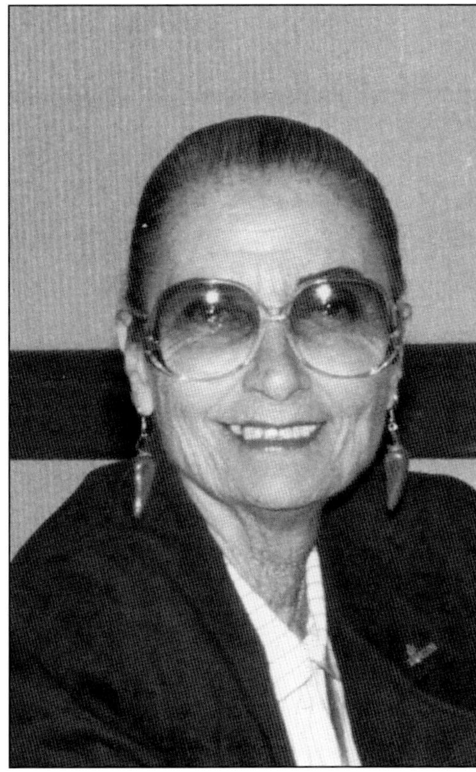

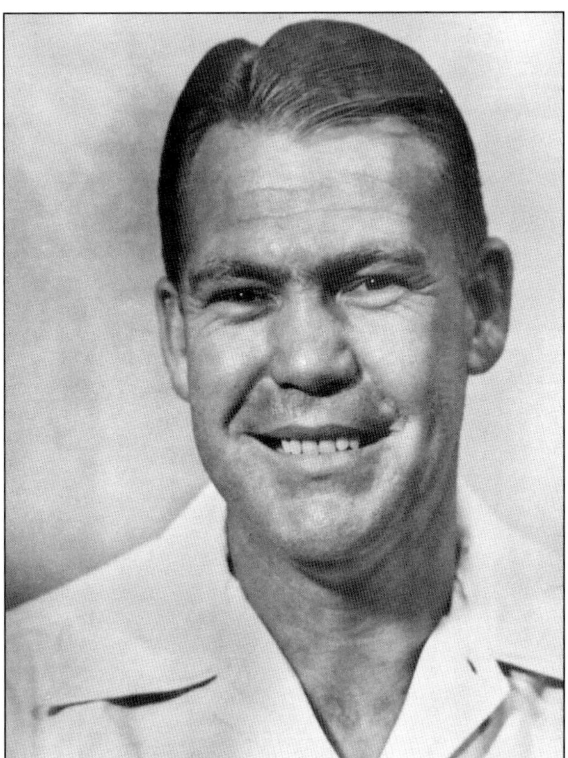

A core group of community leaders saw the benefit of incorporating the town site of Parker, including the consolidation of public services such as water and electricity and the establishment of local representation. Elected the first mayor for the incorporated town of Parker, Glen Strohm served on the town council from June 1948 to March 1953.

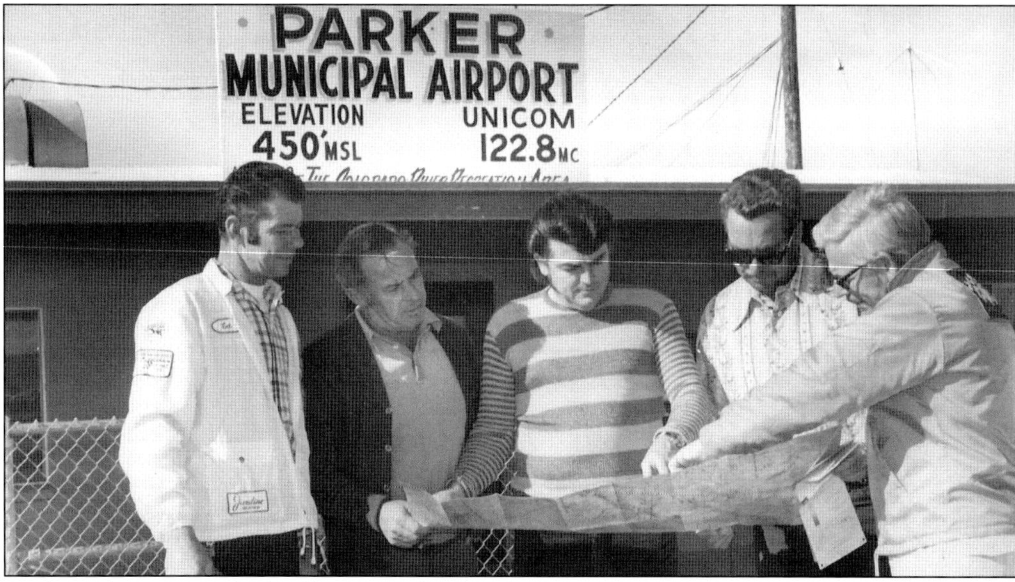

Mickey Thompson, who had been involved with car racing, often vacationed in the Parker area, where off-road racing had existed since 1971. By 1974, Thompson became the official promoter, also visualizing the possibility of an international appeal for this type of racing, which came to be a reality. Over the years, Parker's race has been featured on the television network ESPN. Here, from left to right, Ed Madison, Marion Beaver, Mickey Thompson, and two unidentified men map the proposed course.

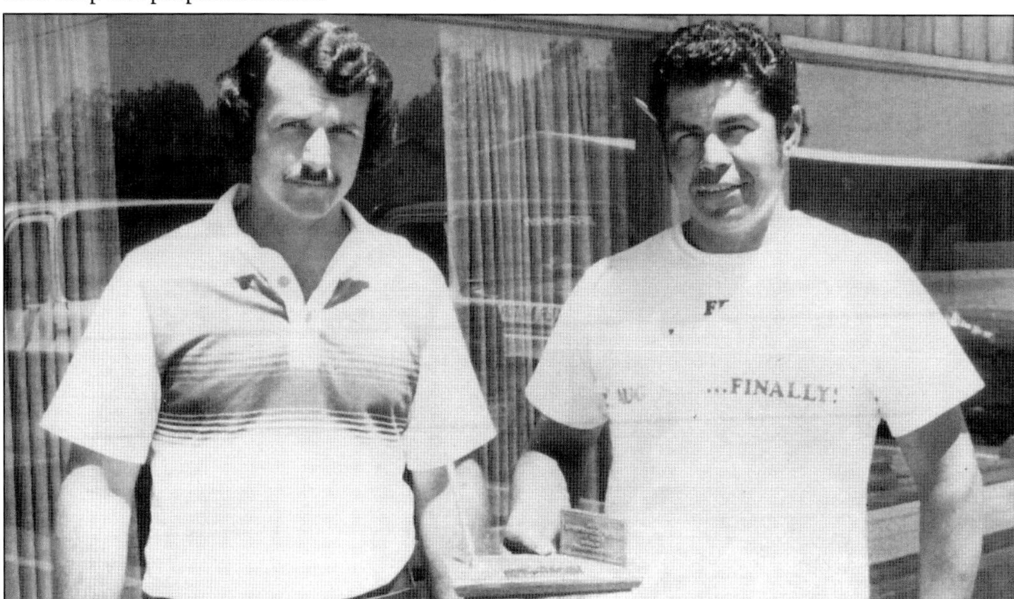

Local Parker boys Danny Beaver (left) and Manny Esquerra started desert racing in 1976. Danny's career as a driver of record lasted 27 years until his retirement in 2003. Co-riders for Danny were his childhood best friend, Randy Hoeft, and Clyde Andress and Taylor Crittendon. Manny's racing career began in 225 Hydroplane boats in 1974. Upon switching to desert racing, Manny became a champion racer and member of Ford Motor Company's Rough Rider team. Co-riders for Manny were his brothers, Tudy Esquerra and Gabriel Naranjo.

Parker's original off-road course encompassed lands in both California and Arizona. The starting line for the Parker Off-road Race has changed several times over the years. This scenic photograph, with the river as a backdrop, shows the starting line when the race began at the Blue Water Resort and Casino. Part of the allure of today's Parker Race is the glitz and glamour of the "Main Street Start" in front of the chamber of commerce. Much time and effort, along with community support, was put into realizing this unique and special feature of the Parker Race.

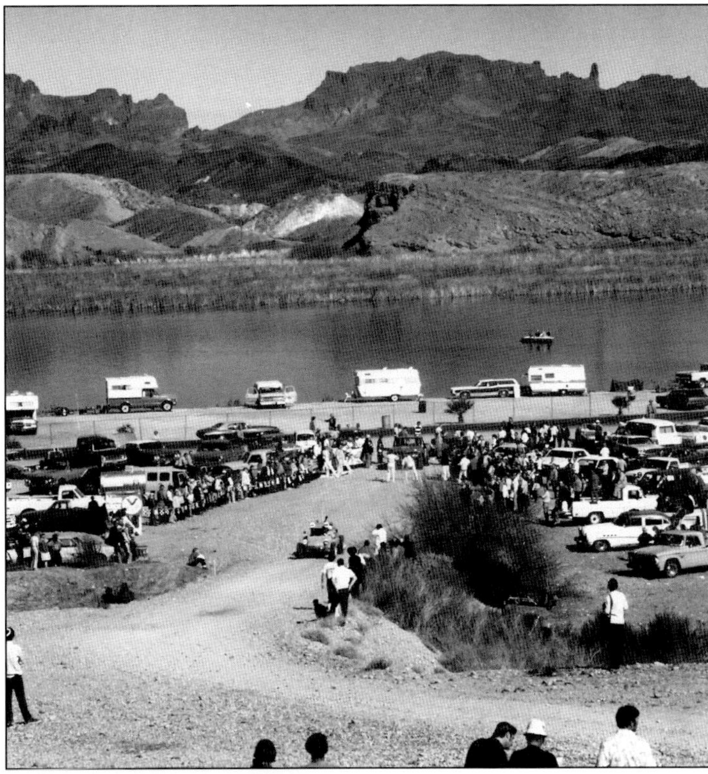

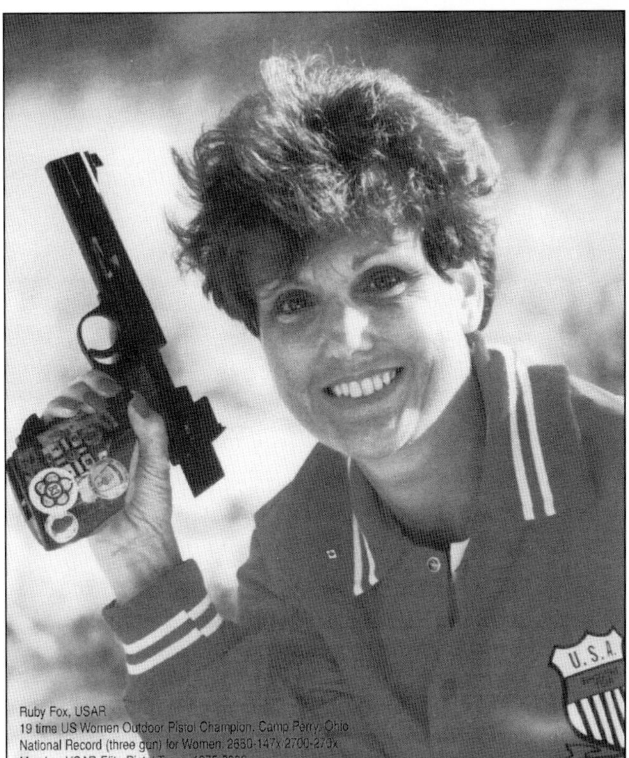

Longtime Parker resident Ruby Finley-Fox is recognized as a world-class marksman in Olympic shooting sports, as well as the NRA 2700 style of shooting. Ruby started shooting pistol in 1968 under the tutelage of her husband, Art. Ruby is most proud of her score of 2660-147x out of a possible 2700-270x.